C0-EFL-209

Books by Victor Ripp

Turgenev's Russia
From Moscow to Main Street

FROM MOSCOW
TO MAIN STREET

FROM MOSCOW TO MAIN STREET
Among the Russian Emigrés

Victor Ripp

Little, Brown and Company   Boston   Toronto

COPYRIGHT © 1984 BY VICTOR RIPP
ALL RIGHTS RESERVED. NO PART OF THIS BOOK MAY BE REPRO-
DUCED IN ANY FORM OR BY ANY ELECTRONIC OR MECHANICAL
MEANS INCLUDING INFORMATION STORAGE AND RETRIEVAL SYS-
TEMS WITHOUT PERMISSION IN WRITING FROM THE PUBLISHER,
EXCEPT BY A REVIEWER WHO MAY QUOTE BRIEF PASSAGES IN A
REVIEW.

FIRST EDITION

Excerpts from "Elegy: for Robert Lowell" and "A Part of Speech" from *A Part of Speech* by Joseph Brodsky. Translation copyright © 1973, 1974, 1976, 1977, 1978, 1979, 1980 by Farrar, Straus and Giroux, Inc. Reprinted by permission of Farrar, Straus and Giroux, Inc.

All of the incidents in this book are true although many of the names have been changed.

LIBRARY OF CONGRESS CATALOGING IN PUBLICATION DATA

Ripp, Victor.
  From Moscow to Main Street.

  1. Russians — United States. 2. Refugees, Political
— United States. I. Title.
E184.R9R56 1984   973'.049171   84-7936
ISBN 0-316-74709-2

BP

Designed by Jeanne F. Abboud

*Published simultaneously in Canada
by Little, Brown & Company (Canada) Limited*

PRINTED IN THE UNITED STATES OF AMERICA

For Nancy

CONTENTS

	Introduction	1
ONE	Homo Sovieticus	7
TWO	Departures and Arrivals	34
THREE	Making It	54
FOUR	Public Institutions	85
FIVE	Politics	119
SIX	Religion	149
SEVEN	Literary Circles	177
EIGHT	The Life of Art	204
NINE	The Structure of Everyday Life	227

FROM MOSCOW TO MAIN STREET

❧ INTRODUCTION

I was on my way to meet Mikhail Baryshnikov at a party in the home of a mutual acquaintance. Though I had been a great fan of his dancing ever since attending his solo debut in Leningrad in 1971, the prospect of seeing him offstage and out of costume was at this moment more fascinating. Beyond his virtuosity as a dancer, Baryshnikov is a historical phenomenon; he is a vivid symbol of the emigration that has recently brought thousands of Soviet citizens to the United States.

I turned off Park Avenue and went up the stairs of a sedate brownstone on the cross street. It was going to be a decorous occasion. My acquaintance had told me that Baryshnikov was a "good Russian," in contrast to Rudolf Nureyev, who was a "bad Russian," given to nastiness and rudeness at social gatherings; the jury was still out on the character of Alexander Godunov, the latest Kirov Company dancer to defect to the West. The standards for these judgments were probably fatuous — my acquaintance moves in a realm of society which is sustained by silly gossip — but it was telling that distinctions of any sort were being made. Apparently enough Russians had descended on America for their blank exoticism to begin to yield individual features.

In the luxurious living room crammed with the bric-a-brac of capitalism, Baryshnikov seemed completely at home, and I wasn't altogether surprised. I had recently seen him on television performing a terrific strut with the gaudily costumed dancers from the Broadway show *A Chorus Line*, giving evidence that he now not only had the artistic freedom denied him in the Soviet Union (his main reason for defecting), but also that he was at ease with the opulence with which we surround our cultural heroes. Nevertheless, he is hardly true-blue American; traces of his heritage tantalizingly linger. I didn't get a chance to talk to him, but as I watched him circulate among the other guests, a distinct image came to mind: a king in exile. It's impossible to look at Baryshnikov receiving fervent tribute in America without remembering that another land had first endowed him with his majesty.

Like Baryshnikov, most of the recent Soviet émigrés command attention because they seem to straddle two worlds. These émigrés are pilgrims from a land long cut off from the community of nations, and they've come to reaffirm our horror of the communist beast; but they also are the offspring of that beast, with some impulses and tastes that are pure-bred Soviet. With such a complex pedigree, the émigrés' entry into American life was bound to set off sparks.

The wave of emigration began in earnest in 1971, when for reasons still not entirely clear the Soviet regime began permitting large numbers of people to leave. For years it had vehemently prevented emigration; now it seemed it couldn't wait to be rid of some of its citizens. The official policy is to allow only those to leave who can prove that going to Israel will reunite them with their immediate family, but the Soviet bureaucratic nets have been whimsically slack as often as cruelly tight, and many with no valid claim have slipped through. Also, some of the most prominent members of this emigration have followed altogether different paths to the West, defecting while abroad, or being exchanged for Soviet spies held in Western prisons, or suffering legal expulsion. However they left, and whatever their original destination, a significant number of the recent émigrés have ended up in the United States. In the decade ending in 1981, more than 250,000 Soviet citizens left their homeland, and approximately 100,000 of these settled in America.

This is, in fact, the last of four large-scale emigrations from Russia in the modern era. True, the people who left between 1881 and 1914 constituted an anomaly. That was the period when thousands of Jews departed the Romanov empire. Because Jews were only contingently a part of Tsarist Russia (enduring various legal restrictions on where they could live and work, and often speaking only Yiddish), once they left, they hardly looked back. They concentrated on the life they intended to build in their new countries: immigrants much more than émigrés.

The accepted usage, therefore, is to begin numbering the successive emigrations with the one following the Jewish exodus. This style of enumeration implies a political judgment. Since the "first wave" left immediately after the Revolution, there is a suggestion that the coming of communism marked the start of a uniquely horrible era. A nineteenth-century pogrom victim, scurrying across the border with murderous Cossacks in hot pursuit, may have failed to appreciate such fine distinctions.

But in one respect the prevailing usage does make sense. The emigrations after the Revolution, the so-called three waves, differ one from another in various ways, but they share a basic feature that the 1881–1914 emigration notably lacked — some lingering attachment to Russia and its culture. Hostility against the forces that caused the departure of these more recent émigrés has not altered their love for their homeland; many continue to regard Russia as their spiritual patrimony, now unfortunately occupied by interlopers.

The first wave's departure spanned the period from 1917 to about 1928, with most people leaving in the earlier years, when civil disorder made penetrating the borders fairly easy. The second wave left after World War II, another chaotic period. Now the third wave is upon us. New York City has absorbed many of these latest émigrés, so many that in some of its neighborhoods, like Brooklyn's Brighton Beach, Russian rather than English has become the best language for dealing with shopkeepers. Every third New York City taxi now seems to sport a driver's ID card with a prepossessing cluster of Slavic consonants. As for the higher reaches of society, one reads almost daily in *The New York Times* of some scientific or entrepreneurial feat executed by an émigré who till recently was wandering through the bleakness of the long Soviet winter. It's as if that fabled creature, the mysterious Russian Soul, had forsaken its habitual northern latitudes and taken up residence down the street.

It's the Russian Soul, moreover, with one very curious item in its baggage: a passionate view of America. What country wouldn't be flattered by new arrivals who have thought through the very details of its social and political life? As it happens, the émigrés' conception of America does not often conform with the actuality of America — not surprisingly, since what they have devised is largely a sort of Russia-in-reverse, a society that would lack precisely those flaws that made their Soviet lives onerous. Yet, though this jerry-built, Slavicized version of America is very much a curio, Americans attend to it. If the third-wave émigrés drastically misinterpret the facts of American reality, they also seem, by some oddity in the cross-cultural ebb and flow, occasionally to touch our national dreams, nightmarish and hopeful ones both.

Thus, Alexander Solzhenitsyn, to take the most flagrant example, regularly anathematizes our institutions, scourges our moral life, all the while pursuing the ideal of a religious, self-sufficient community that is suitable only to Russia (and probably only Tsarist Russia, at that); still, Harvard invites him to deliver its Commencement Day address, *Life* devotes four pages to his teachings. We must sense that valuable insights about our fate lie hidden behind the misapprehensions, a kindred spirit behind the alien appearance. Indeed, in deciding to stalk the tracks of the third-wave émigrés, I assumed I'd be learning as much about America as about Russia, and I wasn't disappointed.

For ten months I sought them out. I went to their cultural events, accompanied them to the social agencies appointed to help them, traveled in their intimate circles. Sometimes I felt like a bull in a china shop, barging against the delicate artifacts of their culture (or, as the equivalent Russian cliché has it, an elephant in a china shop, which seems to imply an even greater uncomprehending awkwardness). But I also found points of common interest with many new acquaintances, and even made a couple of friends.

I also noticed that by the end of those ten months my opinion of Baryshnikov had subtly changed. I realized that his emigration, which traces a spectacular trajectory from Russian fame to even greater American fame, was hardly an adequate symbol for all of the third wave. No individual's life can encapsulate its complexity and variety. On the other hand, neither is the third wave shapeless, an aggregate of 100,000 fragmented destinies; generalizations, hypotheses, tentative formulations are possible, and I have ventured many such.

My opinions, I know, will occasionally exasperate the third-wave émigrés, since they are remarkable for the pertinacity of their own ideas about their historical role. Though I naturally stand by what I have written, I rely as an ultimate defense on the genre I have chosen to work in. This is a travel book (though the exotic culture I visit was in most cases accessible for the price of a subway token), and a travel book customarily filters its subject through the sensibility of the observer. This is a book about the third-wave emigration as seen through the eyes of an American.

Or, more precisely, a second-generation Russian-American. My parents were part of the first-wave emigration, leaving Russia in the confusion of the Revolution's aftermath. But for the accidents of geography, the vagaries of economics, they might not have made it. For services to the Tsarist petroleum industry, my mother's grandfather had been appointed a *kupets pervogo guilda* (merchant of the first guild), an honor that allowed him and his progeny to live anywhere in the empire instead of being confined to the Jewish Pale of Settlement. He kept an apartment in Petersburg for visits, but settled in Baku, in the heart of the oil fields — luckily, since when the Red Army began clanging southward in 1919 in search of the bourgeoisie, there was time for my family to escape. But for the proximity of Turkey, I might have grown up in the same circumstances as the third-wave émigrés had; I might have *been* a third-wave émigré.

As it is, I have a fidgety connection with third-wave émigrés. I was brought up speaking Russian, I assiduously studied and then became a professor of Russian literature, I've visited Moscow and Leningrad for extended periods — but the third wave confounds me. I often feel as someone might feel upon encountering a favorite relative misbehaving at a party, the sense of kinship vitiated by an aghast embarrassment. Their actions and opinions about America appear simultaneously familiar and alien, wise and outrageous, while their marvelously warm and open character (I was welcomed even where I was a complete stranger) often slips in the direction of a lapel-grabbing, overbearing style that I long to escape. At first I was quite willing to let the matter rest at that, just another of life's unresolved ambiguities, but as I continued to run into émigrés here and there, I increasingly saw that my reaction was comparable — congruent, even if of somewhat greater intensity — to that of many Americans. The topic seemed worth investigating further, so I journeyed forth into émigré environs, into their Russia in America.

Incidentally, one sign of my traveler's perspective is already evident in this introduction. Many members of the third-wave emigration would not refer to it as "Russian," since to them that denotes exclusively a native of the Russian Soviet Federated Socialist Republic. Ukrainians, Belorussians, Georgians are Soviets, but they are not Russian; indeed, even some natives of the RSFSR, those that are Jewish, cannot technically be called Russians. Though I have often followed the émigrés' style of precise self-definition, there are times when to do so would have required elaboration not worth the trouble. The third wave speaks Russian, it is the last stage of an émigré tradition that thinks of itself as Russian — for most of an American's intents and purposes, it is Russian. I hope my other instances of cultural egocentrism are as innocent in their implications as this one.

ONE

✣ *Homo Sovieticus*

Russia is a country that people in large numbers have been leaving for a long time, but it does not follow that Russia always inspires absolute revulsion in those who are forced to emigrate. Since the early nineteenth century, Russian émigré communities have been marked by poignant longings for the motherland, and inordinate energy and time have been devoted to plans for returning home. Russian émigrés dream Russian dreams long after they learn to converse and to transact careers according to the conventions of their adopted lands.

As it happens, it is possible to identify the very first official Russian émigré, and his history is instructive. Nicholas Turgenev, a cousin of the famous novelist, was an economist and political theorist who joined the Northern Society, the group of Russian noblemen that contrived the ill-fated Decembrist Rebellion against Nicholas I in 1825. Turgenev was in France on the day the uprising took place, so the Tsarist regime suggested that he live up to the code of a nobleman and return home to face Russian justice. Turgenev declined the invitation (wisely, since six of the conspirators were hanged and many others exiled to Siberia). He was thereupon tried in absentia and a prison term was imposed, its execution to be carried out as soon as he stepped onto Russian soil — which naturally confirmed him in his decision to remain abroad and try influencing Russian politics from afar. In all, Turgenev's case suggests a neat definition of the émigré: someone who would suffer persecution upon returning to Russia, yet retains an intense emotional connection with it.

The third wave has transposed this motif to fit new historical demands, but it's still recognizable. I learned this on almost the first day that I began to inquire into third-wave culture, when I visited the Club of Russian Writers. The meeting was held on Columbia University's campus, but it had a distinctly alien air, as if a bit of Russia had been transplanted to Manhattan's Upper West Side. Most of the twenty-five or so people in attendance looked as if they had just walked in off Leningrad's Nevsky Prospekt or Moscow's Gorky Street instead of Broadway. The men wore the typical Soviet male's uniform of dark suit and tieless white shirt; the women also sported styles of dress which showed traces of the dowdy economy they had recently left behind, though they carried themselves, as Russian women often do, as vivaciously as Tolstoyan heroines.

The guest speaker for the evening was the only person present besides me who was not a third-wave émigré. His name was Mikhail Werboff, a man of about seventy, with a shock of straight white hair, who had come to America in the 1920s. He had been a student of the great Repin before himself becoming a prominent portraitist, and as he strode to the lectern he seemed to have the manner of someone used to attention. He had no prepared speech, no notes. He simply strung together a series of anecdotes from his life, holding them in place by his visible enthusiasm for what he was reporting. He wasn't pompous, just confident that everyone would share his fascination with such a kaleidoscopic life. He rambled on, hardly pausing for logical transitions as he described his relationship with Repin, his brief career as a Hollywood extra, the famous subjects he had painted the world over.

He said, "I painted King Gustav of Sweden on the Riviera in the 1920s, when he used to enter local tennis tournaments under the alias of 'Monsieur X.' He greeted me in his mansion dressed in tennis whites and sneakers, but he was every inch a king."

It was a tale out of another time, with allusions to tastes and attitudes that had to be alien to émigrés from post-Stalinist Russia, but the audience listened raptly. As I was to see many times, third-wave émigrés love every branch on the tree of their native culture; Werboff was a Russian artist and his life, whatever strange events it was filled with, mattered.

As Werboff moved toward his conclusion, there was an interruption. A man rose at the back of the room, looking simultaneously shy and determined, and demanded to be heard. He wanted to read an encomium to Werboff, in gratitude for the joy the paintings had given him. Matter-of-factly, as if encomiums were the order of the day, the audience shifted in its seats to gives its attention to this thin, balding man with a fierce and darting glance. He began somewhat nervously, but soon found his declamatory rhythm.

> *And if people of future centuries,*
> *Having drunk the cocktail of fashion,*
> *Wish to see the face of the twentieth century,*
> *They will come to the subjects of Werboff,*
> *The markings of his brush.*
> *O Werboff, I love you.*

It was, by American standards, wildly excessive, but in the present company it went down smoothly. The reader sat down pleased with himself, Werboff's face expressed gratitude and only a little bemusement, the audience, after a respectful pause, returned its attention to the speaker's table. This gathering apparently could absorb the most extravagant emotions without blinking. Indeed, the evening steadily took on the plain intensity that one thinks of as quintessentially Russian, and by its end, the twenty-five or so members of the club, all recently departed from the Soviet Union, were completely at ease, at home.

I wanted to verify my impression about the tenacious links between third-wave émigrés and Russian culture, so a few days after the meeting of the Club of Russian Writers, I visited its chairman. He lives in a New Jersey suburb, in a large two-story house at the bottom of a quiet dead-end street.

The economic status that his house suggested was unusual for third-wave émigrés, as was the tranquil setting it stood in —

even those who can afford suburban life prefer the city, where their compatriots have created several bustling Russian enclaves. On the other hand, a mother-in-law, a common fixture in third-wave émigré homes, was present. Evgeny Lubin introduced me to her and his wife. He is a stong, compactly built man, his bearing suggesting reservoirs of energy; even his round bald head seemed designed for maximum efficiency. On first seeing him at the writers' club, I had the thought that he had been made chairman for his apparent capacity to keep the proceedings orderly by force if necessary.

At one point during the evening, after the tea and cakes had been cleared away, I asked Lubin why he had emigrated.

He replied, "Many reasons, but one main one. I wanted to get published. I had a good job in the Soviet Union as an engineer, but my real love was writing. It filled my spare time. But I could not get my works published. What I wrote was infinitely better than what the journals printed, but still I was refused. My manner, my way of looking at things, did not fit the Party line."

I asked him why it was so vital to be published.

"A foreigner cannot understand what it means to be a Russian writer. Historically it's always been the most honored profession, and even now in the Soviet Union to be a member of the Writers' Union is to be virtually a god. I'm not exaggerating; I can prove it's true. Listen.

"Once I wanted to go skiing in Kirovsky. As usual there was no hope of getting a hotel room as a simple tourist, so I asked a friend who works as an administrator in the Writers' Union to supply me with credentials for a while. We devised a *kommanderovka* [a trip on official business], and he asked only that I go through the motions of visiting the mayor to announce I was writing some sketches of the locality.

"I get to Kirovsky, a hotel room is waiting, everyone is respectful. Next morning I stop by the mayor's office, I think merely to say hello, but he immediately insists that I tour the region. 'What do you want to see?' he asks. 'The nuclear plant,' I reply, assuming it's impossible to see something so secret. I didn't know what awe a Soviet writer inspires. Next thing I know I'm in a chauffeured limousine, on the way to the plant. The excursion was so unexpected that I had left my identity papers at the hotel, and so had nothing to show the guard at the gate. He hesitates, of course, but my driver shouts to him, 'Don't you know this is a member of the Writers' Union?' So I get a tour of the plant, top to bottom. Can you imagine what I could have done in Russia if I had really been a certified Soviet writer? Do you wonder that I was angry that they wouldn't publish my works as I deserved?"

I asked how it was now, here.

"Here I am published. Only émigrés read me, of course, but still it makes everything worthwhile."

Afterward, as Lubin escorted me outside to my car, I felt in the presence of a contented man. He had finally satisfied his creative urge, he had a good job and a comfortable home; he even claimed, against all expectations, to prefer New York's subway system to Leningrad's sleek, marble counterpart. "Who wants to ride in a museum?" he said. The lush summer night seemed a backdrop perfectly appropriate to his happy lot.

Naturally I was surprised when he started to complain. "It's peaceful here, to be sure. But you know I can still hear the noise, a disturbing noise. Listen," he said, though in fact the highway was a mile off and one had to strain to make out the hum of the tires.

"You should have experienced the quiet I had at my dacha near Leningrad. *That* was quiet, a somehow sweet, perfect silence," he said, suddenly wistful, still nostalgic though all his dreams had come true in America — and nostalgic not even for something palpable, but for an absence, an undefinable air that apparently only Russia breathes.

Nostalgia is a sentiment that besets all people who have left their homeland, but Russians seem to feel it acutely. Perhaps it is because, unlike other national groups, they cannot go home even should they wish to. They are separated from their past not only by time but by a tantalizing sort of geography: they can measure the distance but never traverse it.

And among Russian émigrés, it is the third wave that seems to suffer the worst form of nostalgia, the nagging belief that things easily could have been different. Perhaps it is because they left Russia of their own choice, or because life there for many of them, while unpleasant, was not fatally dangerous, but in any case a surprising wistfulness often creeps into the memories of the third-wave émigrés. Alexander Galich, the immensely popular balladeer who emigrated in 1973, was reflecting a widely held attitude when he said, "I left the Soviet Union; I did not leave Russia." That's an admirably imaginative gesture, thus to separate a country's spirit from its administrative reality, but it also implies deep uncertainty about deciding to leave one's homeland.

The third wave's confusion is compounded by its itinerary. The first and second wave of Russian émigrés went from Russia to Europe and sometimes China, and stayed for long periods. The third-wave émigrés who come to America have only a short layover in Rome. Abruptly surfacing here, without first decompressing in a psychically less potent atmosphere, an émigré can suffer the cultural equivalent of the bends: this country has long occupied a special place in the Russian national fantasy, with a dizzying image constructed of two centuries of misinformation, myth-making and propaganda.

From the beginning, Russians' picture of America had less to do with fact than with symbolism, a consequence perhaps of their abrupt interest after a long period of no concern whatever. The first use of the word *America* in Russian was in 1584, in a translation of the Polish work *A Chronicle of the Whole World,* but for hundreds of years thereafter there was no further written reference to this country. Probably there was no thought of it either. Until the eighteenth century, Russia moved on an isolated course. It hardly paid any attention to adjoining Europe, and a distant British colony was outside its ken altogether.

When Peter the Great opened a window to European influences, intimations of America blew in also, and soon thereafter this country began to spark excitement among Russians. American history struck them as an uncanny replica of their own. Both countries lay outside the staid and perhaps exhausted European line of development; both could still expand, since their borders were not finally fixed; and in both the cities still had the safety valve of large tracts of unsettled land where individuals could follow their adventurous impulses. To a considerable degree, Russia looked on America as a proving ground for its own future, every success here foretelling comparable success there.

As with any idealized vision, Russians' overly tender regard for America implied the chance of a reaction in the opposite direction, and this occurred soon enough. They continued to admire our material wealth and *can do* style, but they began to perceive a despicable thinness in our cultural and spiritual life, an incessant running after money, a brusqueness of feelings. When a character in Dostoevsky's *Crime and Punishment* goes to commit suicide, he announces that he is "off to America." The hyperbole owes much to Dostoevsky's extreme chauvinism, but many Russians equated — and continue to equate — America with the death of human values.

Peter Weil and Alexander Genis, two third-wave émigré journalists on the New York newspaper *Novy amerikanets (The New American)* have written a series of articles about the meanings America holds for Russians. They have touched on topics ranging from Harlem to hobos. On the twentieth anniversary of Ernest Hemingway's death they analyzed the influence of his writings and his life on those Russians who came to maturity in the late 1950s, the period of the post-Stalinist thaw.

Weil told me, "We never read American papers, didn't see American tourists, didn't know the English language. But we read the classics of American literature — and that was enough. We fell in love with America."

To Russians, books of fiction have always been not only a good read but an inspiration to scrutinize the author's manner of life, and this attitude gave Hemingway a headstart toward popularity.

As Weil and Genis had written, "It wasn't to literature that Hemingway owed his status as an idol and a prophet. His life, filled with exotic countries, heroic deeds, love and war, constituted the ideal of a true man. . . . To live in the Hemingway style — this became the slogan of a whole epoch. The Hemingway ideal was so encompassing that even women were expected to become good buddies [*muzhiki*]. Such dialog as the following was not uncommon: 'Hey, good buddy, have you breast-fed the baby yet?' "

Weil is thirty-two, a stocky man with a bearded face, that, when he laughs, evokes Santa Claus, and he laughs often. Genis is a few years younger, more talkative and intense, also thinner. In the Soviet Union Weil worked as a gravedigger, trucker, and fireman, before becoming a journalist for a *Komsomol* [Young Communist League] newspaper in Latvia. Genis worked for a newspaper in Riga, but he also had been a fireman for two years. For some reason, it is their firefighting that is thrown up to them by critics disagreeing with their literary opinions, as if wielding axes and hoses destroys the esthetic sensibility uniquely. They take such criticism with good humor, Genis noting that he wasn't really much of a fireman anyway, never actually seeing a building aflame, and Weil nodding happily at his partner's witticism. In general they converse like some Platonic idea of coauthors, amplifying and underscoring each other's opinions.

Weil said, "Hemingway's picture hung in virtually every young man's room in the 1950s. You had Elvis, we had Hemingway — and which is better?"

Genis added, "The idea that you could have adventures, that you could sleep with someone not your wife — of course we had these dreams before, but now we had a concrete model."

"And also you have to remember that the times were just right," Weil pointed out. "Khrushchev's exposure of Stalin, then the thaw, with the invasion of Czechoslovakia still in the future. There was a feeling of hope."

I'd arranged to meet Weil and Genis at the *Novy amerikanets* offices and then suggested going somewhere for a drink. Surprisingly, they had led me to a nearby McDonalds, but I soon saw the reason for their choice. After buying a large portion of french fries, we sat down at an out-of-the-way table, and Weil produced a brown bag containing a bottle of vodka: possessing this essence of Russian pleasure, what need had we of anything fancy? America's fast-food culture neatly satisfied our ancillary needs, a clean table and a pouch of spuds.

I reminded them that they had somewhere written that it was against the Russian tradition to take food with vodka.

Laughing his Santa Claus laugh, Weil replied, "You misunderstood. It's just that the average Russian nowadays *has* nothing to take with vodka. Perhaps a crust of last week's bread, if he's lucky. Its an economic, not a cultural question, alas."

Genis was eager to return to the question of American literature, and after a moment's thought he said, "You have to understand that from Hemingway we learned not so much a literary technique as a world view, a style. People speak differently in his works, so everyone in Moscow tried to imitate some favorite character. Not only to use American words — *girlfriend* was very popular, for instance — but to talk in broken phrases, with plenty of irony. Every conversation had a subtext."

Weil added, "You can imagine our surprise when we came here. Americans do speak more or less as characters in Hemingway do, but there's no subtext, no reference to something unstated."

Genis explained, "When Hemingway spoke of money, we naturally assumed it was meant symbolically. But now we see that when Americans speak of money, they mean money."

"Just as when Americans send their children to school in dirty jeans, its not high fashion but simply dirty jeans," Weil said. "While we émigrés spend our money on fancy clothes for our children so they won't feel ashamed in front of their schoolmates. It's not America's fault, all these misunderstandings — it's ours. We had too high expectations. We saw America as a land of sincere, sophisticated people, where each person in a few words managed to reveal his soul to the first *sobutylnik.*"

Weil used the Russian word that translates as "a friend made through the sharing of a bottle of vodka," and it may have been an adequate symbol of his disappointment with America that there is no single English word ("drinking buddy" won't do) that is equivalent. Perhaps prompted by his remark, we all took another swig of the vodka, but then hurriedly had to hide the bottle as a roving security guard eyed us suspiciously. We sat quietly for a while, apparently stunned by the weighty implications of our conversation, and in the silence the essences of our encounter seemed to take on a new light. The french fries were, in fact, tasteless; the tables and chairs, far from being functional marvels, were gaudy insults; and drinking vodka at McDonalds probably did not commemorate a reconciliation of two cultures.

"So you're sorry you emigrated?" I asked.

"Of course not," Genis answered. "Leaving Russia was a necessity, and where else would we go? The feeling of living in a country that matters in the world, which for all its faults is something Russia gave to us, this can be duplicated only in America, not in Europe, not in Israel."

Weil added, "I hate to say this, but it's true: when Russia invaded Czechoslavakia in 1968 my friends and I were horrified and ashamed of being Russians, but there was also a twinge of pride. Look at what Mother Russia can do if she wants to!"

"You know the joke," Genis said. "Question: With which countries does Russia share borders? Answer: With whichever ones it wants to."

"America's importance in the world is one of the few good things about having come here. That and the fact that the bars stay open late," Weil said, and then added, "When we were in the Soviet Union, we saw only the good things about America, so perhaps it's natural that now we see mainly the bad. But I don't think we are exaggerating."

Genis said, "What's to be done, we are used to a different sort of culture. Remember in the Soviet Union, in our circles anyway, prestige was a function of intellectual or spiritual capacity. Here it's all money. I've been in American homes, successful and supposedly cultured people, and seen that they have not one book in their house."

I was beginning to feel uncomfortable. After all, in this company I was America's representative, and probably should not be listening with equanimity to denunciations of our moral life. Our little drinking party, begun on such a pleasant note, was turning sour with misunderstanding.

But Weil and Genis pressed their case, down to the barest bones of Russian-American relations. There is a widely held belief that Russians and Americans should be instinctively congenial, that the national characters match; the history of our countries, upstart nations outside Europe's grand tradition, supposedly has fostered a common style of behavior, unbuttoned and amiable. It's certainly true that of all nationalities, Russians and Americans go over the most quickly to a first-name basis with new acquaintances. But that's all a mirage, Genis insisted, a disguising of vast differences of sensibilities.

He said, "In the beginning, when I first met Americans upon coming to this country, their smiles and 'How are you feeling' always suggested to me that I had made good friends. Then I would call them on the phone and they wouldn't even remember who I was."

We walked back out on the street shortly thereafter. The guard wouldn't move on so we could drink our vodka in peace, and anyway the conversation was making me self-conscious. My smiles felt stillborn, my polite phrases resounded with insincerity. Thank God the Russians have a joke for every occasion, and Weil produced the appropriate one, giving us a coda of amiability if not perfect harmony: "For a year Rabinovich goes every day to the visa bureau, pestering the Soviet government to allow him to emigrate. America is his hope, his dream. At last he gets permission and departs in joy.

"A year later he is back in line at the Moscow bureau, demanding a new visa. The official in charge says, 'Rabinovich, you got one visa, why did you ever return to Russia?'

"To which Rabinovich replies, '*Tut gavno, tam gavno — nu doroga!* [Here it's shit, there it's shit — but oh, the pleasures of the passage!]"

The disenchantment with America that underlay Weil's joke was a sentiment I was to hear expressed many times by third-wave émigrés. Very few reject America totally, but many do seem to hold it at arm's length, like a lover coolly regarding the woman he has finally seduced after many years of fervent effort: they'll stay on, but is *that* all there is to it?

Each time I encountered this sentiment, it was a shock, because it registered not only as personal opinion but as historical judgment. The third wave was prepared to love America, but have arrived at a time when we are less than lovable. They came prepared to give homage and participate in glory, but apparently have found only the skeleton of their ideal, some withered traces hinting at the America of their dreams.

On the one hand, refugees from the Soviet Union are merely another group in America's long immigrant tradition; on the other hand, they are very special guests. They have endured a social system that we emphatically proclaim is the diametrical opposite of our own. They are travelers from our negative image.

It's not surprising, therefore, that the third-wave émigrés have been subjected to close scrutiny. Various public and private social agencies have organized investigations, and the University of Illinois is in the midst of a long-range survey that promises a wealth of data. Scholars have also taken up the problem — virtually every conference of specialists in the Soviet area now devotes a seminar to the émigré. But in the manner of many such comprehensive undertakings, the subject, the living and breathing ex-Soviet citizen cannily negotiating his new path, often slips from view.

Dr. Edgar Goldstein is a psychoanalyst who is himself a third-wave émigré, a combination of qualities which suggested privileged insight into the phenomenon, and so I arranged to talk to him. His name had first come to my attention when I saw an advertisement of his services in a Russian-language newspaper. "Treatment of depression and anxiety," it read. "Contemporary methods of treatment and prevention of nervous-emotional disorders and psychological episodes connected with sexual problems, alcoholism and physical insufficiencies. Hypnosis, psychoanalysis, and psychostimulation." The ad had an antiquarian flavor, evoking the days when psychoanalysts had simultaneously to publicize their talents and insinuate an arcane knowledge. This approach was no doubt still necessary within the third-wave émigré community, many of whose members, I knew, found psychiatry a mystifying process — why pay someone to listen to troubles that could be unburdened upon a friend for free?

I found Dr. Goldstein himself to be thoroughly Americanized, speaking English fluently and canny about our practices. He is in his thirties, elegantly bearded and finely mannered. We met in his East Side apartment. On the basis of what I knew about psychoanalysis, I expected him to be reticent during our interview, but it turned out I could hardly get a word in. The topic of the third-wave émigrés fascinated him. We spoke in the living room that doubled as his office, and throughout the conversation he played with the props of his craft, turning the clock to various angles, fingering the levers of his tape recorder, several times glancing at the couch behind him in a way that suggested that he thought some of the individuals we were discussing would profit from stretching out there two or three times a week.

"Third-wave émigrés often expect to be rewarded just for leaving Russia," he told me. "They see themselves as heroes, and of course no one would deny that it is a hardship to live under the Soviet regime. But you know, life under such a system can also be reassuring. There is something to be said for constant police surveillance in today's world, where everyone slips easily into total anonymity."

I remarked that yes, I had a similar sense of ambiguous comfort when I had been in Russia and my phone was tapped: it was nice to know someone cared enough to try and find out where I planned to spend the evening.

Dr. Goldstein dismissed my comment with a wave of his hand. "It's altogether different with a visiting foreigner, who after all knows something about the world. The Soviet citizen has so little access to the truth that he easily gives in to all sorts of fantasies. That's another reason why émigrés have such exaggerated feelings of self-importance. For years they've been listening to Soviet propaganda that tells them that all those who intend to emigrate are in the service of American imperialism. But when they arrive in the West, third-wave émigrés find that their services are not needed by the 'American imperialists' or, indeed, by anybody else."

The words of Dr. Goldstein, who took his American training after having already achieved eminence in Leningrad psychiatric circles, sometimes took on those implications of an inescapable destiny which are common to the language of his profession. He said, "A Soviet immigrant carries within himself a totalitarian state, a system of inner dictates, reinforced by all his experiences in a totalitarian society — inner dictates that are stronger even than those of any neurotic in the free world. Though many of the émigrés hated the society they lived in, they also came to need it. They are Soviets."

Dr. Goldstein went on to analyze the process of identity formation, aggressive attitudes toward society, and questions of adaptation, but in a way what impressed me most was his ability to distance himself from his own former allegiances long enough to formulate his insights.

Later, as Dr. Goldstein was showing me out, I remarked that I had found our conversation very informative, that it was refreshing to meet a third-wave émigré with such cool insight into his compatriots' lives and such a detached perspective on his homeland. But in the days that followed, I began to wonder if I had properly measured the weight of the past. Every time I met a third-wave émigré, no matter how black the cloud of anti-Soviet feelings that was vented, a thin shaft of nostalgia always shone through. Was Dr. Goldstein the single exception to the rule? I got my answer when a few weeks after our encounter I happened to pick up a copy of *Novy amerikanets* and found a letter in it from him to the editor. It was in response to the remarks of an émigré of the older generation who had ridiculed the third wave's continued emotional ties to Soviet Russia, calling them "a phenomenon for study by a clinical psychiatrist." Dr. Goldstein coolly noted his professional credentials, then burst into such passion that I hardly recognized the man I had met earlier:

"For you, it [Russia] is territory, but for me — it's my homeland. A pity she was not the mother one would have liked, but still she was my mother. A pity that she did not nurture us as one would have liked, still she did sustain us. A pity that love and hate for her are mixed, but they are not mixed equally. A PITY."

It is, in fact, Russian émigrés of earlier generations who most often move the third wave to its most passionate outcries. Contact between the various waves of émigrés often seems like a case study in mutual provocation — they have so much in common that every slightly different gesture produces friction, every slightly dissimilar step seems a betrayal.

Though all three waves suffered, their memories of the oppressor are not identical. The first wave's image of the communist regime is stark but lacking detail. Citizens of the Tsarist empire, they were forced abroad before there was much chance to see the New Society at work. The first wave tends to consider the Soviet Union as simply the Enemy, a monstrous Other that has stolen the familial estate.

The second-wave émigrés know the Soviet Union more intimately, but it's the Soviet Union of a special historical moment. Their memories are of the social chaos of the 'twenties and the Stalinist terror and forced collectivization drives of the 'thirties. The Soviet Union was then a society whose sustaining national myths (including the myth of communism) were often sacrificed to exigency. The second wave has a detailed memory of the country they left, but it's the detail of nightmare, everything held together by an encompassing horror.

Though many factors influence the memories of the third wave, the most decisive may be the most obvious: they left Russia in the eighth decade of the twentieth century — which means they left a mature Russia, one no longer in the throes of domestic uncertainty or in fear of foreign attack. It is a stable society, sure of its premises (in both senses of that word). When the third-wave émigrés lived in Russia, they faced an authority that was not only confident but persuasive, and as a matter of course they accepted some of the principles and tastes that were in the air. It's not surprising that after they go abroad they still hover between an anti-Soviet and a Soviet caste of mind, vehemently rejecting aspects of the world they left behind at the same moment they unconsciously embody others.

The histories of the different émigré generations promote different ethical perspectives, but the disputes which rack the émigré community are often triggered by simpler disagreements. The physical circumstances of the émigrés' journey has been one constant irritant. The earlier generation left Russia hurriedly, their lives in danger and with bleak prospects. Though many in the third wave suffered hardship, as a group they travelled in an *à tout confort* style when compared to the first and second wave; they can complain mainly of bureaucratic abuse, official scorn — matters that strike the earlier émigrés as passing and trivial. As a letter to the old-line émigré newspaper *Novoe russkoe slovo* (*The New Russian Word*) noted, what third-wave writers present as tragic seems almost beneath notice to people who left at the point of a gun. "How much can be written," the letter writer demanded, "about the humiliation at *OVIR* [The Department of Visas and Regulation]?"

And the several forms of arrival in America are no less a sore point than are the forms of departure from Russia. To the earlier émigrés, buffeted by cataclysmic events, by wars and ideological passions, America was a haven at the end of a stormy journey, and they felt a commensurate gratitude. Never fully American, of course, many did quickly become genuine Russian-Americans, the hyphen marking a real commerce between the two cultures. One of the most famous among them, Vladimir Nabokov, once said, "I am at least one-third American, *literally*, since I have gained approximately eighty pounds since coming to this country." The whimsy aside, Nabokov's comment defines the earlier émigrés' urge to incorporate American values into their lives.

For third-wave émigrés, America is a desirable place to settle, but few have kissed the ground upon arrival. Whatever affection they feel for their new country is constrained, partly because America has changed, losing its Mecca-like luster, partly because life in Russia, while still bad, was no longer insupportable. The third-wave émigrés tend to congregate in enclaves and to draw upon their old Soviet customs, as hibernating bears sustain themselves on energy accumulated in the past. A surprising percentage of the third-wave émigrés are not eager to enter into the surrounding culture, to blend into the American mainstream.

Noting this tentativeness, the older émigrés infer that the new arrivals are not properly grateful to an America that has saved them from life under communism. Columnists in *Novoe russkoe slovo* have denounced the third wave for cultural insularity, for lethargy, for selfishness — and the shrillness of the charges is compounded by resentment that the new arrivals blithely receive all sorts of government aid such as America did not deign to offer when the first two waves of émigrés came to these shores.

The third wave retorts that its accusers are out of date, and to make this case *Novy amerikanets* reported that the earlier generations do not even fully understand the new arrivals' conversation — it is too studded with the jargon that the prisoners brought back from the camps in the period after Stalin's death. The point, of course, is not only that years spent in America impair one's knowledge of the language, but that they put the crucial events of recent Russian history at an incomprehensible remove.

The first wave consisted of aristocrats, soldiers of the defeated White Army, well-off merchants and businessmen suddenly lacking cachet, all those who were at odds with the new Bolshevik order. After leaving Russia, they settled mainly in Berlin and Paris, hardly entering the cultural life of either capital. (Their main contribution to French life of the period may well have been manning Parisian taxis, which they did in such inordinate numbers that numerous writers mentioned the phenomenon.) They were waiting for the Soviet regime to crumble of its own ineptitude, so they could return home on their own terms. When it did not, many among the first wave moved on to America, hastened on their path by the rise of Nazism.

The second wave is sometimes called the Vlasov wave, because many of its members followed General Vlasov in his attempt to form a Russian division to fight alongside Hitler's troops against the Red Army and communism. But the second wave also encompassed Russian POWs and civilians who had been dragooned into the German labor force — all those, in fact, who for one reason or another found themselves outside Soviet jurisdiction during the confusion at the war's end, and then were unwilling or afraid to return to their homeland. Much of the second wave also ended up in America, often after long stretches in the DP camps. The second wave's harrowing wartime experiences seem to have capped a personality type whose development began in the trying years of early Bolshevism. Its members are more pragmatic and more proletarianized than the first wave, which suggests that it is probably no accident that this is the only one of the Russian emigrations that has failed to produce a writer, musician, or painter of international rank.

The third wave is harder to define. It includes many who felt the sting of Soviet authority, from Leningrad dissidents escaping persecution to Moscow artists seeking more receptive audiences for their experimental creations — and also Tblisian wheeler-dealers who would probably run afoul of the law of any country. The largest segment defies any general characterization beyond that of individuals seeking a more comfortable life for themselves and a better future for their children. Perhaps it is because the third wave is so amorphous in its composition and its goals that earlier generations turn to matters of style when they want to criticize — that is one reason why the way the new émigrés speak has become a point of hot dispute.

When I visited Andrey Sedykh, the editor of *Novoe russkoe slovo,* in his office, almost the first thing he said was, "I am amazed by the vulgarization of language that exists among the third wave. It's not the Russian spirit as I understand it. Perhaps it is because they are more materialistic, more ambitious, than we ever were."

Sedykh's words seemed to resonate in harmony with his appearance. He is almost eighty and distinctly of the old school, with a manner that hovers between courtliness and condescension. He was once an insurance salesman, and he still wears a big-shouldered, double-breasted business suit; its cut emphasized his small head, his heavy-lidded eyes, and his stately posture. He's not anybody's idea of a working editor of a daily newspaper.

Incongruity, in fact, pervaded the offices of *Novoe russkoe slovo.* There was a decorousness and sense of hierarchy that seemed out of place in a newspaper office. Sedykh sat behind closed doors as in a holy retreat. The staff, which was made up mainly of sprightly middle-aged women, emanated a deference that would not have been inappropriate to the scribes and clerks of a law firm in a Dickens novel. Whenever Sedykh ventured out of his room, there was a spasm of excitement. "Good day, Yakov Moyseevich," "How are you feeling today, Yakov Moyseevich?" could be heard from all sides, a sort of celebrative symphony that used as its motif the honorific form of name and patronymic. (The editor's real name and patronymic, that is — "Andrey Sedykh," which is how he is known throughout the émigré community, is a nom de plume.)

In his sanctum sanctorum, Sedykh launched into a diatribe. He told me, "Nowhere is the lowering of taste among the third wave so evident as in language. Of course language must evolve. The Russian language has withstood all sorts of borrowings from German, French and English. With that sort of thing one can come to terms. But we of the older generation cannot abide the incredible coarseness that has come into the language by way of the prison camp.

"There is no need for it, all that *mat*," he said, using the word that connotes an especially strong form of obscenity.

Sedykh has heard, but rejects, the opinion of some third-wave writers that *mat* is necessary if one is to be true to today's Soviet reality, where its use is ubiquitous. "That's just wrong, as theory and as practice. I've been around literature for sixty years and I know realism does not mean giving in to every vulgar tendency. Tolstoy was a realist, so also was Chekhov, but you find no *mat* in their works."

I had caught Sedykh at an inopportune moment; he was on his way out of the office to an uptown appointment. But he suggested that we share a cab, giving us a chance to continue our conversation a while longer. We exited from the *Novoe russkoe slovo* office to a chorus of "Goodbye, Yakov Moyseevich" and went downstairs into the midday crowds, where Sedykh amazed me with his energy: darting into traffic and waving his briefcase like a captain semaphoring across rough seas, he tried to requisition a taxi. Surprisingly, the world complied with his extravagant antics, and we were soon driving off uptown.

Settling back in his seat, Sedykh picked up where he had left off. "No doubt there's a psychological explanation for the new third-wave literature. These writers are suddenly free from censorship, which has been hobbling them for years, and so they look around for ways to express that freedom. It's sad to think that they could imagine nothing better than *mat*.

"There's one writer, whose name I can't bring myself to utter, who has recently published a story that describes the most despicable act, a man ejaculating on the body of his dead mother, as she lies in her funeral casket. That is what they call 'freedom.'

"The third-wave writers complain that the older generation does not read them, that they can't make a living here. Some of them are used to the comforts of being members of the Soviet Writers' Union, of course. Well, they should understand that it is not that the first and second wave do not read books, but that we have cultured taste. We don't want *mat, mat, mat*."

As our taxi cut through Central Park and over to Fifth Avenue,

Sedykh continued to vent his opinions about the third-wave émigrés. Our arrival at our destination put an arbitrary stop to a flood of criticism that clearly could have gone on much longer, but his point had been made: things used to be better; culture everywhere was in decline.

It was impossible to say if it was to exhibit a vanishing standard of behavior or if it was his usual practice, but as he took the change from the ten-dollar bill he had handed over to pay the fare, Sedykh uttered an elaborate, thickly accented "Thank you very much, sir." The cabbie, a young black with a bandana wrapped around his head, started at this form of address, suspecting irony, and gave Sedykh a cool, hard look. But Sedykh was already out of the taxi, ready to dash on to his appointment.

He paused only to shake my hand and offer a final word about the third wave. "They claim they are dissidents, some sort of political heroes. Solzhenitsyn is a dissident. General Grigorenko is a dissident. But not every fellow who participated in a three-man demonstration in Red Square or who was warned not to keep forbidden Western books in his apartment. The third wave, let's face it, most of them were simply normal Soviet citizens."

And that may be the real burden of the third wave's destiny, the reason it enflames the older Russian émigrés and confounds the rest of us. From a distance, the Soviet regime may seem like evil incarnate, an absolute moral blight; but the third-wave émigrés, having endured in the belly of the beast, may compel us to draw finer distinctions. Most of them led unexceptional lives, going on their daily rounds just like their countrymen — did this make them complicitous with evil? Did someone living in the Soviet Union need the courage of a Solzhenitsyn to escape the taint of guilt?

These questions may have reasonable answers, but in the émigré community, at least, reason seems in short supply. The older émigrés, who had a piece of their lives abruptly snatched from them by the rise of the Bolsheviks, cannot be patient with the third wave's tales of strategies of accommodation or of endurance amidst oppression — not when what is being accommodated and endured is the same regime that sent them headlong on their way. When push comes to shove, they are not bashful about telling the new arrivals exactly what they think of their behavior in the Soviet Union. Indeed, when Sedykh was mildly rebuked for his editorial policy by the third-wave *Novy amerikanets*, he characterized his critics as follows: "This collection of escaped convicts, literary failures and Soviet patriots, continually, in issue after issue, tries to teach the editor of *Novoe russkoe slovo* how to put out our paper. I have worked in the émigré press for sixty years.... Can it be that now I must put up with the advice of a former prison guard, who spent his time scrutinizing convicts from his watchtower?"

Sergei Dovlatev, the prime target of Sedykh's invective, lives in Queens, in a section virtually overrun by new émigrés. Go into any grocery store and it is likely that the man in front of you in the queue is doing his muttering about the high prices in his native Russian language, and that the cashier is turning aside his complaints in Russian also.

Recently, a store opened in the neighborhood which purveys Soviet-made goods, imported specially for the new émigrés. Sprats canned in thick oil, jars of fruits floating in opaque fluids, and lumpy liver pâtés fill the shelves. All the items have an acrid, slightly off-center taste, and a foreigner encountering them in the Soviet Union would reasonably assume they had been forced upon a deprived population; now it turns out that they are desirable, the acrid taste much appreciated by the third-wave émigrés. In this, as in much else, the new arrivals have apparently decided to shore up America's bountiful culture with pieces of their Soviet past.

When I mentioned my views on this to Dovlatev, he merely shrugged his shoulders, not changing his saturnine expression. He is a very large man in his late thirties, barrel-chested and tall, and with a crew cut over a low brow. It wasn't hard to visualize him as a prison guard. But though his manner wasn't exactly sunny, he did show flashes of irony abut life's perplexities, such as prison guards are unlikely to exhibit.

Responding to my question, he said, "We *are* all Soviet. I know of only one person among the third wave who escaped Soviet influence while he was there — the poet Joseph Brodsky. And it's probably significant that he wasn't anti-Soviet either. He was somehow outside the system altogether."

Somewhat warily, I mentioned Sedykh's allusion to his former occupation.

"It's true that I served in the *okhrana* [police] for three years," Dovlatev replied "and half that duty was in a maximum security camp. But it's necessary to add that the camp police is now a subdivision of the regular army. One is recruited into it in the normal course of events. To be a member of the *okhrana* can happen to anyone."

These days, Sergei Dovlatev, former prison guard, spends most of his time at home, tending to his newborn son and writing fiction. An almost palpable sense of domesticity pervaded the air as we sat around the kitchen table talking. His wife set out the Soviet pâté and sprats, which she offered as delicacies (and which I hypocritically praised). A silent, elderly woman, the mother of one of the spouses (though, awash in hospitality, I never discovered which), hovered at the stove, keeping the teakettle at a boil and replenishing my glass each time I took a sip. To cap my comfort, I was given a jigger of vodka. Dovlatev pointedly didn't get one — he's on the wagon after years of being a drinker of renown, which is not an easily won distinction among Russians. He's now committed to more placid pleasures.

About life as a prison guard, Dovlatev has written in *Novy amerikanets*, "Life is the same for the guard as for the ZEK [convict]. You awake at the same time, eat the same food or worse. The ZEK has his own property, at least, protected by law, while everyone steals from the guard: officers, warrant officers and their wives, and others too."

Asked about this, Dovlatev suddenly smiled, for the only time during our meeting. "I did write that," he said. "Yet why not admit it — it's not *quite* the same being a guard as being inside. Once my brother turned up as a ZEK in the camp where I was a guard. I told him, 'It's no better for me than for you.' He looked at me in disbelief.

"Eventually I had to 'sit' myself for a while and I found out how wrong I was. I happened to end up in a cell that Lenin had once been kept in — the honor didn't make the time pass any more pleasantly."

Dovlatev did not seem the type to revise his history lightly, and his new view of his former role may have been only politeness to keep an American guest's inquisitiveness at bay. In fact, his most telling comment on the subject of the Soviet citizen's complicity with evil had been made some time before, and it was much more complex, more tragically ambiguous than his remarks over tea. It was in the form of a short story called "Straight Ahead," but there's no doubt that the events happened to him.

The narrator of the story, desperately oppressed by his duties as a guard in a prison camp, goes on a binge, ending up drinking with the trusties. As much for consorting with the ZEKs as for getting drunk, he is ordered to stand court-martial. The officer in charge tells him, "You're supposed to feel antagonism toward the convicts. You're supposed to hate them. Can't you hate them?"

The narrator's best buddy is assigned to escort him to headquarters, and they trek off across the desolate bog. Once outside the camp's perimeter, their usual camaraderie begins to assert itself, and the narrator suggests they detour to the local town for a drink. The buddy hesitates, thinking of his marching orders. Angered, the narrator exclaims, "So that's what happens to a man when they give him an official document and a weapon."

Though the buddy relents for a time, the opposing demands of friendship and duty at last come to a head. At the climax of the story, the narrator shrugs off his buddy's admonitions and walks off to indulge one last whim before submitting to the court-martial's certain harshness; behind him, the buddy clicks the bolt of his weapon, slipping a bullet into the chamber. There is a tense moment of hesitation, but then the narrator stops and turns around, moved less by fear than by a sense of his friend's horrible predicament. He sees a surprising sight, his friend in extreme, almost frenzied, agitation.

"[He] threw down the submachine gun and started to cry and, for some reason, pulled off his sheepskin jacket and tore open his work shirt, all the buttons flying off."

In the midst of encompassing evil, Dovlatév's story implies, the very possibility of ethical choice disappears, and men finally are driven into absolute stalemate. The buddy's mad dance has the pathetic appearance of humanity trying to find a form to express itself. But in the world of the prison camp, as presumably in the Soviet world beyond its walls, humanity is impossible. One can only keep going "straight ahead," trying to disregard the moral implications of one's actions.

Dovlatev told me of something he had once written in *Novy amerikanets*, the description of a sign in a Leningrad food store. "It read, in capital letters: 'The guilty will be punished.' And that's all, not a word more. A threat menacingly emitted into space."

Dovlatev said, "In the Soviet Union there would be plenty of concerned readers of such a sign. Not only those who had already broken the law, or even those who had some criminal plans for the future, but virtually everyone. The Soviet citizen is made to feel his whole life is deserving of punishment, which has been graciously kept in abeyance."

He spoke of *mat*, the obscenities which Sedykh had found such an objectionable element of third-wave style. "In fact, to use *mat* in the Soviet Union is a form of political protest. It's a language that opposes the oppressive language of Soviet officialdom. It may be a feeble weapon, but in the Soviet Union today you use what you can."

It was time for Dovlatev to go downstairs to meet the babysitter who had taken his infant son for a stroll. As we prepared to part in front of his house, I remarked that after his experiences in the Soviet Union, America must seem a godsend.

He said, "It should be easy to make that judgment. In the Soviet Union just before I left, I had been fired from my job on a newspaper. I was about to be sent to prison, or else to work in a factory, which can be as bad as prison there. Compared to that, what wouldn't be better? But in the Soviet Union I at least understood who and where the enemy was even if there was little I could do. In America I'm less sure."

I asked him to explain.

"Take a concrete example. I feel safer in the street in Manhattan than I did in Leningrad. But is that because there are fewer dangers here or because I don't know enough to see them? It's a question of experience, I suppose, and of language. If I saw some guys fighting on a subway, I'd have to hesitate about intervening. I wouldn't understand what it was all about. I might be punching one of them while he was trying to apologize. So I let things pass — perhaps that's why it's safer."

"Still and all," I said, "you must be happy to have come to this country."

"I've got two pairs of shoes and a typewriter, anyway," he said offhandedly. "I've been in worse situations."

Dovlatev's last words sounded an appropriately constrained note. This emigration has foundered after high hopes. Though our news media still occasionally emit a flourish of trumpets to announce the third wave's historical importance in the war with communism, and though at times an émigré still rises to bless American life, the prevailing mood is bafflement.

America has come to expect full-blown gratitude from those it takes in. If refugees leaping from steerage with cries of ecstasy are a thing of the past, today's immigrants from most parts of the world are still patently thankful for America's welcome. How much more so should be the third-wave émigrés, coming from that especially awful hell? They are not, however, and instead, against all odds, even nourish a few warm thoughts for their homeland.

After all the more obvious explanations have been considered — that late-twentieth-century Russia is not evil incarnate, that late-twentieth-century America is not paradise — the third wave's unenthusiastic views of their adopted country remain provocative. What, precisely, in their past constrains them; what, precisely, in our present, dampens their ardor?

TWO
❧ Departures and Arrivals

THE Soviet regime is communistic and oppressive, America is democratic and a land of opportunity: that seems reason enough for the third-wave émigrés to have made their journey. But it turns out to be considerably more complicated. Though at first glance the third wave seems like a resolute brigade flourishing unambiguous banners, closer inspection reveals that it shambles along hesitantly, and its slogans are dotted with interrogatives.

The émigré author Valentin Prussakov has written a novel, called *Proshchay, Akhiney! (Farewell, City of Akhiney!)* which begins to reveal the prevailing mood. It is the story of an emigration from a country called Mandastan (transparently the Soviet Union) to a country called The Government of United Smiles (transparently and wickedly the United States). Prussakov writes:

"Why did I leave Mandastan? Well, why do others leave? About this theme much nonsense has been written. Some speak of the absence of various freedoms and the destruction of the rights of man. All this is true. But the main reason is most likely something else — a psychological reason. People lived for a long, long time in confinement, in Lord knows what suffocating circumstances. And then a window was opened a crack and something new and unsettling entered the country. We are a very curious people and like novelty: new clothes, new women, and new ideas. So, we Mandastanites, especially those who were intellectuals, which is to say those a bit weak-nerved — we began to hop around near the window, and one by one we fell through it. And indeed how was it possible not to fall through the window, or at least to begin hopping around near it? One would have been considered an anti-intellectual, uncontemporary sort of person. And such a slander is difficult to bear."

Prussakov trivializes for comic effect, but uncertainties do cloud many stages of the third-wave émigrés' odyssey. Even their status under United States law, which might be expected to define their condition, only raises new questions. They enter this country as "refugees." Though most held visas to go to Israel, once they passed beyond the Iron Curtain they came under the provisions of our Refugee Act, which defines a refugee as anyone "outside his or her country who would face persecution upon returning to it." That describes their plight perfectly, but it still makes sense that the third wave speak of themselves as "émigrés." "Refugee" evokes connotations too dire.

Certainly the conventional picture of refugees as people fleeing pell-mell toward the border, clutching their belongings in a sack, is inappropriate. Other Soviet citizens in circumstances comparable to those the third wave faced have remained behind, and while their lives may be unpleasant in some ways, they are by no means unendurable. The regime never has proclaimed the third wave a part of a heinous group, all of which deserves expulsion or worse; it is only after a Soviet citizen announces a desire to emigrate that he or she officially becomes persona non grata. In fact, though many endured hardship, few among the third wave suffered the unshackled terrorism of the state. It is a symbol of their experience that they departed on regularly scheduled airplanes, carrying a fair proportion of their goods with them; and upon reaching America, more than a few had second thoughts about their decision to leave. A strange exodus, when the Israelites long for the land of the pharaohs!

No one should expect emigrations to be perfectly rational phenomena, with all features well defined and quickly comprehensible, but by any standard the third wave constitutes a troublesome case. It possesses a quality of moral tantalization. Discussion of the fate of these escapees from a cruel regime seems to demand an invocation of our more heroic ethical categories; but the facts filling these categories often prove only average-sized. And though adjectives like *brave* and *noble* are appropriate, it's usually a low-grade bravery and a spasmodic nobility of purpose that is the most fitting description.

In short, the third wave seems continually to require us to make fine judgments, to separate the merely commendable from the truly admirable. Such discriminations can appear mean-minded under any circumstances, but especially so when executed by Americans living in comfort in a country whose ideology has enshrined the Soviet Union as an implacable enemy. Would that a straightforward calculus existed for measuring the categories of the third wave's moral journey!

Consider the category of politics. Though the third wave, virtually to a man, was at odds with the Soviet government, the degree of resistance varied widely. A few, the very brave, spoke out openly, risking imprisonment or worse. More, though by no means the majority, refused to cooperate in Party activities (which included everything from professional conferences to neighborhood cleanups), and they thereby jeopardized their careers. Most just went along day to day, grumbling quietly. Though simply living in the Soviet Union, with its awesome police apparatus, requires strength of character, the third wave cannot in the main be called freedom fighters. But because by departing they have thumbed their noses at the Soviet state, the urge to render them political homage is strong.

And consider the category of religion. A high percentage of the third-wave émigrés are Jews — Jews in hurried transit, and hence patently part of a long tradition of persecution. In today's Soviet Union, anti-Semitism is a fact of life, blocking careers, hindering entry to universities, occasionally excluding Jews from the black market deals that make the daily round bearable. But Soviet Jews are not fatally threatened, as a few Western organizations imply. The notorious "fifth point" on a Soviet passport, where most citizens declare their nationalities but a Jew must state his religion, is not equivalent to the Star of David that Jews had to sew on their garments in Nazi Germany. Though both practices are onerous, the distinction is worth making.

Given the ambiguity that attends the third wave's emigration, the shades of ethical values it ranges across, it might be expected that the émigrés would tread softly upon arrival in America, taking time to analyze their destiny. No. Apparently some sort of quantum theory of human action has influenced them: finally having made the decision to take the fateful step to emigrate, they moved to a new level of self-assurance, the earlier confusions about their motivations now crystallized into obdurate certainty. They thunder through America like knights upon a mission, beating out a loud tattoo of moral indignation. They claim, quite loudly too, that their odyssey portends the world's misfortune, that the third-wave emigration is the principal part of a skein of events leading to apocalypse. Look at its political implications, or its religious implications, or some other of its implications — and you will see your future, they immodestly declare, quite forgetful of how befogged these matters were at the start of their journey.

It's easy enough to extend a degree of sympathy to them, for they have suffered real hardship; but the third wave seems to be making more absolute claims on America's sensibilities, and that provokes resistance. A high-ranking administrator at one of the agencies that supervises the arrival of the émigrés told me, "They have raised a lot of hackles, caused a lot of irritation. After all, we're used to a humbler sort of immigrant."

I asked if the reaction was in any way justified.

"Of course if you think of the Soviets as a group, disregarding individual cases of tragedy, it is hard to see their plight as one of terrible suffering, as they want to imply. They have been mistreated, but nothing compared to the peoples of Southeast Asia or some countries in Latin America."

The man paused, looking thoughtfully out the window for a minute, as if history's morality might be decipherable in New York's skyline. "But really," he finally said, "isn't it a fatuous question to ask: who suffers most? As if we intended to dole out sympathy in exact proportion to the degree of suffering. The Soviet émigrés were in a bad situation; America advertised its sympathy. Now it's up to us to help those who took us up on that pledge."

It is a puzzle why the Soviet regime ever permitted the third-wave emigration to begin. Perhaps outraged world opinion was influential — though the Soviets routinely ignore world opinion when it suits their purposes. Perhaps incidents of protest in Moscow and Leningrad in the late 1960s and early 1970s persuaded the authorities to make concessions and thus avoid greater disturbances in the future — though the authorities have never hesitated to quell turmoil with force. Another possible explanation is more banal. One émigré mathematician told me that until recently ten of the top fifteen scholars in his speciality were in the Soviet Union, and now seven of these reside in the United States: he reasoned that first one of them was granted a visa by mistake, whereupon bureaucrats all over the country blindly assumed a new policy was in force and followed in step, like sheep.

The uncertainty about why the government permitted them to leave unsettles the third-wave émigrés, who are already uneasy about their motives for having wanted to go. That part of their psyche which should contain an explanation of their fate, painful but at least coherent, instead buzzes with nervous energy — long after they come to America they still seem to want to justify their emigration and define their oppressor.

Zhenya Novokovsky, a computer programmer from Leningrad, wanted to tell me *her* experience of leaving the Soviet Union: she was sure it would clear up any questions. In fact, she was somewhat atypical, being Russian Orthodox, though married to a Jew; but her very atypicality turned out to make a representative point.

I had come to know her through mutual friends, and had met her several times previously. Each time we went to a restaurant or bar, Zhenya complained of American meretriciousness and overkill. Studying one menu, she said, "Overstuffed sandwiches, king-sized drinks? Is this, then, a nation of giants?" To hear her story I took her to a dreary little delicatessen on lower Seventh Avenue, hoping the dirty floor and rickety chairs would calm her with memories of the way things had been in her native Leningrad.

After we sat down, she began, "You know, of course, that as soon as a Soviet citizen submits papers requesting a visa, he loses his job. That's not the law, but it's as inevitable as Lenin's portrait in a bureaucrat's office. An odd job may still turn up, perhaps in a remote district not yet caught up with the latest government bulletins, but don't count on that. You are reduced to living on savings or loans from friends.

"In one sense, unemployment is a blessing. Preparing to emigrate is itself a full-time occupation. Whole days are spent trudging around government offices. Soviet bureaucrats are in any case crude and insensitive, and if they are dealing with potential émigrés they add a dose of malice. For every document they approve, they declare two void."

Zhenya had the Russian habit of reliving the events she was relating. As she spoke, her manner pitched from the matter-of-fact to one of helpless anger, then recuperation and a new attack. All this in Russian, loudly uttered. Several times people at adjoining tables stopped eating and conversing to regard her performance, but Zhenya plunged grandly on.

"For six months after my husband and I put in our application for visas, we spent all our waking hours in government offices — to be precise, in the waiting rooms to government offices. They like you to think that an émigré's problems are not worth bothering about, though at the same time it is they who think up all sorts of documents to be signed and notarized.

"Finally we seemed to be coming to the end of it. One of the final tasks is having all your more valuable possessions examined to make sure you aren't making off with some national treasure. That can include anything from jewelry to old books. The regulations seem to change every day.

"I had a lovely set of old china, originally my grandmother's, which my mother had given me as a wedding gift. I brought it in so the authorities could take a look at it. The official in charge of the inspection was a particularly unpleasant woman, one of those *babas* whose only enjoyment is making people sweat a little. I saw that she would love to prevent me from taking the china with me. She guessed at once how much it meant to me. So she went through one book of regulations, then another, then the first again, looking for some excuse. Finally she seemed to give up. She took out a big rubber stamp; it said 'export permitted' or something like that, picked up one of my saucers, looked at it carefully — and brought down the stamp so hard that the dish broke into ten pieces.

"I wanted to cry. Instead I got angry, which surprised even me. I demanded to see her superior. She just looked at me coolly and said, 'If you have any complaints, when you get to your new home your rabbi there can write an official letter.' "

I asked Zhenya if the bureaucrat couldn't have easily seen from her passport that she wasn't Jewish.

Gathering her things as we prepared to leave, Zhenya shrugged her shoulders, a perfect replica of Chekhovian resignation. "One has to live in the Soviet Union for a few years to understand. Of course she knew I wasn't Jewish. When a Soviet bureaucrat wants to be unpleasant, he or she simply picks up whatever insult is nearest at hand. They don't care if it fits perfectly."

Indeed, especially in the earlier days of the emigration, the regime hardly bothered to check the religious background of those it permitted to depart. Anyone deemed expendable who had in hand an invitation from relatives in Israel — even if the invitation was obviously fraudulent, as many were — was allowed to leave. Non-Jews as well as Jews took advantage of the opportunity. In the eyes of the authorities, the category of Jewishness was extendable to include anyone who did not fit into Soviet society, pariahs all.

One has to credit the Soviet regime with a degree of ingenuity in this. The third-wave emigration presented them with a pressing political dilemma: how to expel a large group of citizens without compromising the myth of national coherence. The idea that life in the USSR is so fully gratifying that no inhabitant even contemplates leaving has been cultivated throughout Soviet history, sometimes to the point of madness — during World War II, the government resolutely ignored the existence of almost a million of its soldiers who had been captured by the Germans, insisting that any member of the Red Army would have died before giving up his person to a foreign power. To meet the difficulty of the third wave, the government simply transforms those who plan on emigrating into beings not truly Russian. By the time an émigré boards the plane for Vienna, official Russia views him or her merely as social debris impairing the nation's ability to function smoothly. Any more individualized characteristics are beneath notice.

The effect on the émigrés is to further cloud what should have been a decisive step. Many of those I met in America seemed to resent that they had been denied a true confrontation with the regime — it would have been more risky, perhaps, but at least it may have crystallized the issues of their emigration. As it is, they have to settle, like Zhenya, for a petty bureaucrat as the chief antagonist of their story. It's hard to construct vivid history out of such shabby material.

In most areas of the Western world nowadays, crossing a national border requires so little effort that the event is hardly noticeable, the precise moment hard to fix. Perhaps there is a tremor of resistance in the form of an impolite customs official, and then you are in a new country. Pre-Soviet Russia approximated this modern condition in effect if not intention. The borders were vast and the police inefficient. Even the most notorious subversives, from Nechaev to Lenin, moved easily on their conspiratorial rounds between the empire and the rest of Europe.

When the Iron Curtain descended in the 1930s, it was a special shock because it altered long-standing practice. In fact, the right of every Russian to travel abroad is written into the Soviet constitution, but that only makes actual circumstances more galling.

The very concept of travel, of visiting foreign parts and forgetting domestic concerns, is nonexistent. Only representatives of governmental policy get to go abroad. To most Soviet citizens, the national border appears an obdurate perimeter, virtually impermeable. It is not surprising that though the Iron Curtain has parted for them, the third-wave émigrés speak of the moment of their departure as a miraculous exodus, a Houdini-like escape from a sealed container.

But, curiously, they also often regard these moments with loathing, as if their triumph had been marred by unspeakable insults. Edward Topol, a journalist who emigrated in 1978, described Sheremetevo Airport in Moscow, which is the most popular embarkation point, in terms more fitting to an outpost of hell than an international terminal. He told me, "One eighty-year-old woman was kept running from official to official until she was ready to drop from exhaustion. Family heirlooms and keepsakes were routinely confiscated. My typewriter was intentionally damaged —not demolished, but just one key broken off, in order, I'm sure, that I should always remember Sheremetevo even after I was abroad."

"Was it so terrible?" I asked, thinking I'd perhaps missed something.

He paused, then answered in a tense rapid tone, as if reading off an indictment. "They pawed through every pair of pants, rapped the tops and bottoms of suitcases and slashed through them with a knife. A customs official took the dresses and underwear of the seven-year-old daughter of my sister and, lifting them high over the table, slowly felt through every strap and seam. My sister began to cry. 'I can't stand it,' she cried. 'Pawing and pulling out our underwear in front of everyone. What am I, a criminal?' And you ask if it was terrible."

Well, yes, surely a scene of discomfort and anxiety, but I still wonder if it was so terrible. The picture really does not, despite Topol's implications, rival Hieronymus Bosch. In one light, indeed, the events at Sheremetevo seem only a more intense example of the battle between passengers and customs officials the world over. No one is tortured, no one dies. If these were not Jews, trailing a centuries-old history of victimization, would we feel even a frisson of anger? If they were not fleeing Russia, archfoe of Western democracy, would their plight begin to compare with that of countless contemporary refugees, for whom toting a typewriter on their journey, even at the risk of having a key broken, is unthinkable extravagance?

And yet, paradoxically, the pathos of the third-wave émigrés may lie precisely in the absence of visible cruelty. They are pushed along their path for who knows what reasons of state. At times, the only rationale seems to be that letting people depart who want to depart will make Russia a little calmer, a little tidier. It's an expression of governmental power at its most abstract, with hardly an acknowledgment of an individual's ideas, his politics, his religion. Though the whining note in Topol's account is not attractive, it is understandable: when something unpleasant is being done to you, you want to be noticed, and if the authorities refuse to notice your nobler disagreements with them, you'll insist on the petty ones.

It made me think of my own experience at Sheremetevo, several years ago. I was enplaning for Vienna after ten months in Russia. Among my suitcases and bundles was a painting by Evgeny Rukhin, an artist whose abstract style had gotten him kicked out of the Union of Soviet Artists. Because of his unofficial status, I had not been able to secure the usual certificate from the Ministry of Culture that would attest to my ownership of the canvas, but Rukhin had told me not to worry, others before me had not been bothered. I was, however. When the painting was spotted, the rest of my luggage was minutely examined and I was marched off to a small room for questioning. Two dour officials sat behind a table; one of them briefly scrutinized Rukhin's fantasy of gauze, varnish, and paint, snorted in disdain, then told me to remove my jacket and shirt, both of which he patted carefully at all the seams.

Motioning at the painting, he said, "Do you know that nothing like this can be taken abroad without a certificate from the Ministry of Culture?"

"It was a gift, not a purchase," I said, falling back on the plan Rukhin had suggested for an emergency.

"Do you know the penalty for transporting anti-Soviet propaganda?"

I felt vulnerable standing half-naked among these buttoned-up officials, but the prospect of an esthetic quarrel revived me somewhat. "It's art, not propaganda, anyone can see that," I said.

The official ignored this and said, "There is a prison term for smuggling, you know. You have nothing hidden in your pants, do you?"

He balanced my passport in his hand, as if gauging its weight. During my stay, I had resisted taking advantage of the privileges that come with possession of a United States passport in Russia, such as access to specially stocked stores, use of restricted library holdings, even hard-to-get tickets to the ballet; it was disconcerting to benefit from an accident of citizenship, as if food and culture had been allocated on a geographical basis. In that little room at Sheremetev, however, I willingly attached my whole being to my passport: faced with the threat of a communist prison, I took my stand on the fact that I was a bona fide American.

Finally, as was to be expected, they let me go. The dictates of grand diplomacy took priority over my transgression; a provocative incident was not needed just then, and I was sent packing.

During the flight to Vienna I felt weak and nauseated. At the time I attributed this to airsickness aggravated by excitement, but now, after listening to third-wave émigrés discuss their departures, I think I detect another etiology. It's dizzying, I see, to have one's fate depend on citizenship. My esthetic opinion about the painting I carried, my views of Soviet life, even my Slavic ancestry — all this and more was completely irrelevant, absolutely weightless when balanced against the abstract, largely accidental fact that I was a citizen of the USA. As it happened, that one feature of my being was given its full measure, and it proved just sufficient for the occasion. The third-wave émigrés, who are stateless at the moment they pass through customs, having been stripped of Soviet citizenship and not yet having assumed their new country's, have not even a prepossessing passport to flaunt. They have only an elemental humanity, which it turns out is a quality easy to ignore.

Indeed, to hear third-wave émigrés talk, it sometimes seems that the evil of Soviet communism lay less in its ideology and politics and economic system than in its bureaucracy. The dictatorship of the proletariat disturbed them less than the scorn of administrators and clerks, and Trotsky's famous "dustbin of history" seems to have appeared a threat mainly as an avalanche of official forms waiting to be filled out. The émigrés' first disappointment with America is the discovery that we have our own bureaucracies.

Most of them encounter American life through the mediacy of NYANA, the New York Agency for New Americans, which provides the newcomers with a bit of material support. A family receives approximately $180 a month toward rent, and each individual approximately an additional $100 a month for expenses. But in return for this support, the third-wave émigré must submit to a whole arsenal of administrative methods and rules.

The bureaucratic onslaught is doubly disheartening because it contradicts the émigrés' idea of how foreigners in a new land are treated. Foreigners in today's Soviet Union stand out because there are so few of them, but they are made even more conspicuous by the red-carpet welcome they receive. A foreign passport, even one bearing the crest of archenemy America, secures its bearer all manner of privileges — and especially relief from the bureaucratic swamps that threaten to envelop the natives. When the Soviet émigrés come to America, they anticipate comparable freedom; instead they must again endure the inquisitiveness of clerks, serve time filling out questionnaires.

The depressing inference is that they may be unwanted guests, and in this context the amount of support they receive from

NYANA takes on new meaning. It measures the warmth of America's welcome and the wisdom of leaving Russia. NYANA's small and grimly furnished waiting room is a hotbed of intrigue and gossip, everyone gauging the amount of his or her allotment and trying to devise new ways to circumvent the regulations. It made sense that the door to the inner offices was kept locked, with a guard in front: some of the émigrés clearly had to be restrained from rushing in with a list of complaints, entreaties, demands. Beyond the door were two long corridors with some fifty small rooms off them, where the Russians met the social workers assigned to their cases. Walking down these corridors, I momentarily imagined that they pulsated, rocked by the power of fifty highly charged interviews compacted into fifty tiny cells.

It is remarkable that all this high drama was constituted by individuals lacking a common language. All communications between an émigré and a social worker passed through an interpreter; anger and disappointment were compressed into neutral tones while the main actors waited impatiently to resume their passionate discourse. I served several times as interpreter and tried to fulfill my duties in the prescribed manner, but it wasn't easy: the charade of cool efficiency we all engaged in threatened to be swept away by a flood of emotions, the Russians demanding more money, more attention, more America.

Mr. Jacobs had arrived from Odessa two months before, and he looked it. He had on the usual uniform of dark suit and white tieless shirt. He also indulged in the Russian male's one conventional stab at flamboyance, sandals over black socks. He was about thirty-five, balding, quickly going to fat on the unfamiliar American diet. But his eyes, which were vivid with apprehension, belied any complacency.

Mr. Jacobs had claimed an emergency, and his social worker had grudgingly granted him a special appointment. As we sat in her office while he was being summoned from the waiting room, she told me, "Watch out for this one. Last week he wanted me to help him get a driver's license. I told him, 'First, how about finding a job, then we can worry about luxuries.'"

The emergency concerned Mr. Jacobs's mother. Ever since she rode the subway from Brighton Beach to NYANA she has felt unwell, headaches and palpitations. She has stayed in bed for a month, Mr. Jacobs said, and now he wanted to know if NYANA would cover the costs if he gets her admitted to a hospital. The social worker was not ready to believe that an hour on the D train causes lasting harm; on the other hand, her profession implied humanitarian concern, and the old woman might in fact be suffering. Something of an impasse ensued, with most of the conversation devoted to a seemingly peripheral but nonetheless intense analysis of an émigré's right to seek a special appointment with his social worker.

Only at the end of the interview, as he was being maneuvered toward the door, did Mr. Jacobs manage to return to his prime concern. He says, "If I go to the hospital, who shall I ask for?"

"It's a hospital," he is told, "not a desert. You will see an information desk."

"And shall I take my mother in a taxi or an ambulance?"

"Mr. Jacobs, please remember, that nothing is free in this country. An ambulance costs seventy-five dollars; a taxi, of course, costs less." Then, perhaps struck by an altruistic spasm, the social worker turned to me and said, "Be sure to add that it is his decision, he knows his mother's condition. He only must remember that if he expects reimbursement, he must justify his expenses."

"Ask her," Mr. Jacobs responded in an aggrieved tone, "if I am supposed to set a value on my mother's health. Do they have a form for that too?"

"They think we give money away," the social worker said, now speaking more to me than to the client. The atmosphere of stern professionalism, which the social workers use to restrain the excitable Russians, was quickly dissipating.

"You're human," Mr. Jacobs told me. "Can you sit there and listen to such injustice?" He seemed to have slipped into a manner worthy of the great Russian novelists, and I was going to be assigned the role of outraged witness. "They are worse than Soviet bureaucrats, who at least make no pretense of helping, don't you see?"

In fact, most of the social workers at NYANA insisted they were not at all heartless, only justifiably cautious. They each could — and, at a drop of a hat, did — cite four cases of fraud to make their point. Tricked too often, the social workers finally resorted to enforcing all the rules to the letter, every case now miraculously open-and-shut. No pleas, not even tears, seemed to affect a decision about financial support. I saw one man denied the subway token he said he needed to get back to Brooklyn. "He's lying, he has plenty of money," the social worker whispered to me. "Look at his shoes, they're new and expensive." I looked, only later marveling at such investigative ingenuity.

The current state of antagonism was probably unavoidable, given the parties involved. The NYANA administrators, Masters of Social Work all, came to their jobs armed with courses on Freud and on Interpersonal Dynamics, and they tended to believe that the émigrés' happiness lay in attaining a blessed condition called "psychological adjustment." One report advised (with no apparent irony) that interviewers present a facade of sincerity, that they "interact informally, openly and enthusiastically with the clients . . . perhaps even sharing one's own experiences about job hunting and living in other cultures." Even office furniture could be made to imply sympathy. "Instead of the traditional decor of desks and hard chairs," the report suggested, "an office that contains a small couch and comfortable chairs arranged in a circle. Such a circular seating arrangement seems especially appropriate for those clients who, when seen in groups on the street, are usually talking in a circle, as if to form a natural barricade against dangerous intruders."

Such ministering strategies, alas, probably only compounded the difficulties. Russians don't like any stranger inquiring into motives or playing at psychology — "trying to crawl into another man's soul," as Gogol famously put it. Someone in an official capacity who tries to do so, especially in a solicitous manner, surely must be pursuing dark purposes.

If NYANA started with an inappropriate picture of the émigrés, the émigrés' assumptions about NYANA didn't advance good relations either. They considered themselves experts in dealing with bureaucracy, their wanderings through the dreary Soviet labyrinths having given them a chance to study the phenomenon close up. They learned how to squeeze out favors, muddle through. Though Soviet bureaucrats are terribly insensitive, they are also very corruptible — though communists, they are part of Russia's long tradition of an Asiatic style of governance, and consider bribery a way of life. When the third-wave émigrés arrived in America, they planned to deal with NYANA as they had dealt with the commissars. Peter Weil, the correspondent for the *Novy amerikanets*, told me, "They wanted to corrupt NYANA totally, an embroidered pillow here, an old samovar there, and everything would be agreed upon."

It didn't work out. Though American bureaucracies are not exemplars of virtue, they have their own styles, which it takes a while for a foreigner to master. The consequent frustration amidst the third wave runs deep and wide, touching even those who suffered greatly at the hands of the Soviet apparatus. Vladimir Bukovsky, who put in time in a Soviet prison (he came to the West in 1972 in exchange for the imprisoned Chilean Marxist Luis Corvalan), has recorded his comparison of the two bureaucratic systems, and his preference is less than clear-cut. "There [in the Soviet Union]," Bukovsky writes, "one could at least give a bribe or exploit a connection [*blat*], which as everyone knows is more powerful than drugs. Perhaps the same is possible here but we don't know how. Moreover, the Western bureaucrat has considerably more independence from his superiors — you don't scare him with [the threat of] complaints. There's no place to lodge a complaint, and no response to a complaint is required."

I interpreted at one interview at NYANA that stays in my mind as a symbol of the third wave's encounter with American bureaucracy. The plot unfolded in the usual manner — the Russian expressing extravagant emotions, the social worker coolly suspicious — but now pitched at a level of intensity that was startling. Mr. Gurev was from Leningrad, about twenty-five years old. The problem was his wife. She had persuaded him to emigrate, against his own better judgment and over the objections of his parents. But when they were safely in America, she had changed completely. She no longer cooked his meals, preferring to watch television all day, and she went out in clothes that would have led to arrest if worn on Nevsky Avenue. Finally she had insisted on a divorce.

"We had an orthodox divorce, because I know that is what my parents wanted. We went to a small synagogue, I'm not sure where. It was recommended by a friend. And for fifty dollars they did it, the rabbis. They held a scroll over her head, mumbled some words, and announced that she was free to go with any man that would have her. Two old rabbis I had never seen before, with beards covering their faces so that it was impossible to tell what they were thinking."

By the time he finished, Mr. Gurev was shouting, but then he immediately subsided into quiet sobbing. It was awkward in the small room, three strangers and one of them suddenly overcome by deep feeling. I hoped Mr. Gurev would resume speaking, and I think the social worker did also. Finally, he said, "And do you know, I didn't even have the fifty dollars they charged us. I had to get the divorce on credit."

With surprising celerity, the social worker spoke up. "Good. You will set aside a little bit from your salary each week as soon as you get a job. Soon you will have paid back the whole sum. Settling a debt will help your self-confidence."

Mr. Gurev, who had been holding his head in his hands, looked up in astonishment. It was hard to tell if he understood, even after I translated. For that matter, it was hard to tell if the social worker believed in her curious advice or was only forestalling a request for a cash advance. In any case, Mr. Gurev stood up, and like an orator addressing multitudes spread his arms over his head. Only he didn't speak; he merely offered his person as an exhibit, as if we should be able to understand his feelings by scrutinizing his pose. All he had, he seemed to say, was his own being, and it should be enough.

After a while, I longed to get beyond the bureaucratic swamps, to some point where America's welcome was undiluted by administrative rules and the new arrivals responded with pure gratitude. But, leaving aside the few instances of famous artists or political dissidents who arrive amidst much fanfare, such a point is not easy to locate nowadays. Since the third wave comes by plane, the traditional moment of immigrant ecstasy — the sighting of the Statue of Liberty — is altogether elided; and it seems that as soon as they ride in from Kennedy Airport, on the bland parkways and alongside the disheveled architecture of Queens, they become enveloped by our quotidien world. If there is a celebratory spark, it flares in unexpected circumstances, at odd times, occasionally after the émigré has been in this country for many months.

My friend Savely is from Moscow. A graduate student of literature there, he became a graduate student here. We used to walk the streets of the Upper West Side discussing the cruel destiny that had assigned him such an unsatisfying fate. As we promenaded, I tried to lighten his mood by pointing out the graces of his new neighborhood. He wasn't much impressed. Central Park was nice but lacked the amenities of Gorky Park; the evolution of Columbus Avenue, slum to chic, roused no interest; the motley crowd at Zabar's delicatessen, enflamed by gourmandizing fantasies, merely startled him. Nowhere did he feel at home: even on the best days, New York City appeared to him like a museum stocked with famous items he'd already read so much about that the originals inspired no curiosity.

One night he called me quite late to continue his complaint about the emptiness of the academic life. I suggested we go to a bar on Broadway, one of those establishments that enjoy a spasm of popularity and then drift along in a limbo of hope that good times will someday return. There was only one other patron at the bar, bent deeply over his drink and oblivious to the world, and the bartender gave us his full attention.

While pouring out our scotch-and-sodas, he declaimed in the time-honored style of his trade. "Can you believe it?" he said to Savely. "Last night there was a mugging almost outside our door."

Savely's English, acquired in Moscow U., is more than serviceable, but he only nodded.

Sufficiently encouraged to continue, the bartender added, "What are you going to do? Goes with the territory. Right?"

To which Savely responded, "Right!"

Subsequently, I learned from Savely, he began to frequent this bar regularly. It reached the point that the bartender would set his standard scotch-and-soda in front of him without being asked. He usually arrived late at night, when the bar was almost empty and the bartender had plenty of opportunity for conversation. As far as I could tell, it never went much beyond the formulaic phrases that I had heard them exchange, but Savely was hugely content. "I'm comfortable there," he told me happily.

In the institution of the neighborhood bar, Savely had finally discovered America's charm — and his case is instructive. Our age of bombastic nationalism has bred its own reaction, a distaste for emphatic cultural symbols; and the third wave, who endured the strident propaganda of the Soviet Union, are particularly suspicious of pomp. (In fact, it's just as well that their itinerary bypasses the Statue of Liberty, since they'd probably react with cynicism: they certainly did when I saw a group of them on an organized tour to Bedloe's Island.) But, by the same token, the third wave is alert to another aspect of our public realm, that ramshackle, unfinished quality that allows pockets of idiosyncrasy to exist quite apart from our proclaimed national myths — like that neighborhood bar, for example.

Indeed, by watching the third wave's response to their adopted country, one can begin to adumbrate a useful map of the public realms in America and the Soviet Union. When the émigrés blandly compare the bureaucracies of the two countries, refusing to register wholehearted approval of America's, we may at first be shocked, but should in time see their point. If our bureaucratic apparatus is infinitely more compassionate and responsive, still it is a bureaucracy, following the cool administrative logic of all bureaucracies. The best of America lies elsewhere, and is still discoverable by those who look. Under the Soviet Union's system of totalitarianism (which word, we should remember, implies an authority that envelops as well as terrorizes), getting beyond administrative rules takes ingenuity and luck, and is hardly achievable at all by the majority of citizens.

THREE
⚓ Making It

Ivan Turgenev was reflecting the opinion of many compatriots when he wrote, "In my view, the greatest poets of today are the Americans, who have pierced the Panama Isthmus and speak of establishing an electric telegraph across the Atlantic Ocean." That was in 1847, but the myth that in America material enterprises routinely achieve sublimity persists in today's Russia, only slightly vulgarized. In very few other nations does the image of American prosperity shimmer as brightly, undimmed by either the facts of our recent economic history or the blasts of Soviet propaganda. Soviet citizens refuse to be deterred from their belief: confronted with contrary evidence, they simply extrapolate to sustain their prejudices. One recent émigré told me that whenever *Pravda* printed photos of America's unemployed queueing up for welfare benefits, the gloating caption was ignored and everyone instead enviously scrutinized the modish clothes that capitalism provided to even its poor.

A hunger for goods and comforts runs rampant in Soviet society, thanks to the oddities of its economic history. Because of its emphasis on defense and industrial production, the Soviet Union achieved modernity without acquiring many of the conveniences of most modern societies; it has developed an economy that whets consumer appetites without yet being able to satisfy them. Thus, when the third-wave émigrés arrive in America, they come with fully primed material desires, with a grasping ambition that is unusual in our immigrant tradition.

But though there is little argument that these émigrés are eager to enter into capitalism's sweepstakes, there is some dispute about how well equipped they are to do so. Some social agencies believe that the attitudes to work which were developed in the Soviet Union are unsuitable for America, and must be changed. I heard that a vocational center serving Russians in New Jersey ran group meetings on this issue, sort of quasitherapy sessions about the mysteries of salary and accrued vacation time, and I decided to go and have a look.

In a small room furnished in a spare institutional style, three rather bewildered Russians were sitting around a table. At the head of the table stood the vocational counselor, an earnest young woman with the no-nonsense air of a nun. Behind her was a television camera and screen; at odd moments she pressed a button and an image of one of the émigrés would flash onto the screen. The aim was for them to see themselves in formalized action, thus instilling confidence for job interviews; but the effect seemed largely daunting, a doubling of their insufficiencies as they observed themselves struggling to put their thoughts into English.

The first question that the counselor asked was "What is more important to you, a job that is exciting or one that offers security?"

She was answered by a computer specialist from Moscow, a woman of about thirty-five and with such an energetic manner that she stood when she spoke, as if elevated by enthusiasm. "Security is not so important. I had a secure job in the Soviet Union and learned what that can cost. My area of specialization is called information retrieval and I worked for a computer research institute. Do you know what a research institute is in Russia?"

The counselor, to whom the question was addressed, kept silent, but the other Russians nodded happily, as if at an old joke they recognized. The woman then continued, "At an institute they let you do most of your work at home, coming in once or twice a month only. As long as we fulfilled our annual plan, our director was satisfied and let everyone alone. But in return for that sort of job we had some very unpleasant tasks. Every once in a while we had to review the journals and periodicals published that year. We were looking for ideological deviations. It was like being an informer."

The television lit up with the image of the woman's face, which was contorted by both the effort of speaking English and unpleasant memories. When she saw herself on the screen, the woman fell silent, subsiding into her seat. The counselor said, "Let me ask my question this way. Do you want your job to be satisfying, to give you personal pleasure and fulfillment?"

A statistician from Leningrad, in his late forties, answered. "In the Soviet Union, you don't speak of such things, they don't make sense. I had a good job, very good for the Soviet Union. But there were always problems with my supervisor. He was a Party member, I wasn't. He was always talking to me about American imperialism, saying that it made it necessary for us to fulfill — overfulfill — our Five Year Plan. I wanted to tell him to look around a bit and not believe all our propaganda. I would have preferred to leave that job, but if you leave a job, it goes on your record. You may eventually get another job, but it will be in a factory in the provinces or perhaps sweeping the streets. So I stayed, and worked without thinking about anything but my own tasks."

"But that's the way *everyone* works in Russia," exclaimed a vegetable store manager from Odessa. "Let me give you a good example. My wife and I went to a movie, and typically it was three and a half hours long and quite boring. That night I did not want to see again how the Red Army defeated Nazi Fascism. We get up to leave, we go out into the lobby — the door to the street is locked, bolted shut, and no one is around. A woman had the job of not letting anyone *in* during the performance. It was not her business if someone wanted to get *out*. So she locked the door and went off to have a beer. We had to watch the movie to the end."

The television screen, which was beginning to acquire a sinister aspect, now lit up again, bringing silence to the group. The counselor said, "So in Russia, you were not fulfilled by your job, you could not express your feelings in your work?"

The statistician said, "How can one talk of being fulfilled? In Russia there's always something to make you hate your job. If it wasn't the Five Year Plan, then it was a new directive from Brezhnev to work harder for the glory of communism. Or else a *subbotnik*. Do you know what a *subbotnik* is?" The counselor shook her head grudgingly, not wanting to lose any authority. "It's the voluntary work everyone does one Saturday a month, voluntary but required. The second Saturday of every month I had to report to a vegetable depot on the outskirts of Leningrad at four-thirty in the morning, dress up in old clothes and big rubber boots, and push around mountains of potatoes with a dirty shovel. It was supposed to show that in the Soviet Union even intellectuals do manual labor. Instead it showed me two things. One, that the potatoes in our cafeterias were probably filthy. Two, that some intellectuals have to take orders from other intellectuals, who at four-thirty on Saturday mornings are home in their warm beds."

The store manager said, "Don't worry, there are no *subbotniks* here in America, only these meetings."

Everyone laughed except the counselor. After the laughter had subsided, she looked up sternly and said, "Tell me, tell me honestly, how would it be if in a Russian marriage, the woman had a job and the man was unemployed? Would that cause friction?"

Silence greeted this question. The Russians stared morosely ahead. The counselor at last spoke up, taking another tack, a question about how much vacation time one could expect on an American job, and the discussion resumed its course.

Afterwards the counselor took me aside and said, "Russians *never* answer that question about the wife working and the husband not. They won't get into matters they think are too personal. They simply don't realize that some personal matters can affect one's professional success. They have no notion that they may have to sell themselves, since nothing like that was expected of them in the Soviet Union. Cultural differences!" Her voice dropped to a whisper. "I think I've heard it all when you come to so-called cultural differences. You know, for a while employers were calling me and saying that the Russians we were sending to them for jobs were unacceptable because they *smelled*. Apparently, they bathe on a different schedule in that culture than we do in ours. We finally had to begin to show films about hygiene to our groups. They were insulted, but it was for their own good."

But however many problems their hygienic practices cause, it's certain the émigrés' attitudes toward work cause more. They have come from a country where the concept of work was continually and insistently glorified by the regime. Especially during the early days of their rule, the Bolsehviks struggled to wrestle to earth some Platonic idea of labor, intending to make it the standard of each citizen's worth. Exertions that mankind had long despised as arduous and dull were to be transformed into something joyous, a balm for the spirit. It's a measure of the early Bolsheviks' audacity that they included in their canon of inspirational literature the novel *Cement*, the title of which refers not to some metaphorical bond but to the gritty stuff bricklayers use. (It is, by the way, not a bad book.)

Emigrés, almost to a man, insist that Russian history since 1917 is a series of abject failures to live up to the Revolution's proclaimed principles. Work has not been spiritualized. Indeed, under the dictatorship of the proletariat, labor appears more alienated than ever, because hopes were raised only to be dashed. "*Tashchi s zavoda dazhe gvozd / ved vy khozyain a ne gost*" ("Steal from the factory even the nails. / After all, you're the owner and not just a guest") runs one popular couplet, reflecting the bitterness of workers toward the false promises of communism.

Nevertheless, it cannot be said that the Bolshevik experiment has been entirely without effect. In today's Soviet Union the category of work has attained a remarkable distinctiveness, a shapeliness quite unlike its ragtag existence in most Western countries. To work means to fulfill certain precise requisites, to participate in definable civic tasks. The intense attention to the forms and meanings of labor have left an impression even on those who mock the official ethos most vigorously. A joke that was current recently in dissident circles in Russia goes like this. A new factory has been built that will convert double beds into triple-sized, so that everyone will be better able to live up to the slogan that is affixed to almost every billboard, "*Lenin vsegda s nami*" ("Lenin is always with us"). The laugh of course depends mainly on the image of Lenin's bald pate popping up from betwixt the sheets as lovers pursue their pleasures; but the joke would not work completely unless the listener also accepted the implication that Russia is a nation that routinely converts abstract principles into material processes. To instill such a belief was one of the early Bolsheviks' prime goals.

The air in today's Soviet Union is so thick with exhortations to participate in the national task that no one can ignore them. The public realm displays itself to the citizenry as a honeycomb of jobs: each cell must be filled by an energetic worker or the whole edifice will collapse. The jobs may be unproductive, or deadly boring, or the make-work scheme of a bureaucrat, but jobs there are. Every Soviet citizen is thus made subject to a nagging sense of obligation, even those who find the announcements of communism's glorious future to be pure sham. In a full-employment economy, it's not easy to stay home or go fishing.

The Russian culture of work may be summed up best in the status of older women, women who in America would be living idly or in some form of sequestration. Whenever snow falls in a Russian city, teams of women in their fifties or older, bundled up like Tsarist peasants, are out at dawn sweeping the streets with anachronistic birch brooms. At the foot of every escalator descending into a Russian subway it's an elderly woman who sits for hours at a stretch, on the alert for a mechanical breakdown. (It never comes, Russian subways being models of efficiency.) The throngs that assault the *garderobes* of public buildings, where everyone must check his coat even if entering for only sixty seconds, are placated by patient old women behind the counters. All these women look as if they should rather be home baking cookies for their grandchildren, and they might as well be. The jobs they do are the equivalent of light dusting: they keep the nation tidy and neat, but it's hardly crucial labor, or something that could not be done by a force a tenth their number if properly organized. But since everyone in Russia works, they work.

For a while, every time I saw one of these creatures battling dirt and disorder, I felt sympathy; but sympathy was probably inappropriate, as I learned one day when I saw an old woman at work on one of the more squalid battlefields, a busy public toilet in Leningrad. The stench of the place was stupefying. Instead of urinals there was only a large blank wall with a shallow trough along the bottom, against which a great press of men relieved themselves.

The woman, tiny and with Asiatic features, wandered along with a mop and a pail, trying to keep sanitary conditions above the level of the inner circles of Dante's Inferno. Her presence stunned me, practically halting me in the act of unzipping. Russians usually treat bodily functions with Victorian circumspection in public — a man asking for directions to the nearest toilet will whisper into another's ear as if disclosing a shameful secret, and euphemisms often have an impenetrable elaborateness ("I'm looking for the place where even the Tsar had to go on foot" totally befuddled me on first hearing). But the woman flung her mop around with vigor, oblivious to her surroundings.

Moved by her predicament, I smiled congenially at her as I exited. I think I believed that a sign of human warmth would help her get through the day. She was clearly taken aback; then her face contorted in anger and she yelled at me, as if responding to an insult. I retreated hurriedly, and for the rest of the day cursed the Russian character, incapable of recognizing kindness. But later, after thinking things through, I reconsidered. I had introduced emotions incongruously; the woman devised her day as a series of cut-and-dried mechanical tasks, and here was I cheerfully inviting her to recall that every life could have its joys. Perhaps her anger was justified.

In the Soviet Union, the realms of emotion and of work are absolutely distinct. The old woman in that Leningrad toilet, as indeed most Russians, merely sojourned in the workaday world, a displacement of the body which satisfied the regime's demand for labor but kept the spirit intact. Only at home or in the company of friends does one smile and get smiled at.

And how will people with such a history fare in the United States, the country that one of their authors has designated "The Government of United Smiles"? How will they fit into our late capitalist economy that puts a premium on congeniality, on employees, whether waiters, telephone operators, or corporate executives, who can tell clients to have a nice day and seem to mean it?

Somewhat surprisingly, the answers to these questions seem to be: quite well. A survey conducted by the University of Illinois found that about 75 percent of the men and 55 percent of the women have held at least one steady job since their arrival (and there's even some evidence that the women, at least, tend to stay at their jobs longer than their American counterparts). Such figures compare very favorably with those of other immigrant groups, past and present.

One factor contributing to the good performance is the third wave's high level of training. The Soviet Union, after all, is no underdeveloped banana republic; it has an efficient educational system and a complex economy. (One area in which the émigrés have done particularly well is our computer industry.) But technical knowledge cannot be the whole story; there must be some explanation of worker psychology: the third wave's background as part of the Soviet labor force should have handicapped them, rendered them unfit for the American eonomy, yet it did not. I wanted to know why.

There are so many differences between the idea of work in the United States and in the Soviet Union that talking to a third-wave émigré about the topic should best be accompanied by some sort of oral equivalent of footnotes, whereby alien terms and attitudes could be glossed while the main discussion unfolds. For example, in the Soviet Union, Anna Bor told me, she had been an engineer, and it struck her as unfair that she had been offered no work in her field in this country. But "engineer" may be the most prominent example of the Soviet habit of exaggerating job descriptions. It can connote everything from master builder to movie projectionist, and even the manager of a local grocery occasionally takes shelter under its stylish auspices. As a result, it was hard to judge the merit of Bor's complaint.

When she couldn't find the job she wanted, she went to work for a small firm in Manhattan's garment district. After five years as a seamstress on the assembly line, she has worked her way up to forelady, but it's still a grinding job. I met her just after she got off her shift. "At the end of the day I feel as exhausted as a Stakhanovite," she told me, referring to the shock-troop workers who set the Party's standard for labor in the Soviet Union.

I remarked that her invocation of this official symbol of communist labor to describe a job under capitalism might be taken to mean she was disappointed with America.

"To a degree. After the awfulness of the Soviet Union, I think I expected America to be a perfect opposite. For example, you know how there everyone keeps private feelings for friends and family, absolutely never showing them on the job. I thought my coworkers in America would be different. But though everyone smiles and chats about the weather, no truly personal matters are ever discussed. I was amazed — no one even bothered to ask why I had left the Soviet Union.

"For the first year on the job I walked around very serious, never smiling, because I was very nervous and had a lot to learn. One day a fellow came up to me and said, 'Why don't you ever smile?' To be funny I answered with the cliché, 'Life is hard.' I meant it as a joke, but the fellow took off like the wind, afraid I might burden him with my problems."

Bor is in her early forties, both her parents were killed during the Nazi invasion, her husband died while on a scientific expedition to Siberia — she's grown accustomed to the darker side of life and wasn't going impetuously to applaud American flash. When I asked her if her American salary hadn't noticeably improved her lot over what it had been in the Soviet Union, she smiled sourly and said, "As the Russian peasant said when asked how life was going, '*Nechevo — korovo u soseda cdokhnula: meloch nu chto-to.*' [Okay, my neighbor's cow died: it's not much but it's something.] Of course I get a fairly good salary, but I find I'm constantly comparing it with everyone else. When I was in Moscow, I thought getting a Ford would be marvelous, but when everyone else has a Cadillac it takes the pleasure away."

But, I said to her, you should think of it in a different light: you do get to buy more things in America, you do own more possessions than would have ever been possible in the Soviet Union, and it's thanks to your job.

"True, but I'm not sure how much *feelings* about work have changed. For example, there we had to steal on the job just to make ends meet. Here many émigrés continue to steal because they feel that's the only way to keep up in society. You know, we call the habit '*otstatki sotsializm,*' " she said, ironically alluding to the phrase *otstatki kapitalizm* [vestiges of capitalism] that Soviet bureaucrats use to explain away all problems of their young system.

"So," I said somewhat desperately," working in America is just like working in the Soviet Union."

"No," Bor said, "it's better, of course. But it's not paradise."

I was to encounter Bor's paradoxical blend of attitudes — simultaneously efficient in her job and dismissive about its psychic rewards — in so many émigrés that I began to wonder if that wasn't the best explanation of their success in America's workplace. The harsh experiences they had with their work in the Soviet Union prove beneficial here; not expecting any deep psychological returns from their job, they move with ease through our economy, on the alert for the best chance, taking on tasks others may consider too risky or too degrading. It is not that Russian émigrés have a weak sense of self-worth — even brief contact with them confirms that these are people with an amazingly powerful, even overbearing will. Rather, their personalities are so strong that it seems that any occupation (including, sometimes, living on welfare) suits them, since a job can only slightly alter their considerable self-esteem.

A passage in one of the most popular third-wave novels, *Eto Ya, Edichka* (*It's Me, Eddie*), by Edward Limonov, neatly encapsulates the attitudes of many of the émigrés. He is describing his job as a busboy:

> At seven o'clock there appeared the first customers — usually they were stiff, gray-haired men of middle age, who had come from the provinces for some sort of professional conference. I remember that from time to time all of us had a paper tag glued to the lapel of the red jacket of our uniforms, with something like the following inscribed: "Greetings, dear participants of the conference of pulp and paper producers: the personnel of the Hilton Hotel welcome you and invite you to have a traditional piece of the Big Apple. My name is — Edward."

Eddie does not feel in the least diminished by the circus-like aspects of his job — that side of life is trivial, as easily put aside as the tag the Hilton forces him to wear. His real, authentic existence lies elsewhere, in the realms of private sensibility. Paradoxically, Eddie's unconcern with the workaday world yields a practical reward, the freedom to exploit opportunities recklessly. As the mood takes him, he drops out altogether, or performs menial chores, or stumbles on a cozy sinecure. (The extreme example of how his aloof view of work propels him through our marketplace is his decision to become a male hustler: though he hardly comprehends the emotions or even the mechanics of homosexuality, he makes quite a success of it.) Eddie wants money, a slice of America's pie to sustain him as he pursues his personal dreams; he does not expect a job to give him "fulfillment." How different from the natives, who have encumbered their idea of work with the fancy rituals of "interpersonal relations."

Yuri Radzievsky was the first third-wave émigré to make a million dollars in America's business world, so his views about economic success have weight. He told me, "Though one naturally didn't know it, many of us had pretty good training for American life while we were in the Soviet Union. Life there is a survival trip, so you develop a hunter's instincts. If your refrigerator breaks down, there are no repair shops, no spare parts. You do what you can. If you want a car, it's pointless to go through official channels, since that takes years. So you find unofficial networks, figure out some barter arrangement, some black market deal. As a result of all this, a man finds he acquires entrepreneurial skills, even though he's living under communism."

In the Soviet Union he had been an engineer and, later, the host of a popular TV quiz show. He was not badly off materially, but still he felt he had to leave. "It was no life," he said, managing to imply with three words a whole world of constraints and misfortune, such that asking for details would have been impolite.

He arrived in America with his wife, young daughter, and very little money. He told me, "For a Russian newcomer to America there are traditionally two occupations — taxi driver and translator. Those who fail their driver's test go into translation."

For a while, Radzievsky struggled along as a low-paid translator for a large firm, but he soon hit upon a scheme that raised him well above the status of hired hand. Learning that the firm was about to bid on a substantial contract with an American manufacturer, he adroitly submitted a lower bid of his own. The client was impressed, but suspicious of the capacities of this new company of which he had never heard before — not surprisingly, since it as yet didn't exist. The client asked to inspect the offices, which caused a problem since Radzievsky had been negotiating out of a phone booth.

Radzievsky quickly rented premises in midtown, and with the help of friends painted the walls, toted in furniture, and installed an impressive-looking reference library of Russian books — all in twenty-four hours. (The reference library in fact consisted of Radzievsky's Tolstoy collection, but no American was likely to know the difference.) When the client arrived, the office was bustling with activity, secretaries at typewriters, administrators running between rooms with memoranda.

Radzievsky said, "The man was impressed all right — until he tried to use one of the phones and saw it had never been connected. The charade fell apart. But we still got the contract. He liked our energy and imagination."

From there it was success after success. Nowadays, Radzievsky is chairman of Euramerica Corp., which specializes in adapting advertising to foreign locales, for example suggesting that when "Drink Pepsi-Cola" appears on Soviet billboards it should fit into Russian's infernally intricate grammar. (In this case, Radzievsky's efforts went for nothing, since Pepsi-Cola ruled that its sacrosanct trademark would never succumb to the Russian accusative case.) We met in Euramerica's swank Fifth Avenue office, in a room guarded by a small platoon of secretaries and administrators. Seated in an oversized wingbacked chair, behind a prepossessing fortress of a desk, Radzievsky appeared at ease, just like any other captain of American industry indulging in a brief respite from his labors. He wore a natty suit of continental cut, exposing flashing white shirt cuffs, had neatly coiffed hair, and showed a remarkable mastery of the lingo of our business community. Only occasionally, when his faint Russian accent gave the trendy platitudes an unexpectedly gentle turn, did intimations of a whole other world appear.

I asked him to enlarge on the topic of the preparation Soviet society gave for entry into the American economy: it must have been, I said, quite a jump from backwardness to efficiency.

"Efficiency? We émigrés did, it is true, expect that America would be a highly efficient economy, like a perfectly tuned Swiss watch. But the reality is different." Radzievsky smiled, signaling a joke. "It's not chaos either, of course. Let's say, given the true powers in today's international market, that it's more like a Seiko watch."

I said, and what about the style of American business, had that been a surprise?

"At first I understood nothing of the way people communicate here. When I went looking for a job shortly after arriving and was told with a friendly smile, 'Don't call us, we'll call you,' I'd rush home to my wife and tell her I was on the verge of being hired. Only gradually did I get the hang of the way Americans feel obliged to mix polite gestures with their business life, a purely conventional friendliness.

"It still surprises me, in fact. I was recently walking with the vice president of Mack Trucks through their plant and a janitor yelled to him, 'Hey Joe, how's it going.' That sort of thing wouldn't fly in the Soviet Union, believe me. People at work have to conform to certain rules of behavior."

Is that better? I wanted to know.

"Better, worse, who knows? You can't say that the Soviet style gets more productivity out of the workers. Still I guess it's good for everybody to know that work means work, not fun and games."

Whereas, I ventured, off the job with friends and family, anything goes, the sky is the limit?

"Oh that," Radzievsky said. "The theory about the division between work and personal life which every American sociologist proclaims. But I suppose it is true that we Russians give great weight to friendship. Two weeks ago, a friend of mine called me up at two in the morning to ask if I could come over and help him park his new car in a space that was too small for him to maneuver into by himself. It didn't matter to him that I had an eight o'clock meeting that day. Talk about how much Russians demand from friends! I helped him, but grudgingly. I'm getting used to American ways."

No vestiges of your Soviet past? I asked.

"As you see," Radzievsky replied with a wan smile. "Mostly Americanized. Still, I admit, occasionally I need a dose of the old ways. To take a few bottles of vodka and go to some forest with friends, perhaps find some birch trees to remind us of home. Or go off to a Russian restaurant in Brighton Beach where I can take my tie off, drink till morning, get up with a microphone and sing."

As he said this he became more animated than at any time

during our conversation, but the excitement passed quickly. Perhaps the weight of those million American dollars was a drag on his Russian buoyancy. He said, "Those are the old ways, all right, but I now want them only very occasionally, and never two days in a row, thank you."

Radzievsky's remark about émigrés' affinity for the taxi-driving trade is hard to verify but appears likely to be correct. The occupation is something of a Russian émigré tradition, beginning in the 1920s when many deposed aristocrats and former White Army generals took the wheels of Parisian hacks. Vladimir Nabokov noted the phenomenon and expressed his generation's view of it in a line in *Lolita:* "There were thousands of them," he wrote of his first-wave émigré compatriots, "plying that fool's trade." The most buffoonish character in the book, an émigré forced to drive a cab to survive, is dubbed by Nabokov "Mr. Taxovich."

Among third-wave émigrés, there is less onus attached to the occupation, presumably because many of them are of humbler origins. Also, these émigrés construe driving a taxi as a single small step from owning one, which in today's New York City would mean getting a leg up on capitalism in a big way. Lyova Feldshtein has realized the common dream with resplendent flourish, since he now owns not one but three taxis.

I was early for our appointment at his base of operations, a storefront on Tenth Avenue which also served six other entrepreneurs like him. In the narrow room there was a single row of desks, with a minor magnate behind each, at work controlling his small empire and receiving petitions from drivers needing a day's work. Responding to my question, the man at one desk said, "Lyova? You mean Leon? He'll be right back, he went to get something to drink."

Apparently as a concession to Americans' inability to get their tongues around the Russian language's thickly palatalized vowels, Lyova had Westernized his name, and when he entered a minute later I saw he had Westernized his person also, from his cowboy boots and designer jeans to the bottle of Perrier he held in his hand. He was so much at ease in his role, in fact, that he could not comprehend why anyone should care to discuss it.

But I pressed on. I had heard persistent rumors of arcane fiscal maneuvers by third-wave émigrés, wonderfully profitable sleight-of-hand transactions, and I wondered if I didn't have an example of these practices in front of me. (One common variation is for an émigré to leave his accumulated rubles with individuals in the Soviet Union who have relatives in the United States, the latter paying off in dollars when the émigré arrives here: because there are so few items on which to spend money in the USSR, some of the émigrés built up quite a nest egg, and even at the black market rate of seven rubles to the dollar they could look forward to a nice sum when they arrived in this country.)

I asked Feldshtein how he managed to acqure the money to buy a hack medallion so quickly. His answer was disarmingly simple. "Some luck," he said, "and some hard work."

A typical American success story? I asked.

"I don't know what is typical for America," he answered laconically.

Still searching for a sociological nugget, I said that perhaps he had managed so well by relying on experience gained in the Soviet Union.

"Hardly. I was an engineer there," he said — which comment at least invited me to look at still another instance of that remarkably capacious Soviet category.

In general, however, Feldshtein was disinclined to make himself an object of ethnographic curiosity. All memories of anxious peregrinations seemed to have been replaced in him by the calm belief that his present situation was as natural as the sunrise. In this, he may have been a symbol of the third wave's future, when their Soviet past will have assumed the manageable status of legend, instead of continually pricking them into doubt and irritation; but for now he was too atypical to be of much interest to me, and I made ready to leave.

Just then a driver passed by on his way to the back of the

office, and Feldshtein pulled him in by the elbow. "Here is a better source of information," he said. "Mark Lansky, genuine Russian taxi driver."

Lansky was large, swarthy, and mustachioed, a sort of overstuffed Omar Sharif. He was wearing a blue sweatsuit — the uniform, in fact, that virtually every man in the Soviet Union dons upon returning home in the evening, to save wear and tear on regular clothes. The third wave must have been delighted to discover that their lounging gear was in high fashion here, but there's some vestigial embarrassment about displaying in public what was formerly strictly dishabille, and Lansky primly buttoned up his covering raincoat when he stopped to talk.

"I like driving here. A taxi driver sets his own hours and doesn't have to report to any *khozyain*," he said, using that roomy Russian word that encompasses everything from landlord to capitalist boss. "Of course the hours are long and there are dangers. A friend of mine was robbed and shot in the mouth by a fare. You have to develop an instinct for whom to pick up."

What are the guidelines? I wanted to know.

"You look at a person's clothes, at the way he signals for you to stop, that sort of thing. And then," Lansky said, adding a sly grin, "then you try to calculate your affinity with his ethnic group."

Rousing himself from his silence, Feldshtein interjected, "That's a fine approach, of course, except one shouldn't forget that Russian émigrés themselves are not such wonderful fares. They think they own the world."

Lansky considered this information for a moment, then said, "That's probably true. A week ago a guy got into my cab and without even hesitating announces his destination in Russian. I say, 'How did you know that I understood Russian?' He answers, 'I didn't, but it's the only language I know, so I took a chance.' Actually, with the number of Russian cabbies these days, his odds were pretty good."

I asked if driving a cab here is different than in the Soviet Union, in terms of the respect a driver gets from his fares.

"What a question!" Feldshtein exclaimed, and made a show

of withdrawing again from the conversation, going back to reckoning his accounts.

"It *is* an interesting question," Lansky said, adjusting his heavy features into an approximation of thoughtfulness. "For example, yesterday a young woman gets into my cab and immediately lights up a cigarette. I point out the 'no smoking' sign. She says she'll open the window. I say, no, it's raining. Finally she shouts, 'I paid to ride; I'll do as I like.' In the Soviet Union a passenger would never light up without politely asking permission. Passengers treat drivers as equals, not as their servants. That's why they always prefer to sit up in the front seat, instead of riding behind like some lord."

And tips, I asked, how do they compare?

Without bothering to look up from his papers, Feldshtein announced, "Better here, definitely."

"Depends on how you look at it," Lansky said slowly, not willing to dismiss the issue too facilely. "In the Soviet Union there are a lot of people who won't give anything, since legally you are not supposed to. But there are also quite a lot of people with loose cash in their pockets and nothing much to spend it on, so sometimes you get quite a grand tip. In America, aside from some out-of-towners who don't know better, there is pretty much a fixed scale to tipping. It's OK, average, but nothing to get rich on. After all, who rides taxis here? The wealthy have their limousines, the poor ride the subway. Taxi riders are the middle class, with their bourgeois habits."

As I left I thought: apparently Marx was right — always trust the worker and not the owner to provide the best analysis of capitalist relations.

The third-wave émigrés have virtually taken over the Brighton Beach area of Brooklyn, and have given it a new distinctive stamp. Walking down Coney Island Avenue on a bright day, one is assaulted by the noises and smells of a robust mercantilism, of capitalism in its ascendent phase. Fish vendors display their glossy catch on the backs of pickup trucks, clothiers push racks out onto the sidewalk to free up their crowded stores; everywhere merchants haggle vigorously with buyers, unashamedly eager for the sweet sound of coin slapping against palm. It's like a frontier town on the make.

From one end of the five-block stretch to the other, Russian merchants now own the stores. The culture of the neighborhood's older Jewish residents lives on at a few odd spots — for example, Mrs. Stahl's knish store, reputedly the best in town — but mostly it's Russian services and even Russian goods, offered by Russian-speaking tradesmen. The restaurants and gaudy nightclubs have Russian names and offer Russian fare, and often indulge the Russian practice of making a customer wait an hour for his meal. The Black Sea Book Store stocks Russian books exclusively: the esthete Nabokov and the political firebrand Solzhenitsyn compose a curious duo in the display window, evidence that here, at least, the category of Russianness can transcend all differences.

The grocery store on one corner neatly measures the sea change of culture that has taken place: it previously belonged to the family of Marv Albert, a local TV sports announcer given to faddish suits and Jewish–New York–style wisecracks, but now it retails *prostokvasha* and *kefir* and other delicacies for the Russian palate.

In his office in the Coney Island Bank, the head of the Brighton Beach Board of Trade told me, "The arrival of the émigrés improved the neighborhood immensely. They have invested over one and half million dollars in commercial enterprises, and all the property values have shot way up. I've been here long enough to know something of the history of this area, and I can tell you it was dying. Now things are beginning to look up.

"Russians are hardworking. I see some of them opening their stores at six-thirty in the morning, sweeping off the sidewalks. They put in a full day, and they don't take no crap. If any riffraff comes in, shoplifting or any of that, the Russians really go after them.

"But it's not all good. They are very clannish. It's Russians for Russians. They hardly bother catering to Americans. In some stores, if a customer can't make himself understood in Russian, he won't be waited upon. We've tried to bring Russian merchants into the Board of Trade, but so far without success. They're suspicious of any organization. It reminds them of communism, Party meetings, that sort of thing. We've got to get them to work with the older merchants, but so far it's no go, and we're suffering economically."

That's the view of the *ancien régime* of Brighton Beach, the class in retreat before the onslaught of the émigrés, but it's not the whole picture. In an émigré-owned coffee shop, where I stopped for a cup of soup, two other aspects of the Russian adventure in American capitalism were on exhibit. At a table near the door three middle-aged men discussed their prospects, planning an escape from the taxi driver's trade. They had been tailors in Odessa, they would be tailors here, but on a broader, more American-sized, scale. It would be necessary to rent premises for a factory, and buying a truck or two to transport material was not out of the question. Licenses, tax regulations, and union rules were acknowledged facts, but the intricacies surrounding them could be mastered ad hoc, once the ball got rolling. Capital for an initial investment? Perhaps they could advertise. It was an interesting spectacle, entrepreneurial energy with virtually no knowledge of America's entrepreneurial system. Life in the Soviet Union had fostered capitalistic dreams but had provided little concrete experience that would help in realizing them.

Behind the counter was the second panel of the diptych that could have been entitled "The Innocents Encounter the Dollar Economy." The proprietress, a fiercely red-haired woman in her forties, was conducting business in a way that recalled the inept style of comparable Soviet establishments. One sale was lost because there was no opener to uncap a bottle of juice; when paying the bill, another customer had to accept an unwanted candy bar in lieu of change that was not available. I half expected to see that fixture of Soviet stores, an abacus for reckoning payments — many shopkeepers there, after all, are only a generation removed from life on the farm. The abacus was absent, but the proprietress had brought along the typical mien of Soviet shopkeepers, which is to imply that every transaction is an annoyance, every customer an intrusion.

The style of service had evidently led to less than great commercial success, for the proprietress was complaining to anyone who would listen about the state of her business. The day before, moreover, the Board of Health had cited the premises for violations, and today the mortgage was due. Her husband, who should be helping her, instead had taken to mocking her openly, thus driving away the few customers who did wander in. The woman's tone was mordantly quiet, but occasionally she let loose some notes of operatic shrillness. In the middle of one such aria she abruptly stopped herself, walked to the phone on the wall, and proceeded to place in the local newspaper an advertisement to sell the shop. Presumably she had been considering the action for a while, but it appeared like sheer impulse — a sudden, total abdication of concern with mundane detail, the legendary Russian leap into the existential abyss. The three men discussing their tailoring business might have taken the woman's defeat at the hands of American capitalism as a cautionary lesson, but they paid her no mind.

Walking back toward Coney Island Avenue, I struck up a conversation with the cop on the beat, asking how he found the neighborhood had changed since the émigrés arrived.

He said, "Before I was on duty in Bedford-Stuyvesant, so this is like a holiday for me."

Is there much crime? I asked, still pursuing the question of occupations under capitalism.

"There is a Russian Mafia forming already, though it's hard to know exactly who is involved and what is getting done. These people learned pretty well in Russia how to live outside the existing system."

Could he define the character of the people? I asked.

"These days a New York cop has to be more sociologist than police officer," he assured me. "First of all, I have to say I like the Russians. I admire them. It's true that Friday and Saturday nights things get a bit wild, drunken brawls in the streets, knifings in their nightclubs, but I accept that. These people work hard all week, some of them twelve, thirteen hours a day. They're ambitious, out for the buck, and if that means they're cutting corners a bit, doing things slightly illegally, still you have to like their energy. When the weekend comes around, they want to relax, let off steam — and they know how to do it. I may worry whether a meal costs fifteen or twenty dollars. They go for broke, spending as if there were no tomorrow. Then Monday comes along and they're back on the job, in some factory or selling fake driver's licenses, whatever."

This description of the émigrés had a faintly familiar ring — give or take a few details, such as vodka instead of whiskey, didn't it evoke images out of our own history, when our entrepreneurial and acquisitive spirit was at flood tide? America has settled down since then, constraining its old buccaneering energies under heavy layers of "life-styles," sublimating naked desire for goods and comforts into strategies to pamper the "self." Émigrés, so far, mainly want money. The simplicity of their goal may help them to achieve it. They will ignore our culture's gauzy and embroidered explanations of what it takes to lead a satisfying life and head right for the gold. There are bound to be failures among them, but the Soviet system has, completely unwittingly of course, created a personality type that has a powerful edge in the American marketplace.

It is indeed tempting to assume that whatever occupational difficulties the émigrés face at the moment, they must all have made the right choice in coming to America: how could they not be better off than in the Soviet Union, where everyone's job was low-paying and as boring as the Siberian tundra? But though this rule of thumb applies in most cases, it is not universally true. Soviet society does work, after all, if not smoothly, at least adequately, and not simply because the populace is driven by terror. That wouldn't keep the lid on rebellion for very long, even granting the regime's brute strength. Soviet society functions because it offers its citizens jobs that satisfy their needs — in most cases, only barely, but for some considerably more than that.

Many Soviet scholars, for example, lead a good life. They receive good pay, enough to put them in the upper economic brackets, and they command general respect. Even shopgirls, who are rude on principle, treat them with the deference shown a priest in Rome. Equally gratifying, scholars participate in a vibrant intellectual community. Certain topics of inquiry come covered with an impenetrable Marxist-Leninist goo, and others are out of bounds altogether, but the remaining area is often explored with zest and with the conviction that the discoveries matter. Even among humanists and social scientists, there is little of that feeling of irrelevance which haunts American campuses.

A Soviet émigré scholar expects to find at least as much pleasure in pursuing his career in America, and his hopes at first glance appear entirely reasonable. Knowledge is universal coin, after all, and America has signaled its eagerness to get in on the bidding. In 1974 the Program for Soviet Emigré Scholars was established with the help of a grant from the Ford Foundation. Its aim, as stated in the annual report, was "to prevent as far as possible the loss of talents and skills of the Soviet émigrés" — presumably for America's benefit as well as the émigrés'. But, though there have been individual successes, the high hopes attending the program's inceptions have faded. American universities have not found a reserve of grateful and capable workers. And many émigrés have soured on America's academia, deeming it mean-spirited and culturally barren. (The last complaint comes especially from émigrés in the "hard" sciences: in the Soviet Union, these fields attracted the most intellectually inquisitive, since Marxist-Leninist dogma could not easily penetrate there — while in the United States, these people argue, most students of science have very narrow interests.)

The Ford Foundation, perhaps unhappy at not backing a winner, has withdrawn support, and the program now operates out of offices on lower Lexington Avenue which are just a cut above shabby. Mary Mackler has the title of Executive Secretary, but except for one bored receptionist, she is the whole show. A cheerful, informal woman in her forties, she breezed in fifteen minutes late for our appointment, exclaiming in mock horror about the midtown crowds that had impeded her progress at every step. After we settled down in her small office and she took out her lunch from her briefcase — graciously offering me an apple — she related her experiences with the program.

Apparently, the difficulties the émigré scholars face in America are only partly the result of peculiarities in the substance of their education: the style they are used to also is an obstacle. In the Soviet Union, the formal proprieties of East European academe obtain, and émigrés are startled by that casualness on American campuses among colleagues and between professors and students which keeps our university life bubbling along at typically moderate heat. University life in the Soviet Union is hierarchical, almost medievally so. To advance, one needs a mentor to whom one defers in all things; once up a few rungs on the ladder of one's career, one becomes a mentor also, with respectful underlings of one's own. The hearty give-and-take of American professors, that democratic bonhomie that disguises ambitious urges, is a manner that Soviet scholars generally have difficulty comprehending. Point them to the source of power, they say, so they can orient themselves accordingly.

Mary Mackler remarked, "They are all sure they deserve good jobs right away, of course, and if they are told that none is available, they say to me, 'Perhaps you should talk to the chairman, or the president of the college.' To get a job in the Soviet Union, you went to the most powerful man you could reach, so it must be the same here."

The group of émigré scholars for whom it is easiest to find positions in American universities has been, not surprisingly, mathematicians. They work on a level of knowledge that allows them to skip lightly over national borders; a Soviet mathematician and his American counterpart share a language long before they learn to chat about the weather. Only slightly more difficult to place are the natural scientists. The Soviet Union lags in the development of the practical tools of these disciplines, laboratory equipment and the like, so there is a period of adjustment for émigré scientists coming to America. By and large, however, it's a relatively easy transition. The only question regarding all these scholars, indeed, is why the Soviet Union allowed them to leave in the first place.

By contrast, émigrés who work in the social sciences have great difficulty adjusting to the American intellectual community. Their fields were most corrupted by the dogmas of Marxist-Leninism. The intellectual task of many of these individuals was only to repeat in new phrases explanations of social phenomena that were already contained in Communism's Holy Writ. Even those who resisted the Party line while in the Soviet Union arrive with a distorted perspective — after all, if an aborigine rejects the tribal totem, he becomes not a freethinker but an antitotemist.

Then there are the engineers, that extraordinary Soviet group. Like members of some ragtag provincial army, they often display the insignia of authority without having the training that should go with it. And even when they prove to be bona fide engineers in the Western sense, émigrés find adjusting to America difficult. The Eastern Bloc nations have a set of measurements and specifications uniquely their own. This is good military strategy, since an invading force will have its rolling stock clang to a halt on the Soviet railways and will find no spare parts for its machines. The émigrés, traveling in the other direction, suffer their own sorts of difficulties as a result of the incongruities. Though the Soviet regime could not have anticipated this result, it is doubtless happy to be able to reach beyond its borders to continue to annoy its former citizens.

Finally there is one more group of émigré scholars, whose encounters with the American academic community have been so awkward and abrasive that I had already had occasion to witness the resulting sparks. These are the Slavists and the historians, experts on the Soviet Union's cultural life, and, as such, individuals who often think of themselves less as scholars bearing information than as witnesses or even embodiments of the facts they profess. When a historian describes the GULAG, he may be describing what had been his home; when a linguist analyzes the harmonies of the language, examples of Russian in its purest form come out of his mouth; when an émigré professor of literature recites Pushkin, his sensibility resonates with the lyrics as can that of no American professor of Russian literature. No longer simply votaries of Russian culture, émigré Slavists and historians occasionally think of themselves as halfway to godhead. Consequently, if they are not offered a job in an American university, many feel that more than their intellectual credentials are being questioned: their very being has not received the respect it deserves.

I met Igor Komorsky a few weeks after visiting the offices of the Program for Soviet Emigré Scholars. In Moscow he had been a successful author, writing prolifically about Soviet culture, and he expected to get an academic position in America which matched his talent and experience. It hasn't worked out. When I visited him in his Brooklyn apartment, he said, "More than one American professor has come to sit in that chair where you are sitting. They come to ask me all sorts of questions about the Soviet Union. Of course, because I *know* the Soviet Union. But though they keep coming, not one has offered me a job."

Komorsky is well into his fifties, a scholar (as attested by his well-stocked library in the den where we sat), and with aristocratic manners, but he is hardly sedate. He seemed constantly to be suppressing some explosive urge. Even when sitting, his bearing was reminiscent of a soldier on parade, and his eyes fixed a guest with a steady stare, sentries on alert for attacks and transgressions.

He announced, "Instead of a job in a university, I work as a loader in a warehouse. Every day I put in eight hours of hard physical labor, then come back here to write."

His tone was designed to forestall sympathy, but he appraised my reaction nonetheless: having mapped out the coordinates of America's injustice, he seemed curious to determine exactly how far my citizenship had carried me into the enemy camp. In that small room lined with learned tomes and looking out over a dreary shaftway, there seemed to be an atmosphere of heightened meaning, every slight gesture scrutizined for marks of hostility. Even his wife, who entered to deposit a tray of tea and cakes, moved apprehensively. When I put two spoonfuls of sugar into my cup, I felt Komorsky scorning my weakness of character.

He said, "When I first came out of the Soviet Union, I was asked what I liked about the West, and I answered: the politeness of the policemen and the availability of Xerox machines. I thought, what else does a writer need except freedom from the intrusions of the state and the possibility of reproducing one's manuscripts? But I didn't realize I would be given no way to support myself except by doing manual labor."

Komorsky pushed a plate of candies in my direction, as if it were a chess piece probing an opponent's defenses. When I picked up a chocolate, he nodded as if registering a fatal chink in my armor, then resumed talking. "Perhaps," he said, "if I were more of a diplomat, more ingratiating, I would get the job I deserve. But I am an honest man. If someone deserves to be scolded, I scold him. If someone deserves to be criticized, I criticize. A man must do what is right."

He poured me a second cup of tea, ignoring my protestations. He said, "If necessary, I will continue to work as I am working now, in order to support myself and my wife. A woman leans on a man, and a man must be strong. That is a biological law. I am not going to be like those American men who let their women work while they stay home washing the dishes and sweeping the floors."

Komorsky is now writing a book about the ideological role of sports in the Soviet Union. He read me a portion he had completed that day, about the rigors imposed on preadolescent gymnasts.

"Do you think an American professor could know anything about these matters?" he demanded. "But they are the ones who teach these subjects while I work as a loader."

When I reached the street a half hour later, the New York sky looked unusually immense, my reaction, no doubt, to having been crammed into a small room and jostled by an imperious ego. Komorsky is an extreme case, to be sure, but his attitudes nonetheless say something about a significant fraction of those émigrés trying to participate in the American economy. This is a fine country for the majority, who were thoroughly dissatisfied in the Soviet Union, working at jobs that hardly engaged their attention, let alone their interest: contemporary America, with a workplace that provides a panoply of roles, jobs of every description for those willing to bend and fit into the available niches, seems a golden opportunity. But for the émigrés who had a measure of occupational satisfaction in the Soviet Union, America appears as a cruel joke. Like Komorsky, they must often perform jobs that distort who they really are, follow a daily round that keeps reminding them that their authentic selves — that shapely Russian soul nurtured over centuries of hard effort — must get its sustenance elsewhere.

The question is: where?

My friends Regina and Dmitry Frydberg intended to celebrate the end of the workweek, and they invited me to join them for dinner at a restaurant. They both hold down responsible and well-paid positions — he's a mathematician, she's a computer specialist — and they work hard, often staying past closing time. Comes the weekend, they like to reap the rewards of their labor. As Regina told me more than once, "All work and no play makes Ivan a dull boy."

As we drove to our destination, pressed together in the front seat of Dmitry's pride and joy — a new Oldsmobile (with Turbodrive!) — I proclaimed my determination to exploit the moment by interviewing them about the idea of work: since we had covered that ground twice before, they groaned in mock horror, and Dmitry added that he'd prefer to discuss the merits of his power steering. But finally they acquiesced.

Dmitry said, "Really, many of the problems of adjustment are purely technical. Regina and I both worked on computers in the Soviet Union, so we thought we were well prepared. In fact, we had to spend months retraining. Compared with American computers, the Soviet ones are prehistoric, virtually dinosaurs."

Regina said, "But it's not *only* technical. It took me a long time to become accustomed to the way work is organized in my company. In Moscow, when I was working on a project, I had to check with my superior at every step, five or six times a day. Here I may not see my superior all week. At first it was really frightening. I kept hoping someone would appear to tell me what to do next."

Braking robustly as we came to a traffic light, Dmitry said, "Yes, but you get used to such things soon enough. An adaptable people, we Russians."

"That's true enough," Regina responded. "But some things still astound me, and will always. The way everyone at my job keeps saying, 'Enjoy!' I leave for lunch, my secretary says, 'Enjoy!' When my boss gives me my paycheck, he says, 'Enjoy!' When a colleague gives me a new project, he says, 'Enjoy!' What an idea, this hope for constant enjoyment! Russians know you are put on this earth for two things — to suffer and to die. If you find occasional pleasure, it's through luck and hard effort."

"Well, then, onward with the quest!" Dmitry exclaimed happily, accelerating so quickly when the light turned green that the tires screeched. He took the curves of the Central Park transverse road in Grand Prix style and even managed to cut off one abashed taxicab on Amsterdam Avenue, all the time keeping up a grandiloquent commentary on his driving skills. By the time we reached the restaurant and tumbled out of the car, our mood verged on hilarity. Russians have a real talent for enjoying themselves, treading a fine line that divides merely toying with social proprieties from absolute chaos — on this night, Dmitry seemed to be striving for a condition roughly comparable to an uproarious rugby scrimmage.

Regina had invited another émigré to join us, but our party actually expanded by four. The woman had brought along her two teenaged daughters, who in turn had invited one of their boyfriends. We entered noisily, like an invading army bent on plunder. Dmitry grandly demanded the best table, though in fact all the tables of this informal establishment were equally unprepossessing. His irony may not have been apparent to all, and we were seated, instead, at a table cramped up against the kitchen door. If this was a slight, it passed unnoticed by the members of our party — they were too rollickingly determined on having a good time.

Dmitry bid the various courses (including, in one case, dessert) be brought to the table simultaneously, prompting an enthusiastic sharing of dishes. With the vodka flowing freely, and everyone talking loudly and even occasionally singing, we soon resembled revelers around some knight's sumptuous medieval table in old *Rus*.

When a waiter approached to replenish our supply of vodka, Dmitry grabbed him by the arm and offered the following bit of instruction. "Do you know that for purposes of export the Soviet vodka industry manufactures bottles with conventionally grooved necks, which permit the cover to be screwed on and off? But for the domestic market" — here he paused dramatically — "for the domestic market, the bottles are made with smooth necks, so that once the cap is off it cannot be put back on. And really, why bother? Can you imagine that a Russian would not finish off his vodka to the last drop?"

So it went, for more hours than I care to remember. When we finally staggered out of the restaurant and onto the sidewalk, I only hoped I could make it back to the comfort of my bed without mishap. I was naturally amazed when Dmitry proposed that all of us return to his apartment for "more drinking and singing and discussing the meaning of life."

"The night is young!" he exclaimed. "We have to make full use of the hours we have before we return to our dreary labors on Monday morning."

The evening, when it was finally over, left me with a gigantic hangover, but also with a new perspective on the question that had been nagging me. In our society money still talks, and the émigrés are more than willing to listen, but have they really been taken in completely by capitalism's intricate spiel? In fact, though

America's perennial grindstone — pursuit of cash, nourishment of ambitition — has polished some of the émigrés' rough Slavic edges and fitted them to our society's available niches, it has not totally worn away their old ways. The Russian soul countenances our workaday world; but it rouses itself to vibrant flight only in after-hours America, replenishing itself through pleasures very like those that existed in Moscow and Leningrad.

FOUR

❧ Public Institutions

On a cold and blustery December evening, my émigré friend Misha and I set out in the taxi he had recently been licensed to drive. We were bound for Brooklyn via the East Side Drive, to sample the nightlife of Brighton Beach. The excursion had a special air of adventure because Misha was behind the wheel illegally: his insurance did not cover off-duty trips. Suddenly the car in front of his braked to a halt, to avoid an aluminum lamp pole that the wind had deposited onto the highway. Misha drives with the erratic nonchalance of many third-wave émigrés, for whom a car is simultaneously a giddy capitalist dream come true and no more than a just reward for choosing America — and so he didn't come close to stopping in time. We demolished a Volkswagen and inflicted a grievous wound on an elegant Oldsmobile.

When, several weeks later, Misha's case was called in Manhattan's Small Claims Court, he asked me to accompany him. He was not certain that his English would bear up under the weighty legalisms he expected to have hurled at him. More important, he said, the prospect of entering an American hall of law, all proceedings fixed according to impersonal codes and rules, was daunting. It brought back memories of the Soviet Union's brisk forms of justice and of a lifetime trying to avoid the attention of authorities. When we entered the large hall, which was packed with row upon row of sullen defendants and plaintiffs, all supervised by several stern bailiffs, Misha became quite nervous.

He needn't have worried, as it turned out. Small Claims Court is dedicated to the principle of making the best of things; better some rough justice, if quick, than the endlessly fine grinding of the higher courts. Common sense and the mutual good faith of the disputing parties serve as the basis of judgment.

As soon as he got the lay of the land, Misha said, "This is like our *Narodny sud* [People's Court]," referring to the early Bolshevik effort to do away with bourgeois procedures and substitute a more humane, more informal type of justice. (The institution still exists in today's Soviet Union, but in name only, all its innovative substance having long since withered away.)

The parties involved in the automobile accident were summoned before the judge, then ushered into chambers to settle the matter through negotiations. To Misha's happy surprise, his lack of insurance proved a problem less to himself than to the two claimants, who now had to devise other means to collect damages from him. In addition, his fairly impoverished condition, which he had feared would put him at a disadvantage, proved to work in his favor, since there were few possessions to confiscate in lieu of cash. By the end of the proceedings, he had discovered the important principle that his legal person was distinct from his actual one, and he brandished the knowledge with the cunning zeal of a disarmed warrior abruptly handed a new weapon. After it was agreed that he should pay damages in small monthly increments, he slyly inquired, "And what if one month I decide not to make my payment?" When the two claimants and the judge turned on him with angry disbelief, he allowed, "Of course I'm just speaking theoretically."

Several weeks later I was in Misha's apartment when another émigré came to visit. Volodya had his own story to tell about his encounter with American justice, beginning with a short preamble.

"My first weeks in America I was so completely innocent and in such a daze that I would go into the subway carrying my money in one hand and my wallet in the other, like a schoolboy on the first day of school. I was robbed soon enough. Thereafter I tried never to use public transport, so when I had to go out to Long Island, I borrowed a car from a friend, even though I didn't have a license yet. As I'm driving along the highway I realize that I've gone past my exit, so I make a quick U-turn. Unfortunately I didn't see a car coming in the opposite direction. Boom! An accident. It wasn't a good situation, me without a license and the other fellow insisting on calling the police. So I took off, I panicked. The cops tracked me down, trapped me in a dead-end street."

Misha brought in some tea for us from the kitchen, his eyes vivid with excitement. Tales of confrontations with the agents of the government invariably stir these fugitives from the Soviet police state. He picked up the narrative where Volodya had left off.

He said, "Since by now I was an authority on United States traffic laws, I went with Volodya to his trial. It was held in Mineola, and it was the last case of the day. He was nervous and I tried to assure him that in America not having the proper automobile insurance could be a blessing. As it turned out, not having any driver's license proved even better. The judge was left with the choice of imposing a real harsh sentence, as if dealing with a real criminal, or ignoring the whole thing."

Volodya added, his face merry as a child's on Christmas morning, "Of course he chose to do nothing. Why make a Soviet émigré suffer needlessly, especially after all we've already been through."

Misha continued, "Yes, when the judge found out we were Soviet émigrés, he stayed for a half hour after the court closed to talk to us. He lectured us on the American system of justice, telling us how good it was in comparison with the communist system. We just kept nodding and agreeing. Why not — hadn't he just let Volodya off?"

That sequence of events, from Misha's accident on the East Side Drive to Volodya's appearance in a Mineola courtroom, describes a path by which immigrants from many countries have traditionally learned to deal with America's rules: passing on experience from friend to friend until it forms a fund of common knowledge. But the third-wave émigrés also alter the pattern, by the astonishing rapidity with which they learn to maneuver through the maze of our public institutions. The facility comes from their long exposure to Soviet practices. Years of enduring in that rigidly ordered society produced an exquisite sensitivity to any loopholes; encountering America, with its much more flexible habits, they are likely to see it as nothing but loopholes. That civic structure of implicit norms and tacit limits which we pride ourselves on often escapes their notice altogether, as if it were actually made of the thinnest gossamer.

Peter Rabinovich possesses a singular perspective on America's public institutions. Once a member of the Moscow bar, he recently was certified to practice in America. Though a few young émigrés have passed through American schools to become working lawyers, Rabinovich is the only third-wave émigré to have had to adapt the experience gained under the Soviet's strict legal system to America's more fluid and rambunctious practices. He did it by taking a few bar review courses and cramming from law books — a task made still more difficult by his not knowing any English when he arrived.

Rabinovich now works as legal counselor for an agency that administers reparation claims against Germany by victims of Nazism. It's an important position, reasonably well paid by American standards (and stratospherically well paid by Soviet standards), and provides offices with a nice view across Madison Square Park to the Flatiron Building; nevertheless, in some ways the job represents a falling-off. In Moscow, Rabinovich was a very prominent lawyer, used to being at the center of urgent debate. Here he has become a cog in a machine that has for thirty years been trying to extrude satisfaction for grievances committed half a world away, and will probably continue doing so for thirty years more. His desk was covered literally end-to-end with briefs and claims, and he looked a bit weary as he surveyed the Sisyphean task that the jumble of papers portended.

In response to my question about his Moscow practice, he said, "There I defended people charged with all sorts of crimes. I defended murderers, rapists, thieves, as well as people charged with antistate activity. There were also a lot of personal injury cases, though, as you might expect, the damages that were awarded were much smaller than in America. In one way that doesn't make much sense. Here a person makes money through sweat and talent, then can lose it all in court. There the people who have money have made it through bribes and graft, yet are protected by the law."

Rabinovich is fifty-eight, with hair combed sideways over a high forehead, and with bifocals that give him a donnish air. He was well versed in the finer distinctions between Soviet and American law, and was ready to express his opinions; but he often accompanied them with little shrugs and ironic glances that implied all his insights should be taken with a grain of salt — the weight of knowledge gained from close observation apparently had deflated some of his airier assumptions. I had heard of Rabinovich when I read an article in *The New York Times,* which quoted him in praise of the American Constitution and the jury system ("the greatest invention of mankind"), but by now he had acquired some reservations.

"I speak as a foreigner, of course, so my views are impressionistic. Still, it seems to me curious that the most successful lawyers in America are not the wisest but those who know how to make use of technicalities. The Soviet legal system has many insufficiencies, but at least it moves quickly, directly. It provides a justice that usually has something to do with reality. I sometimes think that American laws were devised by a few old Jews sitting in an out-of-the-way yeshiva, who never looked out into the street to see the consequences of what they had done. Nowadays people are afraid to go out at night, and soon they will be afraid to go out during the days also."

He glanced out the window, as if intending to confirm his analysis. Indeed, in the center of Madison Square Park the statue of the Civil War admiral David Farragut could have acted as a handy barometer to measure our social climate: gathered right nearby, several youths were hawking marijuana to passersby, as oblivious to the inspirational inscription on the pedestal as to the stern visage and rectitudinous bearing of the champion of our Union's cause.

He said, "American liberals tell me, 'Better that one hundred guilty men should go free than that one innocent man should suffer unjustly.' That principle was fine in the past, when societies were different, when not every second person had his own gun. America is trying to live as if it were two hundred years ago."

Rabinovich delivered his judgments more in sorrow than in anger. Only occasionally did some sign of passion flash in his eyes, and even that vanished so quickly it seemed it may have merely been light striking the bifurcation of his glasses at an odd angle. "Its a matter of respect for the law," he pronounced. "If people know they won't be punished, they will of course commit crimes. In the Soviet Union, if you strike a policeman, you are in deep trouble, so no one does. Here a police killer goes to prison for a year or two, which is almost a vacation. I've seen American prisons. The inmates sit around all day watching color TV and eating fried chicken."

I remarked that it seemed strange to hear an escapee from the Soviet Union calling for harsher punishments — did he want America to turn into a police state also?

Rabinovich shifted in his seat, passing quickly through an attitude of exasperation before resuming his decorous calmness. "I didn't say America needed harsher laws, only that those which already exist should be properly enforced. And don't forget, countries are not just laws. People read books, go to the movies, fall in love, raise families — a thousand things that have nothing to do with the law. And in that area America is very good indeed. That more than makes up for the flaws of the legal system. But still it would be nice to have a proper legal system also."

Later, as he was showing me to the door, Rabinovich told me a historical anecdote — Russians can't resist a picturesque tale even if the punch line contradicts their main argument. "In the old days, the Tsar would hold public beheadings in Red Square, at the *lobnoe mesto,* the executioner's block. The population was expected to attend and watch, the hope being that the horror of the event would induce honest behavior in all. Yet, it is said, right during the execution, as the ax fell, pickpockets would circulate through the crowd, working their trade while everyone was distracted by the spectacle."

But then he gave a final eloquent shrug, as if to put matters into a durable perspective. "An American liberal might say that this shows that punishment never deters criminals. But the executions in Red Square were hundreds of years ago; things change. Today society has to defend itself."

Rabinovich's enthusiastic digression on pickpockets in the course of his plea for law-and-order shouldn't have been a surprise. The professional criminal fascinates Russians. He's also a figure that underscores their deep ambivalence toward public institutions.

On the one hand, most Russians strenuously affirm the rule of law. They insist that without strong civic restraints profound anarchy would envelop society, and of course history has given them cause to worry. "God preserve us from a Russian revolution, senseless and merciless," Pushkin wrote when he contemplated Pugachev's bloody peasant rebellion at the end of the eighteenth century, and the chaos that was released in 1917 is still a living memory for many Russians.

On the other hand, a succession of tyrannical rulers has made Russian law appear as nothing more than an instrument of the privileged. The Tsar's claim of a divine right to a life of feudal splendor was bad enough, but the Soviet regime's practice of sanctimoniously invoking Leninist doctrine to justify policy is in many ways worse, since communism presents itself as preeminently rational. The show trials of the 1930s, those charades where judges, prosecutors, and defendants danced their minuets of proper jurisprudence while all the time the executioner's gun lay already cocked, shows the Soviet legal system at its extreme; but the principle that the state and the law speak in a single harmonious voice persists, grating the consciousness of every Soviet citizen during the most mundane activities. That may really be the definition of contemporary Soviet communism—not cruelty or terror (though these exist), but the smug insistence that right is invested in the national bureaucracy, which the average man assails at his own risk. Given the oppressive burden of Soviet law, illegality has come to imply political resistance, and in fact some criminals have achieved legendary status. Mention Benya Krik, the king of the Odessa underworld who was immortalized in Isaac Babel's stories, and a Russian's eyes light up in admiration.

The figure of the professional criminal becomes more unsettling to the third-wave émigrés in America, where illegality loses much of its political coloration. The initial reaction upon hearing of a crime is unconstrained aversion; if the accused is one of their own, there is also disbelief. It is not surprising that recent speculation in the New York City press about a third-wave organization engaged in protection rackets, arson, and drug dealing aroused the émigré community inordinately. (The style of reporting may have intensified the anger — it was unclear if the point was to gloat that the Soviet Union fostered illegal impulses or to take perverse pride in capitalism's capacity to corrupt.) Responding to *The New York Times* description of a Russian Mafia — an FBI agent was quoted as saying that one existed, although its structure was, for the time being, not so coherent as the Italian counterpart's — the Russian-language newspapers loudly complained that it would have been fairer to have also noted that most third-wave émigrés are law-abiding. And *The New York Post* account of the arrest of eleven Soviet émigrés on narcotics charges provoked hoots of anger and irritation.

But elements of pride and chauvinism were mixed in also, albeit coated with irony. When the *Post* quoted a New York detective as saying that the several émigrés who had recently been arrested for drug dealing constituted a gang that "could at a moment's notice obtain, besides drugs, machine guns, rockets, and even tanks," a *Novy amerikanets* journalist responded, "In the light of the USSR's fivefold superiority in the number of tanks, such people [the émigrés under arrest] should in every way be encouraged, for who knows if they are not our best means of defense."

Inquiring about this topic, I was told by several people to visit one émigré who had particularly strong opinions about crime in America, and after a while I went. Alec lives in a pocket-sized walk-up apartment in Washington Heights, with so many books stacked along the walls and on the floor that it resembles a stalagmited cave. The works of William Buckley, Thomas Sowell, and other stalwarts of conservatism were especially well represented, sending a spasm of ideological claustrophobia through me, some fear that political bombast would crowd out the small amounts of air that remained in the room. But Alec, who is in his forties and speaks fluent English, was affable. Only occasionally did an edginess arise which proclaimed that special version of the foreigner — the one who knows America so well that complaint gets raised to a bill of indictment.

I asked his opinion of crime in America.

He had received me in jogging shorts and a T-shirt, and he took the time before answering to rearrange his spindly and very white limbs into a new posture, as if seeking a system of bodily punctuation which could underscore his meaning. His response was similar to what I had heard from other émigrés, though I was taken aback by its detail. He invoked statistics from the U.S. Census Bureau, opinions from *The Wall Street Journal,* a knowing tone borrowed from *The National Review,* and tied them all together with some irony. He said, "Crime is essentially caused by a small, hard-core set of individuals. Of course, American liberals keep thinking up theories to explain this phenomenon. They say some groups suffer special economic deprivation, as if that were an excuse to commit crimes. How much do you think I earn?" He gesticulated at his cramped apartment. "But I don't go out and rob."

He eyed me coolly, less to appraise any reaction, I thought, then to align me more exactly in the gunsights of his criticism. He said, "It's all thanks to American liberals' unusual sense of guilt. They think they have to keep paying for wrongs committed a hundred years ago. They should better ask themselves: were the actions in the past so bad that it is worth perpetuating crime a century later? Americans won't ask themselves this question, they feel too guilty. But I can ask it, if only because my ancestors were serfs, who lived in conditions as bad as a southern plantation."

And what, I wanted to know, was the remedy?

Alec rose, whether to find a more impressive oratorical pose or simply to make himself more comfortable, I wasn't sure. But the effect was to lend emphasis to his answer. "The remedy? Simple. More prisons, tougher laws. Americans have all been raised in a commercial atmosphere, so they are constantly looking to compromise. But in this area compromise is a mistake. The law has to be enforced by all necessary means — that's an old-fashioned idea, no doubt, and to defend it at a party of New York intellectuals would mean that one's social life thereafter would suffer. But it's the truth."

Thinking I sensed a contradiction, I asked if he would apply the same standard to third-wave émigrés, like the ones recently arrested for drug dealing?

"If those guys broke the law, as the police claim, then I say 'get their ass.' There's enough crime in America without Soviet émigrés adding to it."

Trying to get to the crux of things, I asked him if there was such a thing as a "Russian Mafia" in America.

"Perhaps there is, though who knows for sure? I will say this: Russian criminals aren't going to sit still while you ask them about their organizational affiliations. They're not like those American gangsters who are so eager for attention that they'll chat with every interviewer. Get too close and you'll get your face smashed up."

Coming after all the law-and-order theorizing, this struck a note of unexpected respect, an intimation of pride that "some of our boys had made it" into the big leagues of crime. Though I wanted to be sure I had interpreted his drift correctly, I found myself stymied because his tone implied that it might be dangerous to discuss the topic further, even at our seemingly safe distance. Indeed, his few well-chosen words kept recurring to me over the next few days, triggering a frisson of nervousness up my spine and making me want to glance around to check that no one was sneaking up.

If it is sometimes difficult to get a grip on the third-wave émigrés' sense of civic responsibility, this may be because civics comprises not only laws but psychology, which in their case can be highly erratic. Their way of life before emigration developed attitudes toward authority which were simultaneously respectful and resentful. Soviet society imposes an intricate network of bonds and allegiances on its citizens, and while this may be oppressive, it's also gratifying to feel part of the community. As Genis and Weil, correspondents for the *Novy amerikanets,* have written, "We were always the compositional elements of some group or other: the kindergarten group, the school group, the factory union, the brotherhood of socialist republics, the progressive forces of humanity." Breaking these bonds and allegiances may seem an exhilarating prospect, but it may also seem risky, a free-fall with social oblivion as the end point.

Not surprisingly, given their past, third-wave émigrés are especially struck by the American phenomenon of the bum, the hobo, the bag-lady, all those society has dismissed. It couldn't happen in the Soviet Union, with all its social safety nets, and the sight leaves them aghast. Most fearful of all, of course, would be the sight of one of their own in such a predicament.

Nonna Osipova is not yet reduced to the most extreme circumstances, but she may be on her way. She has been evicted from her apartment and doesn't even have a place to store her belongings. Every day, rain or shine, summer and winter, she sits on a ramshackle folding chair on Fifth Avenue between Fifty-third and Fifty-fourth streets, by the steps of St. Thomas' Church. Several times, she told me, other third-wave émigrés have walked up to her and scolded her, claiming she was giving them all a bad name. But it seems possible that their motive may have been less rational — the anxiety that her status portended their own future.

At Osipova's side is a table covered with stacks of brochures, broadsheets, and mimeographed pamphlets, all for sale. They provide her only income, and not many people stop to buy. A large placard announces the collection as "American *Samizdat*." Osipova, who has the detached manner of someone used to dealing with all sorts of questions, from the sympathetic to the impertinent, explained the meaning of her exhibit to me. "*Samizdat* is a Russian word meaning 'self-published,' manuscripts that are uncensored, usually some sort of protest literature. Of course one understands its function in the Soviet Union, but it is necessary in America also. Publishers refuse my works. The New York Public Library will not buy them, even though that building is filled with nonsense and pornography."

Osipova, who is fifty-eight, came to this country in 1972. Her English has become fairly fluent, but she still speaks slowly, making sure that her message is fully understood. Combined with her broad, grandmotherly features and old-fashioned wire-rimmed spectacles, this gives her a schoolmarmish air, redolent of some one-room country school. It's a bit of a shock to look around and see the teeming Fifth Avenue crowds, but Osipova never loses her genteel bearing.

She told me, "Only in the winter does it get very uncomfortable. Especially my legs. I had to construct some leggings to keep them from getting frozen. But I've survived a Russian prison, where they put me for anti-Soviet activity, so I can survive this also."

She's had her share of misadventures in America, she tells me. The rector of St. Thomas', unhappy that she had set up shop directly outside his church, vigorously tried to make her move on. Several times, passersby have harassed her so violently she is sure the KGB had a hand in it. And in 1980, in what was the most startling episode, she was arrested for illegal peddling.

"A policeman, almost twice my size, confiscated all my books and pamphlets, though they are my only source of income. In

America you need a license for this sort of thing, he informed me. As if that weren't bad enough, he then forced me into a patrol car, pulling my hair and sitting on my head as he did so."

She relates these events in a remarkably cool tone, as if reciting passages from famous historical documents. In fact, she has written down accounts of all her disputes; the literature she sells is mostly devoted to cataloguing years of claims and counterclaims. There's such a long list, presented in such elaborate detail, that her table fairly bends under its burden of grievance.

Her particular bête noire is her landlord, with whom there has been a running battle of several years' duration. Presumably there was once a clear point of contention, but it's buried under mounds of pettiness and squabbling, often of a Kafkaesque turn. Osipova told me that in the most recent skirmish the landlord accused her of turning her apartment into a commercial plant-growing establishment, including a watering operation that had purportedly ruined the ceilings of the apartment below hers. He sued for eviction; Osipova countersued for damages due to harassment and nonmaintainance of premises.

When she showed me the papers documenting this battle, I noticed that the landlord's name was Slavic, so I asked if their common heritage had not inclined him to leniency.

"Oh yes, he's a third-wave émigré just like me, but first of all he's an American landlord, which means he intends to suck his tenants dry."

I had met Osipova at a critical juncture in her dispute. Three days previously, the landlord had been empowered to have marshals evict Osipova from her apartment. To mark this turn of events, she had crossed out her address wherever it appeared in her pamphlets and had substituted the handwritten word *homeless*. In fact, she told me slyly, though she had removed all her belongings, she still retained a key to the apartment and sneaked back in at night to sleep.

"What will you do when they change the locks?" I asked.

"I will sleep on the frozen sidewalks, like I slept on the frozen floors of a Soviet prison. Or I'll perish. You know there's a shortage of apartments in the Soviet Union, but at least no one has to sleep in the streets. Here they make people sink to the level of animals.

"And when you try to get justice," she continued, "when you go to court, you find that everyone from the judges on down is on the side of the landlord. Even the court guards are against you if they see by your clothing that you are poor. In Russia, everyone is poor, so you are not mocked for that. Even in a Soviet prison I got more respect than I get here."

You almost sound sorry to have emigrated, I said.

"What can I say? For a criminal, like my landlord, it's certainly better in this country. For an honest person, it's bad everywhere."

As we spoke, passersby in the noontime crowd occasionally paused to regard Osipova's large placard or to crane their necks to contemplate the literature laid out on the table, but few actually picked up any items, and no one bought anything.

Osipova glanced around with a wary and practiced eye. "Oh yes, they stop to look, but they're afraid. Look how they keep their distance. I tried once to start a petition in defense of my rights. After two weeks only ten people had signed it.

"Only after the experiences that I've had in America do I begin to understand certain aspects of life here, such as simply do not exist in Russia. For example, all those bombs that people put in shops and offices, all this violence. I thought at first, why kill people? I still do not approve, but I'm beginning to understand. You suffer injustice," she concluded with an oddly pleasant smile, "till at last you feel you must do *something*."

Several days later I spoke to Osipova again. We were in the corridor of the New York State Supreme Court Building, outside the Appelate Term, where she had just been pressing her complaint against her landlord — namely, that instead of paying him three thousand dollars for legal fees, as the lower court had ordered, *she* should be paid for all the inconveniences she had suffered.

"I wrote all my own briefs, did all my own research," she told me. "I don't bother with the Legal Aid Society. They have so few lawyers. Why should I deprive someone who is illiterate and truly needs help? Instead I do my own work. I go to the Federal Court Library, one of the few American institutions that makes sense. The people there are very helpful. I've learned about American law, about the American Constitution. It's a great document — if only people lived up to it."

Osipova's day in court had been disappointingly undramatic, because the opposing party had decided to file papers instead of appearing for oral argument. But the court did permit her to make a brief statement. She approached the designated place in front of the bench, from which low angle one could see only the heads of the three stern-faced judges, against the backdrop of a large American flag. Some in the audience, which was composed almost entirely of lawyers in pinstripes, momentarily glanced up at the unusual spectacle of a client arguing her own case — or perhaps they were bedazzled by the bright polka-dotted slacks that Osipova was wearing for the occasion — but soon enough they returned their attention to shuffling papers and scribbling notes.

Osipova was unprepared for the turn of events, and she was able to pronounce only one sentence to the court. "I only want to know why I am being treated so unjustly," she said.

In the corridor, afterward, she told me, "The chief judge said they would take my papers under consideration, but he said it very, very *drily,* you know. They won't really bother. Their job as judges is to keep things just as they are. They look at me, a poor person, and decide in advance not to disturb the system on my account. So what if I perish?"

She didn't speak any louder than she had on Fifth Avenue, but in the hall with its marble floors and ceilings her words echoed. Some twenty feet away, four well-tailored lawyers, lately adversaries but now deciding where to eat lunch together, looked up at her last words.

A good place to live is an integral part of the third wave's American dream. Housing in the Soviet Union was uncomfortable for most of them in various degrees, and a good number endured in the sort of dwelling that has taken on the status of nightmare symbol of the Soviet condition in general: the communal apartment. Emigrés tell stories about communal apartment life as if relating war stories — the cunning required to commandeer the single stove shared by four families, the dreary siege outside the occupied bathroom, the dulling of feeling and proprieties from being quartered in two small rooms with several generations of one's family.

In fact, even when neighbors and family members were the most proximate irritants, the government bore the brunt of complaint. An encyclopedia of complex rules, regulating everything from footage of living space per individual to justification for living in an urban center, has created a huge bureaucracy that seems continually to provoke the citizenry. It's no accident that one of the most popular books of the 1970s, *The Ivankiad* by Vladimir Voinovich, details a heroic attempt to acquire a good apartment in the face of officialdom's meanness.

The third wave expected better in America, but to many it appears that only the face of their tormentor has changed, in accordance with their passage from socialism to capitalism. "Landlords in America exploit the émigrés terribly," I was told by Alexander Zayats, who works for the Coney Island Neighborhood Association. "Anything to make a dollar, no human feelings enter into it."

Zayats is himself a third-wave émigré, but he speaks fluent English and thinks of himself as at least half Americanized, so he tries to keep things in perspective. "It's not that there's some flaw in the American character. No. It's the social system. In fact, even those third-wave émigrés who have managed to become landlords themselves are now as bad as American ones, if not worse. I told one of them, 'Don't you remember how you struggled, don't you see how you are mistreating your own countrymen?' He answered, 'This is America, that's the way things are done here.' "

Zayats works out of a makeshift office in a corner of the Coney

Island Bank, divided from the rest of the lobby by two glass partitions and with two desks and a jumble of chairs inside. During receiving hours, émigrés stream in steadily, seeking advice and, not infrequently, solace for their housing problems. Zayats deals with these briskly and formally, but glimmers of pity continually enliven his bland expression. In an interval between clients, he told me, "These émigrés move into apartments that are usually in terrible shape, because American tenants hardly considered them as homes. They know they'll be moving on very soon. But for a Russian, an apartment is part of a dream, a place of their own at last, and they work hard to improve them. They paint, put up wallpaper, and so on. By now landlords know their habits, so they don't bother doing any upkeep or renovation of their own."

Zayats interrupted our conversation to tend to the problems of an elderly pensioner from Kiev, whose landlord refused to accept governmental rent subsidies — though the amount would be the same as he got directly from the tenant, he didn't care to depend on the bureaucracy. "It's a common problem," Zayats told me. "A little delay in getting his check means more to the landlord than the fact that a poor man will be denied financial assistance."

He made a series of phone calls, all brief and apparently unsatisfying. "Normal procedure," he said, shrugging his shoulders. "It takes about an hour to find someone in the Housing Authority who will take the responsibility of answering a question. The bureaucracy here is fragmented. In the Soviet Union, at least you knew to whom to complain, even if it did no good. The government there isn't very helpful, but it doesn't hide."

He picked up the phone again, ready to resume the task of tracking down the responsible official, then stopped in midaction. "I see I'm complimenting the Soviet Union. Well, why not admit it — while it was pretty bad over there, there were good points too, certainly as regards living arrangements. Here people, like the ones you see today, come into my office all the time. They are old and poor, and they have to live behind locked doors and are afraid to go out in the street. Their American neighbors, who they may see every day for months in a row, never say more than 'hi.' Is that the way people should live? In the Soviet Union, at least there is some human warmth, a sense among the people that they have common problems."

He paused, then said, "The really sad thing is that since they've come to America, this sense of collective spirit has vanished from among the émigrés. The only way to fight the landlords, we've found, is to organize, to have tenants' associations, rent strikes. But émigrés associate all such organizations with politics, with party duties, and they had enough of that in the Soviet Union. No more meetings, they say. In America we want our time for ourselves."

I walked outside with the pensioner from Kiev, who was eager to continue venting his complaints against his landlord. It turned out to be a complicated story, and to stay warm during its unfolding, we retreated to a McDonald's on Coney Island Avenue. I was surprised by its pronouncedly Slavic ambience, as much Odessa café as American fast-food joint. Though the patrons sat in the carefully measured insularity that is decreed in all these establishments, more or less anchored in place by the ingenious design of the tables and chairs, they warred against these restraints. Indeed, it seemed as if some demon of rambunctious congeniality possessed them: food was passed from table to table to be sampled, children circulated continually, to be cosseted as if by close relations, exclamations of greeting punctuated the arrival of each new customer. When a man dressed in what looked like a cut-down blanket arose and incoherently shouted something about a threatening letter from Con Edison, people did not look away or slump behind their newspapers, as native New Yorkers might, but instead listened patiently to his ravings, and offered advice and sympathy.

In this setting, with the Russian manner at least faintly resurrected, my companion's final remark before he departed struck a harmonious chord. "I have a friend who knows someone whose wife works at City Hall," he told me. "He will speak to him, get his wife to do something that will make my landlord listen to reason. It may cost me three or four bottles of vodka, but it will be worth it."

For centuries that's been the Russian solution, and the ascension of the Soviets did little to alter prevailing practices. Where once Tsarist officials ruled, now it's commissars who must be placated: in both cases, the state was the arbiter of power because it was the only effective force on the social landscape. There was, and is, no choice except to turn to it for relief; and if legal petition fails, then bribery and the exploitation of connections must be tried. Many third-wave émigrés haven't noticed that finding redress in America means running a more circuitous course, because our social landscape is more varied.

In fact, Russians have always been rather amazed by America's bent for clubs, volunteer associations, professional societies: all those agencies that can mediate between the individual and the state. Alexander Lakier, whose journey in 1862 was the first extensive tour of this country by a Russian, noted about New Yorkers that they habitually acted not through the government but "privately and through organized societies, through books distributed to the people and through agitation at public meetings." He was astonished; and to a large degree such intermediate agencies remain alien to the Russians who have arrived in the 1970s and 1980s. If they must deal with the government (most prefer not to), they want direct contact.

Of course, the history of the Soviet Union is the twentieth century's great object lesson that it is better to keep the state at arm's length. The communist regime has embraced the individual only to suffocate him; solicitude comes insidiously mixed with control. That's the accepted view, yet nevertheless, when third-wave émigrés talk of their past, they occasionally sound notes of exhilaration at having been on such intimate terms with public institutions; and, most remarkably for these fugitives from a police state, they often complain about the treatment our American democracy provides. Of course they are grateful for the money and aid they receive, and they don't intend to bite the hand that feeds them; but if they had the opportunity they would certainly rehabilitate the spirit that moves the hand that feeds them. They don't like the *manner* in which our public institutions deliver their services.

One arena where the third wave's irritation is daily expressed is the Coney Island Hospital, which serves the Brighton Beach community. As a public hospital, it must treat everyone who applies, and the outpatient ward is always crowded with the ill and the crippled. Most of the people look sullen as they wait to be examined, and they're not much happier when they leave. It's a typical public institution for the urban poor, a smell of despair as palpable as the acrid disinfectant. But the émigrés often stand apart from this picture of depression and hopelessness. They have specific ideas of what treatment they require, and are not shy about making these known.

One case I saw symbolized their behavior. Dmitry was in his early sixties, but appeared as robust as a sailor just back from a voyage. His color was ruddy, his hair windblown, and he had the rolling gait of a man used to a careening deck. In fact, he told me, he had been a director of a Palace of Culture in Kharkov. That is one of those misnamed Soviet jobs. Little administrative ability and no cultural taste is required, since the "palace" usually consists of two rooms meant to provide a place for government hacks and factory foremen to make inspirational speeches. The only necessary credential is membership in the Party.

"I joined the Party because I had to," he told me by way of introduction. "What could I do, only Party members get anywhere. Of course I could have been a hero, refused to join and ended up sweeping the streets to make a living."

As we sat in the dreary waiting room, I asked him to compare American health services with Soviet.

"The doctors are better trained here, of course, no question. But the American bureaucracy is terrible. A hospital administrator here is like a dictator."

I remarked that I had heard that the Soviet bureaucracy was no bargain either.

"Oh, it's terrible, all right, but you can get around it once you see how it operates. Perhaps a bribe in the right place. Or a threat of complaint. If a doctor treats you badly, you can report him to his superior and he will be called to account. You can do nothing like that in America. It's all arbitrary, with petty tyrants at every level. Last time I came to the hospital, the nurse on duty was an Italian whose father had died on the Russian front in World War II. When she found out I was Russian, she refused to examine me. As if it were my fault her father had died. But there was nothing to be done until another nurse came on duty."

Finally Dmitry was summoned into the examining room, and I was called shortly thereafter to offer translation. As soon as the doctor, a young man probably still doing his internship, pulled the curtain closed to form a cubicle of privacy, Dmitry launched into a narration of his medical history. He punctuated his tale by displaying empty containers that once held prescribed medicine, a spectacle designed to prove both that he had followed doctor's orders and that these orders had been inadequate to overcome his malady. The doctor listened with the sort of immobile pose that is meant to imply rapt attention, but it was clear from his glazed eyes that he looked forward to the conclusion of the tale, and to hearing Dmitry's present complaint.

This proved to be a rash. Perhaps, Dmitry heartily suggested, it was venereal. The doctor flushed slightly, then asked when was the last occasion of sexual congress. Many, many years ago, came the merry answer, as if the question's only point had been to rekindle fond memories. Though the doctor thereupon declared that the problem could not then be venereal, Dmitry was not mollified. He had a nine-year-old granddaughter whom he took daily to the park, and he did not intend to endanger her. Even as the doctor began another line of inquiry, it was clear that Dmitry was still worrying about his possible infectiousness.

The doctor, satisfied with his diagnosis of a simple heat rash, began to write out a prescription, and at this point Dmitry became especially excited. "Tell him," he said to me, "that he should examine me."

The doctor considered the proposal briefly. "It's not necessary," he said.

"No, he must, he must," Dmitry insisted, getting to his feet and mimicking the action of removing his pants, lest something had gotten lost in my translation.

Dmitry's exuberance seemed to disconcert the doctor, and he only shrugged his shoulders. Dmitry took the gesture as a sign of acquiesence and hastily dropped his pants. Smilingly he advanced upon the doctor, energetically manipulating himself to reveal the area of infection. The doctor hardly had any choice but to comply with Dmitry's wish for a close examination, and though he repeated his original diagnosis, he seemed to speak in more measured tones, admitting an element of doubt — he appeared eager to satisfy Dmitry's picture of a proper hospital visit, if only to be rid of him.

Afterward, as we made ready to exit from the examination room, Dmitry said to him, "Please tell me your name so I can ask for you specially next time."

The doctor mumbled a reply, grudgingly.

"And your first name," Dmitry persisted.

"That won't be necessary," the doctor replied, and hurried to take refuge from Dmitry's attentions by turning to a nurse to discuss the next patient.

Outside in the waiting room, Dmitry told me, "He was really very sympathetic after all, not what I'm used to here. I think he must have been Jewish, don't you?"

All in all, one might call the episode a small triumph of the third-wave sensibility, the establishment of a beachhead for the sort of direct, personal contact they prefer; but the extremity of the effort also measures the discrepancy between what the émigrés expect and what America usually offers.

To get a broader perspective on the issue of health care, I talked with an émigré doctor — a designation, by the way, that in itself announces an individual of more than average energy and dedication. There are many hurdles to negotiate before someone trained as a doctor in the Soviet Union receives certification here, many subjects to review and examinations to pass. What's more, there's a whole new sociology of medicine to master. It took Dr. Gennady Lifshutz, who had been a leading cardiologist in Leningrad, about eight years to achieve comparable status here.

We met in the East Side apartment where he lives with his wife, ten-year-old son, and a much pampered Scotch terrier. Lifshutz is in his forties, with curly hair, a broad face, and the spark of someone who was always the smartest in his class. He has a forthright manner, and clearly had given the topic of medicine in America and Russia much thought.

He said, "The main differences are obvious. First, American doctors are better trained than Soviets. The technical level of medicine in a large Russian city is approximately two decades behind current American practices. It's not even worth speaking of what goes on in the provinces of Russia. On the other hand, Soviet doctors know how to treat their patients with much more respect. We were taught to regard a patient as if he were a close relative."

Was there an explanation for this different approach?

"Partly it's because people who become doctors in the Soviet Union are from the most cultured circles, people who try to understand the world philosophically as well as technically. The most talented students go into medicine because it's an area that is relatively untouched by politics. Whereas in America, doctors are often only technicians, nothing more. An American medical student came to my apartment once and saw my set of Mark Twain that I had grown up with. He said, 'Who is that? A Russian author?'"

Perhaps, then, I said, a broadening of America's medical school curriculum would alleviate the problem.

"It might help, but the problem of doctor-patient relationships is really a social issue. It is a question not only of what the doctor thinks of his patients but what the patients think of the doctor. In the Soviet Union, a doctor is highly respected, and not only as someone who can cure physical ailments. A doctor is someone to turn to for advice, someone who can be trusted. Here in America it's more of an adversary relationship. I suppose it's the existence of malpractice suits, which have made patients in this country suspicious and aggressive. But equally important, in my opinion, is the popularity of psychoanalysis. In the Soviet Union, an individual uses a visit to the doctor as an occasion to discuss all sorts of personal problems, with the result that the doctor gets a much better picture of his patient. But here patients reserve all such talk for their psychoanalysts."

Lifschutz paused, furrowed his brow, petted his dog. His self-confident manner momentarily wavered. Then he said, "It amazes me — and most émigrés also — that Americans actually pay someone to sit and listen to them talk, even if that person does have a diploma on his wall and calls himself a psychoanalyst."

We continued to talk for a while longer (till even the dog grew weary of lying in comfort and ran off), and during that time Lifschutz analyzed other differences in the medical systems of the two countries: the greater camaraderie among Soviet doctors, the American doctor's greater willingness to tell a patient the truth of his condition, the different approaches to sexual problems in socialist and capitalist cultures — these and other topics he adroitly explained. Only psychoanalysis baffled and exasperated him.

His reaction was not that surprising: after all, psychoanalysis is probably the most striking example of the American penchant for formalized displays of feelings, a phenomenon that often throws the third-wave émigrés into confusion. They find it hard to resolve such spasms of intimacy with the habitually brusque and uncaring relations that they believe prevail in American society. Thus, when they do encounter public congeniality, many émigrés are certain that they have stumbled on only a simulacrum of humanity, an area (like psychoanalysis) that has been set aside for merely conventional expressions of concern while the heart of society remains as cold as ice.

Nowhere is this reaction as evident as in the third wave's

dealings with our government bureaucracies, and it is a measure of the émigrés discontent that some claim to prefer the Soviet apparatus. "Most officials in the Soviet Union were bastards," runs the typical comment, "but at least you knew where you stood." The message seems to be: a society should keep its own face, not trying to mask the administrative nature of its goals. Then if one does happen to encounter an act of kindness in the public realm, it is pretty certain to be genuine, rather than a ploy to promote bureaucratic efficiency.

It's easy enough to say that the third wave's cautious view of our public realm is the result of their bouts with the Soviet regime — but such a phrase hardly begins to convey the *feel* of their former lives, its prickly and suffocating texture. Only a native can fully know the constraints of daily life in the Soviet Union, but I had an experience once that gave me an inkling. It was in Leningrad in the early 1970s, by which time the *druzhinniki* were fully active: these were the neighborhood volunteers who Khrushchev had decreed should help the police by taking care of minor transgressions. The theory was that citizens under communism should learn to handle their own disputes, with the power of the police gradually withering away; but the practice was less benign.

I was walking home from an all-night New Year's party, and the early-morning streets were deserted except for two sailors passing in the opposite direction. Presumably they were coming from their own night of revelry, for they were quite drunk. They were arguing good-naturedly about their last remaining cigarette. They began to push a bit at each other, then to threaten, but it was still nothing serious, just two pals momentarily at odds.

Suddenly, a fat, gray-haired *baba* ran out from a doorway, blowing on a *druzhinnik* whistle for all she was worth and shouting for the police to come and arrest the pair. The sailors ran for it, hightailed it around the corner — and, what's more, so did I. I was infected by their fear. It was as if we were fleeing a scene of murder and mayhem. That's the way it is in the Soviet Union:

agents of the government can pop up anywhere, and what was merely a private squabble gets transformed into a prosecutable offense.

There is no American equivalent of the *druzhina* (though some of our neighborhood patrols and vigilante groups sometimes seem as if they are heading in that direction). Our police have to do the job themselves, but they have developed an updated arsenal of techniques that includes the weapon of "community relations." The jurisdiction of the Sixtieth Precinct includes Brighton Beach, with its approximately 25,000 ex-Soviet citizens, and Bill Selwyn, an affable man in his early forties, is the officer in charge of maintaining a liaison between this group and the police. He took me for a tour of his bailiwick.

Driving out from the shadow of the elevated tracks that blanket Coney Island Avenue, Selwyn pointed out groups of elderly residents who had deployed their folding chairs to catch the sun's warmth. He told me, "This neighborhood was much more unsafe before the Russians came. They like to be outside, walking around or sitting in the sun like those people over there. That makes the streets safer for everyone."

Looking for a parking space, we drove down the side street toward the beachfront, with Selwyn keeping an eye cocked on the bustling activity around us. He said, "It's a good neighborhood, but I'm not going to say its perfectly law-abiding, with great cooperation with the police. If there's a crime, Russians often will try to deal with it themselves, or forget it altogether, instead of calling us at the precinct. That's a habit they picked up in the Soviet Union, where the police are always the bad guys. Often when we come along to investigate a crime, it's monkey see no evil, hear no evil."

We passed the Coney Island Baths, famous for its swimming pool, shuffleboard arenas, and the passionate gin rummy games of Jewish pensioners. Selwyn nodded in that direction and said, "The club took a group of émigrés on a tour of its facilities, and they were really impressed. Then they found out they had to pay for membership and they just walked away. You get these things for free where they come from. If they haven't changed their thinking about things like that, I guess there's no reason to expect they'll quickly change their attitude to the police either."

We looped back onto Coney Island Avenue, still with no parking space in view. Selwyn pointed out a dilapidated storefront. "That's where our community action group is. They help the émigrés with housing problems, welfare, things like that. Last year they handed out free surplus cheese and there nearly was a riot. So many émigrés pushing and shoving that they broke the glass door. They're a physical people, and besides, it stands to reason that the Soviets let out a lot of people who weren't perfectly law-abiding. It was a good way to lower the crime rate there, shove off their problems onto us. So far it's mostly small-scale stuff around here, burglaries and so on, and mostly against other émigrés."

We finally found a parking space down by the beach. Selwyn expertly maneuvered the car into it, then got out and dropped a coin into the meter, shrugging in resignation as he did. "You think that a Soviet policeman has to drop money into a meter when he parks?" he said with a grin. "No way."

As we walked up the ramp toward the boardwalk and the spectacular vista of Sheepshead Bay, Selwyn said, "Some of the Russians take to America pretty quickly, but for a lot of them it's quite a shock. We try to help by educating them about the ground rules of American society. For example, the precinct holds classes describing basic precautions against crime, watching out for purse snatchers, not opening your door without first securing a latch chain, that sort of thing. Attendance at the classes has been pretty good, but it could be better. They don't like to come to the precinct, so we have to go out into the community."

On the boardwalk, the bright sun did not fully offset the blustery December chill, and there were only a few people about. Three teenagers strolled toward us, one hoisting a blaring portable radio. "They're Russian," Selwyn told me. "I can pick them out even if they're wearing American jeans and leather jackets. Something in their walk. By and large, the émigrés are good kids.

We do get some juvenile delinquency reports from the schools, but it's usually for small things like truancy. The parents keep the kids in line. They brought them over here to make good, to have a future, and they don't want anything spoiling that."

We passed a windowless storefront on the boardwalk, with a flimsy door that flapped open to emit two jovial and probably inebriated men in their fifties or sixties. Selwyn remarked, "Their private club. A lot of drinking, some gambling. We don't bother them as long as they keep things in bounds."

He maneuvered me into the luncheonette next door. "You should see this place in the summer. Packed to the rafters. A Russian owns it, but everyone comes in — Puerto Ricans, blacks, Italians, you name it. The boardwalk in the summer reminds me of what New York used to be like. Sure, there are some fights, and the Russians are as much into defending their own bit of turf as anyone. But basically Russians want to enjoy themselves, live and let live if at all possible."

For a certification of these views, Selwyn wanted to introduce me to the luncheonette's owner, a jowly man who stood behind the counter methodically washing and wiping several hundred glasses, arranged in glittering platoons.

But all my attempts at conversation elicited only mumbles and sour grunts. Selwyn told me, "What are you going to do? They're suspicious of outsiders who come around asking questions. Especially since in that trenchcoat you look like the FBI — or the KGB."

Actually, I noted, the proprietor was not that willing to talk to Selwyn either. The sight of an amiable policeman eager for a chat must have diconcerted this refugee from the Soviet Union. The presence of *druzhinniki* in every doorway is unpleasant, but it may seem only marginally more comfortable when the authorities pop up continually, supposedly just to pass the time of day.

In the Soviet Union, tracking the government's intentions was fairly easy, since it moved against its citizens at a consistent, ponderous pace. Though a noisome force, it was comprehensible, which is more than one can say about how civic authority functions in America. The government here is like a boxer who alternates elegant jabs with sweaty clinches, a whirling dervish of feints and fancy footwork: the third-wave émigrés, who don't know that the threatened roundhouse right is rarely if ever delivered, sometimes look as if they will get TKO'd merely from the anxiety of anticipation.

If the third wave's perplexities about America's public realm are to be resolved, it will be the result not of persuasion or logic but experience. Our institutions have a deserved reputation for absorption: even while newcomers remain unconvinced by our rhetoric, they may look up and find they've become part of our civic life. Schools are probably our most efficient instruments of Americanization — there's nothing like the hurly-burly of adolescent peer pressure to rub off alien corners and ethnic angles.

The process disquiets the older third-wave émigrés, many of whom have very tidy ideas about the meaning of education. One of them, once a teacher of English in Odessa and now a teacher in a Manhattan public school, told me, "Melting pot? Perhaps — though these days the Hispanic influence is too strong to melt, in my opinion. Which means noise and more noise. When I walk down the school corridors, I can't hear myself think because of the students' shouting. In the Soviet Union, they'd be walking on their tiptoes and showing respect for teachers. Say what you want about the Soviet Union, its terrible ideology and so on, at least it provided good schools."

To avoid having their children sucked into America's roiling mainstream, a fair percentage of third-wave parents have sent their children to yeshivas, though they care little about religion and know they are thus imposing the extra burden of learning Hebrew in addition to English. Some other parents prefer schools affiliated with the Russian Orthodox Church, where all the instruction is in Russian. A third choice is the bilingual program offered by the New York Public School system: students follow the regular curriculum, but several periods a day are devoted to Russian literature and grammar.

South Shore High School, in Brooklyn's Flatbush district, is one of the schools where the bilingual program is offered. It's a working school, which is high praise by today's standard. Students go to class and generally sit in their seats, even though the attention span of some is measurable only in milliseconds. When a teacher makes a request, students don't argue, and usually even comply. As I walked down the empty corridors toward the Bilingual Program Office, a ball of paper sailed out a classroom door some twenty feet ahead of me, described a gentle arc, and settled beside a discarded candy wrapper; there had been no specific target and no accompanying whoops of battle. That's South Side — if the sense of decorum seems continually about to vanish, the pandemonium that threatens is at least not sinister.

In the office I met Azari Messerer, a recent émigré who teaches in the program. He told me, "It's ironic. Emigrés in American schools are often taunted by their classmates, who call them communists, and yet many of them emigrated before they could fully understand what it meant to be Russian, let alone communist. In this program they can learn about their native culture and still get in touch with American life. It's a good compromise."

In fact, at first glance the Russian students at South Side appeared thoroughly Americanized, and not merely because of their jeans, Adidas sneakers, and leather jackets. In the corridors between classes, they shoved and mixed with the rest of the student body, shouting out all the latest colloquialisms with gusto and no accent.

I approached one girl who stood out because of her spectacular outfit of red, skin-tight pants and a sweater emblazoned with the face of a rock star, and asked her how she enjoyed studying the literature of her native land. She shrugged in response. "I don't know why my parents make me do it," she said. "It has nothing to do with my life."

In an aside, Messerer whispered to me, "She's not typical; she's incredibly brazen. I once asked her in class what she thought of Chekhov and she replied, 'What do *you* think of him?' But I must admit that many Russian students behave badly. They imitate the worst aspects of American life, sometimes going further than the worst Americans. An American will always have an intuition about limits, but an émigré lacks this sense. We can only learn these things after we've lived here for some time."

We proceeded to the classroom for the Russian literature lesson. The students spilled into the room, still scuffling and exchanging exuberant insults, most of which, I noticed, were now being delivered in Russian. If the prospect of a bout with their native culture inspired no reverence in the students, it at least induced most of them to transact their tumult in their native language. One straggler found himself locked out in the hall, not to be admitted till Messerer finally noticed his absence. "You are sick!" the butt of the joke shouted in English at his jeering tormentors as he made his way to his seat, and the epithet sounded slightly incongruous, a piece of Americana that did not fit the newly established Russian tone.

Messerer announced that the period would be devoted to a student report on a story by the twentiety-century writer Andrey Platonov. He added that he had purposely given the assignment to Sasha, who was from Leningrad, and thus could appreciate Platonov's tale of how Peter the Great had insisted on that city being built on swampland, at the cost of thousands of lives. Sasha, still a bit excited from the byplay around the door, took his place at the desk at the front of the room. He was fifteen or sixteen, with the beginnings of a mustache, and somewhat hulking, as if his considerable size had come upon him unexpectedly — in general, indistinguishable from some American counterpart. But the Platonov story had apparently sparked some synapse of the cultural unconscious, bestowing enthusiasm and even grace. Speaking at the typical machine-gun pace of a Leningrader, he related how Peter brings in an English engineer for help in building a canal, how the project ultimately fails, how the engineer is forced to walk all the way to Moscow to accept his punishment, death. By the time Sasha finished, the class had become completely attentive.

To open the discussion, Messerer gave his opinion of the story. "Platonov's point is to show what happens when a tyrant tries to impose his will on the people. Peter is like those dictators of the twentieth century, who knew they could achieve their distorted goals only by using the threat of death."

Messerer's words galvanized the class. Though the story in fact can support his interpretation, the class was having none of it.

"Why 'tyrant?' " one blond girl demanded. "The times required leadership, and think of all the things that Peter accomplished as a result. There wouldn't even be a Leningrad today if not for him."

And an amiable giant, who till then had seemed to be drowsing, roused himself to say, "A strong leader can only be good. Think of Stalin. Of course there was hardship during his reign, but those were remarkable times also, much got built. Railroads and factories and houses for people who before had lived in huts. Not to speak of how he held off the German invasion."

Messerer, seemingly a bit taken aback by these comments, beat a strategic retreat. "Of course," he said, "it's a point people can argue about, how much a nation's progress is worth in terms of individual suffering. Still, think how many innocent Russians have died because of their leaders' cruelty. Millions and millions."

"But why pick on Russia?" another student remarked. "Innocent people are killed everywhere."

There was a brief lull, as if everyone were surprised the discussion had revealed such a sharp opposition between teacher and students. Far from being too Americanized, most of the class stood revealed as passionate Slavophiles; Messerer, who had proposed to guide them gently back to the landmarks of Russian culture, seemed left in the dust of their galloping nationalism.

Breaking the embarrassed silence, the young man who had been locked in the corridor suddenly spoke up, his surprisingly deep voice lending his remark gravity. "I have a point to make.

I must say that Sasha, for all his good intentions, fails to get to the truth. Perhaps it is beyond his capacities."

To which gibe Sasha replied, "See me in the corridor after class, and I'll show you a bit of the truth."

The class laughed uproariously, and as the bell ending the period rang precisely at that moment, they spilled back into the American area of South Shore High School already prepared to partake in its riotous joviality.

Afterward in his office, Messerer showed me the yearbook the students had compiled. The title, *Na yuzhnom berege,* is a straight translation of *At South Shore,* but the Russian strikes a more plangent note, a crib from Russia's great poetic tradition, and this is occasionally echoed in the text. In a section devoted to the query of what the students expect from life, there was the usual mixture of plans to become doctors or lawyers, but also several expressed hopes for "happiness" and one for "spiritual calm," dreams more suitable to the legendary Slavic soul than to a teenager of jazzy South Shore High.

Messerer also pointed out a five-page story that turned out to be a marvel of cultural schizophrenia. Though the author was a senior from Leningrad, she attributed the narration to an American girl; indeed, the main point of the story is the American girl's effort to comprehend the behavior of a Russian classmate, as the two sit together at a concert. "What could I expect from this girl?" the narrator wonders. "What does she think about?" The displaced perspective reveals the extent of the author's anxiety: other people's opinions add up to one huge interrogative.

The narrator says of her Russian companion, "She admitted that in class she missed much of what was said. And it wasn't because of the language barrier but because of the abundance of information. That's why she sometimes seemed lost while all the other students were enthusiastic. But this time [at the concert] she was carried away by the music."

That last line underscores the depth of the desire to blend in, but it also indicates an acute sensitivity to the obstacles — only on the nonverbal, emotional level of music does assimilation seem possible. Apparently even émigré teenagers, who among the third wave are the most open to new influences, find it hard to enter fully into American life.

It makes sense, therefore, that the third wave keeps a measure of its allegiance to its homeland, and continues to admire Russian history and Russian heroes — even to the extent of including Stalin in the pantheon. The émigrés' past is filled with cruel and oppressive events, elements which distort the human spirit, but it is *theirs*. It would be foolish for America to try to extinguish their memories and their traditions very quickly, before the émigrés have created substitutes.

FIVE
❧ Politics

THIS is the emigration of the dissidents. They lend the third wave a brave political coloration even though the majority of the émigrés did not actively oppose the regime. The acts of Solzhenitsyn, Ginzburg, Bukovsky, and a score or so of others are so courageous that their luster rubs off on all, a sort of grand background music that makes the prosaic shuffles and skips of the average man seem a graceful dance.

I wanted to see a dissident in public action, so on a cool October evening I made my way to a symposium that included on its panel Valery Chalidze, who had been the editor of the underground journal *Chronicle of Current Events*. The symposium was sponsored by the Helsinki Pact Watch Committee, it featured a Yale professor of international law, and it took place in an imposing building located just off United Nations Plaza. In other words, the event portended decorum, if nothing else; but in actuality it proved slightly indecorous, in a way characteristic of political discussions between Americans and Russian émigrés. Not that there was any outright antagonism — Americans and Russian émigrés have common political ideals, after all — but the geniality that can paper over slight public disharmony was absent.

The audience consisted mainly of Americans, an elegantly dressed and obviously educated group that had come to "explore the issues," as I overheard one gentleman sitting behind me express it. But amidst this tranquil congregation there were points of palpitating anxiety, Russian émigrés who stared at the speakers' table as if momentarily expecting a disclosure of their destinies. And, by themselves, in the front row, secluded as if by quarantine, sat two men more closely resembling out-of-training boxers than interested students of grand diplomacy. Throughout the proceedings they pointed a tape recorder at whoever was speaking. They were, it turned out, correspondents from Radio Moscow, whose call letters in this instance were certainly KGB.

Leon Lipson, the Yale law professor, spoke first. Standing up and pulling down his pinstriped vest in the same abrupt motion, he launched into an unbroken fifty-minute disquisition on the meanings of the Helsinki Pact. Strategies and counterstrategies, demands and counterdemands, he itemized them all. It was a dizzying journey across the treacherous terrain of international law: yes, he concluded, the Soviet Union behaved monstrously at times, and yes, its record of honoring treaties was laughably poor; but the only way for the American government to hope to influence the Soviet's treatment of its citizens was by continuing such negotiations. Ergo, though the Helsinki Pact was flawed, it was valuable.

Lipson sat down, acknowledging the applause for his dextrous performance, and Chalidze prepared to begin. He had rounded shoulders and a short neck, but sharp, almost exquisite, facial features, as if the head of a Greek statue had been placed on the body of a bear. After two or three awkward sentences in English, he switched to Russian, pausing periodically to allow Lipson to translate. He spoke softly, but it was clearly the softness of imposed restraint, and he allowed himself to become progressively louder. Soon he seemed on the verge of jumping to his feet, passion incarnate, if it would help him make his case.

"America is a great, great country," Chalidze said. "But America is a bit blind also, a bit too trusting. The Soviet Union today is not a country with which to sit around a table, drink some toasts and talk abstractly about human rights. It is a terror-ridden, criminal nation. Americans should not be so naive."

Before translating some of the sentences, Lipson paused and looked with dramatic quizzicality at Chalidze, as if to emphasize that the words about to come out of his mouth did not originate in *his* mind.

Chalidze continued, blind to Lipson's miming. "You must write to your congressmen, to your senators. Tell them that behind the Iron Curtain there are men and women, my countrymen and countrywomen, who are everyday being falsely imprisoned and punished. America cannot sit back, signing a treaty every now and then, and expect things to change. We are grateful to America for letting us come here, but America can do more, much more. America must resist communism, and instead it is sitting back and getting fat and lazy."

Putting Chalidze's ideas into English, Lipson now occasionally tried to add a weak smile in his own right, a puny attempt to keep his distance. Chalidze hardly noticed his interpreter's discomfort and rolled like a juggernaut toward his conclusion. It was a startling performance, certainly to American eyes. Instead of the expected political analysis, we were invited to contemplate an incarnation of righteous anger, some fierce fire of the human spirit — and, surprisingly, some of this fire was being directed at us.

History is partly at fault for the contretemps, no doubt. Russians have for a long time equated going abroad with securing a respectful hearing for what they have to say. Emigration is their bully pulpit. The tradition goes back to the sixteenth-century boyar Andrey Kurbsky, who broke with Ivan the Terrible, crossed to the safety of Poland, and from there directed a stream of critical letters at his erstwhile lord. Surprisingly, Ivan read the letters attentively; more surprisingly, he responded, in part trying to justify himself. By the nineteenth century, the custom of authority paying heed to dissidents abroad was so well established that radicals living in Europe could publish open letters to the Tsar in their journals in full confidence that they would be read.

Though today's dissidents burn with the same critical fire, the target at which they direct their imprecations has altered. The regime the dissidents left behind is stable and confident: it pays less attention to criticism from abroad and is more efficient in preventing the citizenry from even hearing it. Even world-famous Solzhenitsyn often seems to feel that the comments he addresses homeward only float away in the wind. "This letter," he wrote in the preface to his *Letter to the Soviet Leaders*, "was sent to the addressees six months ago. Since that time there has been no response or reply to it, nor any gesture toward one. . . . But even now I cannot regard it [the regime's refusal to answer] as irrevocable. It is never too late for repentence."

Despite his gracious willingness to attend to any reply, Solzhenitsyn still has gotten no answer. Other dissidents, with less reputation than Solzhenitsyn, suffer still more acutely the silence emanating from the Soviet Union. A smug monolith, it seems equally impervious to curses and blandishments. In these circumstances, it is perhaps not surprising that dissidents vent their fervor on the more proximate audiences of their host countries, if only to vent it somewhere.

But it makes for odd encounters. Listening to Chalidze's outburst, the émigrés in the audience seemed to swell with a sympathetic anger, while many of the Americans lapsed into slight embarrassment, like distant relatives come to a house of great bereavement: a disproportionate concern with the Soviet Union's criminality moves the two parties, the unbridgeable difference between a native's intimate acquaintance with the horror and the foreigner's intellectualized interest. I may have been wrong, but as I left it seemed to me that the two men from Radio Moscow were smiling at the confusion and missed signals in their enemy's camp.

Though Efraim Sevela is not as famous among Americans as some other third-wave authors, he is, barring Solzhenitsyn, the writer most popular with his fellow émigrés. His novels sell out almost immediately, and then are passed from family to family like valued icons. What accounts for this? Sevela informed me, "I give my readers what they want. For the third wave, my literature is their bible. People stop me in the streets, women embrace me, saying, 'Live long and keep writing such books.' When I arrived in Paris in 1972, Marc Chagall read my book about Jews in the Soviet Union and told me, '*This* is the vitamin that Soviet émigrés absolutely require.' " On the other hand, when I asked one third-wave literary critic about Sevela, he only shrugged and said, "He is our Harold Robbins."

As with the merits of his fiction, there is some argument concerning Sevela's place in the history of the dissident movement. Some insist his activity was limited to one bravura act, coming after years of political unconcern and followed by more years of negligence. Sevela describes a grander scenario, with antecedents and consequences fitting naturally into his most majestic moment. That occurred in 1972; here is how Sevela reproduced the event in his novel, *Stop the Airplane, I Want to Get Off*:

> On that freezing day, twenty-four Moscow Jews accomplished an incredible feat: under the nose of the Kremlin, on Manegé Square, they seized the Reception Hall of the Supreme Soviet of the USSR — the highest organ of Soviet authority, and settling themselves in they issued an ultimatum to the government: they would not leave voluntarily until that time that they had assurance from the highest officials that all Jews who wished to go to Israel could do so. . . . President Podgorny himself gave his word that Jews would now be allowed to leave for Israel.

There's an element of wishful thinking in this picture of Soviet leaders caving in to personal heroics, and a bit of self-aggrandizement also, since Sevela ignores the fact that the pressure to force the authorities to permit emigration began well before 1972 and involved individuals who were even more daring and long-suffering than Sevela and his twenty-three colleagues. Still, the sit-in marked a significant historical moment, and was acknowledged as such on both sides of the Iron Curtain. Four days after the event Sevela was expelled from the Soviet Union; and on his arrival in Paris he was hailed as a fighter against communism's injustices. *L'Express* put him on its cover, acclaiming him as "The Slavic Christ" (an odd expression, surely, for a Soviet Jew —

but perhaps the editors were swayed by Sevela's beard of biblical cut), and Baron Edward Rothschild invited him to stay at his manor.

These days Sevela has no fixed address, preferring to travel widely and to stay with friends as the mood strikes him. I had tracked him down to Connecticut, where he was house-sitting for the summer in a friend's cottage. Following the directions he had given over the phone, delivered confidently but with a garbling of detail, I took several wrong turns before ending up on an unmarked dirt road. Just as I was making ready to return to the highway and pick up the lost thread, I spied a man of about fifty striding along in sandals, shorts, and a shirt that was opened to the waist. He had a beard, and also, I decided, the distracted air of an author just risen from the rigors of composing a plot. It was indeed Sevela. "I had to walk down to the main road to my mailbox, my car is broken," he told me. "Have you noticed how a man without a car in America is like a castaway on an island? Utterly helpless." It was the first of many pronouncements on America I was to hear that day, and among the milder. After we got back to the cottage and settled ourselves on the small patio, Sevela got down to business in earnest. He has a streak of the actor in him, he admitted, and his conversational style was slightly larger than life. He carved broad gestures in the air and also had the trick of emphasizing key words by drawing them out syllable by syllable. "Most critics are idiots. Id-i-ots! My books have been translated into I don't know how many foreign languages, French, German, English. Sixty-two separate editions, all told, which I think says more than any critic's reviews. Why am I so popular? Because I write like an artist, not an excess word, no fancy twists and turns. Not like some authors who are like a man who, when his left ear itches, has to reach around his head with the right hand to scratch it." Sevela mimicked the action he had described, contorting his features into a buffoon's expression. "Charlatans, that's what they are. Char-la-tans! Ask any third-wave émigré who they prefer."

And what, I asked, trying to get our interview back on track, were his impressions of America? If Sevela were indeed the third wave's spokesman, his opinions might be more than ordinarily pertinent.

"Impressions? Oh yes, I have impressions," he said with a bit of menace creeping into his tone. "I've been all over America, so I know it well. I'm constantly being invited to give talks about the third-wave emigration. Why me? Once Americans hear that you've been on the cover of a news magazine you are considered an expert. And they must at all costs have an expert.

"And there is much I can tell them. To be frank, every schoolboy in the Soviet Union knows more about America than one of America's so-called Sovietologists know about Russia. These scholars like to talk about a 'Russian Man' — they write books on the subject, argue on TV, and even get paid money for this. They say, 'a mysterious sphinx, the Russian people, it will arise in time and have its day.' This makes me laugh. These Sovietologists are just idiots, id-i-ots. The Russian masses will never do anything against their regime — it may be a dreadful and bloody regime, they say, but it's *ours*."

Yes, I said, but what about Americans' views of America, how did these strike you?

"I don't want to give advice; after all, I've not been in this country very long," Sevela replied, but after a pro forma pause launched into a disquisition anyway. "Americans are so naive, really like children. Tell them something serious, vital to their interests, and they forget the next day. They refuse to see that the Red Army is just around the corner, waiting, ready to strike. America's future is hanging by a thread — any Soviet émigré can see that clearly, but Americans are blind.

"You know, I met Nixon when he was still President. I saw at once he was a useless man. But you know who was a wise politician, very keen? Agnew. He understood the world. He read one of my books and told me he had learned a lot."

Sevela's broad and colorful conversational style, swallowing whole worlds in a single gulp, made it hard for me to keep my bearings, and to reestablish the coordinates of our position I asked him a direct question: would he say he liked America?

"*Like* is the wrong word. You cannot *like* America. It's a confused country, a rich, crude country with strong muscles and a weak head."

"But one can live comfortably here," I ventured.

"I said it was a rich country," Sevela replied. "But is that enough? There are no beliefs, no values. What can you say about a country where people commit all sorts of crimes and are not punished? Believe me, a civil war is coming in America, and it will be worse than anything that occurred in Russia."

This broadside sparked my dormant patriotism — in my encounters with the third wave I'd taught myself to adopt a stoic, almost somnambulistic pose when discussing America, but Sevela's clangorous phrases roused me. Even if our public life left something to be desired, I announced to him, our private circles had many excellent virtues.

"Of course, there are cases that support your claim," he granted. "But in general, the people here lack spirit. Even with all their money, they don't know how to relax, how to enjoy themselves. Family life means watching TV, and a party is a group of people discussing the weather. Look at Americans' eyes. They are always busy and unquiet, unsure about what tomorrow will bring."

Did he see no hope, no hope at all?

"For a while I thought Israel was the answer. I fought in the Yom Kippur War, and I would even today go back and fight if Israel was attacked. But I can't say I am any longer a great enthusiast for that country. I found that Israel is just like Russia. Russia was taken over by the Bolsheviks, Israel by the Mensheviks. What was done in Russia by blood was accomplished in Israel by American dollars. It's a negligible difference."

I was ready to call it a day, but wanted to ask one last, strictly historical, question, which might let me quit the premises under an aspect of purposefulness and decorum. What, I asked Sevela, were his thoughts when he agreed to participate in the sit-in at the Supreme Soviet?

"Before that day I was not a big supporter of Israel or even of the emigration movement, but I had a name in Moscow as a movie director, and so those who had organized the sit-in knew I would be useful. I took part when other Jews turned aside in fear. I took part even though I knew it might mean twenty years in Siberia or even the death sentence. They came to me in the middle of the night and asked me to join them and I did — because I would have been ashamed not to, as a *man* [*chelovek*]," he said, stretching out the last word so that it seemed composed of not three but seven syllables.

"Are there men like that here in America, who will act on principle? Very few, very few. America is in trouble, believe me. I have come to see that the only thing that may save it is a takeover by the military, government by strong man. If not that, there will be disaster."

To be a man, to live by a strict ethical code, to enforce correct principles by strength if necessary — Sevela probably construed these injunctions in extreme fashion, if my hours spent with him were any guide, but it's a fact that many émigrés invoke ideals of a roughly similar sort. Theirs is a politics based on morality, on manifestations of the will, probably because many believe that Russia is in its present awful condition precisely because of a collapse of individual values. The 1917 Revolution was not a historically necessary event, set in motion by economic or social forces; it was first of all the result of failure of nerve on the part of the intelligentsia, who, many of today's dissidents feel, could have resisted the Bolshevik putsch, but were too timid, too spiritually self-divided, too constrained by feelings of guilt for the masses.

Solzhenitsyn, in many respects the exemplary figure of the dissident movement, sums up the political attitudes of many with the last lines of his novella *Matryona's House*. Of his heroine, he writes, "We had all lived side by side with her and never understood that she was the righteous one without whom, as the proverb says, no village could stand. Nor any city. Nor our whole land." Not political activity is important, but righteousness, the power of the spirit. Though many émigrés disagree with aspects of Solzhenitsyn's program, most accept his emphasis on the need for a national morality.

It's not altogether surprising that when third-wave émigrés size up America's problems they invoke the same moral standards they use in interpreting Russian history. Habit predisposes them to this form of thinking, and so also does another factor — a political vision based on moral principles does not require much knowledge of the details of American development, which in fact many émigrés do not possess. They measure America not in terms of its ethnic balances or its labor-management conflicts or any other concrete social phenomena, but rather in degrees of national willpower. Indeed, the Vietnam War, which is invariably described as proof of America's loss of nerve, seems to be even more prominent in the third wave's memory than it is in that of Americans.

The drive home from Connecticut felt like an escape. I saw that my attempt to discuss the fine points of American life with Sevela had been a bit like a man trying to dance with a bear — the etiquette of the encounter soon gets lost amidst the mauling and pummeling. I wondered: did Sevela, as he claimed, indeed reflect the thinking of the third-wave emigration in general?

I decided that it paid to go see some émigré who had thought through his political position carefully, someone who had analyzed the entry of the third-wave émigrés into American life instead of swashbuckling through every unfamiliar phenomenon.

While in Moscow, Valentin Turchin had worked closely with Andrei Sakharov in the most Western-oriented bloc of the dissident movement. His background was in mathematics and computer science, and he often brought to bear on political questions a cool, analytic eye. Most important for my purposes, Turchin, unlike many of his fellow émigrés, had given careful attention to

American political life as well as Russian — he's written a book, *The Inertia of Fear* (1980), that scrutinizes the problems of our technological society. His bona fides suggested he would be just the man to see.

When I phoned to arrange a meeting, Turchin was at first reluctant and evasive. He'd seen enough of reporters, analysts, and sociologists, he'd said all he wanted to on the subject of the third-wave emigration. As with many émigrés, he had initially been surprised and flattered by America's attention, then grown wary that it was all in the service of some fatuous "publicity." (Significantly, there's no equivalent word, and no equivalent concept, in Russian.) But when we finally did meet in his office at City College, in the Department of Computer Sciences where he teaches, Turchin was very forthcoming. His nature is lively and amiable, and could not long be suppressed. He is about fifty, but his eyes literally twinkle, making him appear much younger; one could almost discern some boyish self, Turchin as he had been as a young activist in Moscow.

He said, "Oh yes, I love America, I appreciate the freedom and the opportunity I have here. But allow me to say that America is in deep trouble. There is too much freedom, with everyone allowed to live according to purely individual taste. There is simply no consensus about national purpose — it's as Dostoevsky foretold in *Brothers Karamazov:* 'Everything is permitted.' Every émigré, from Solzhenitsyn on down can see this clearly, though Americans seem blind to their own calamity.

"Why? Because a Russian knows that such a thing as Truth exists. In Leningrad and Moscow people sat around for hours every night discussing the meaning of life. Its not that we expected to discover the answer in the course of one evening, but we knew that the concept of Truth existed, and that it made sense to struggle toward it.

"Perhaps we behaved that way because in the Soviet Union every thinking man must be something of a philosopher. Every day you are confronted with the profound question — do you follow your conscience or pursue your career quietly? That can make a philosopher of you soon enough, give you a sense of right and wrong.

"But in America it's apparently *undemocratic* to say there is such a thing as Right, that there are values everyone should acknowledge as correct. 'Values are private matters,' I am told; 'They cannot be imposed.' Of course I am not suggesting enforcement or persecution of those who don't agree, but still there should be an established national consensus, some sort of institutionalization of values. When I mention this, the next question always is 'And who will formulate this consensus?' The implication is that I am after something profoundly illiberal. That is because Americans believe that liberalism means everyone has an equal right to state their preference, that everyone's opinion should get equal weight. I believe in equality of opportunity, but equality of ability is rubbish. Some people are better able to get at the Truth than others, intellectuals, for example.

"But that is one of the things that astounds émigrés when they come to America — that there is no such thing as an intelligentsia. Hippies and blacks and almost everyone else see themselves as distinct groups, but not intellectuals. They are ashamed of speaking their minds on philosphical issues. As a result, Americans pay as much attention to TV comedians as to college professors. Today's Soviet Union is a terrible place, but to be an intellectual there is a respected position.

"Americans eventually will have to choose, either the exaggerated form of democracy that now exists or a society with a coherent set of values — the two things cannot coexist. Some sort of metaparty will be necessary to rise above the petty squabbling and establish a set of norms.

"I see that, and other émigrés see that, but Americans seem to have a total inability to think in such general terms, in some manner that rises above the next day's tasks. When in my classes I try to raise a question of value or philosophy, I see that the students' eyes turn blank, or they even laugh at me as if I had done something extraordinarily stupid.

"I am sure America used to be different, better. When I was

growing up, the idea of America was exciting to us, vibrant and alive. Of course we thought of Americans as terrible pragmatists — the expression 'Time is money' was to us an American invention. But we also believed it was pragmatism with a vision. Americans seemed always to be rushing about, looking for new inventions, new economic ventures. The country appeared to agree on what was the right way to live.

"Now America is in decline, in confusion. As Hamlet put it, *'Zapakhlo gnilom v danskom emperii,'*" Turchin concluded, using as a coda to our talk Pasternak's famous rendering of 'Something is rotten in the state of Denmark.' This citation served to remind me that this genial man, looking exactly like any American professor, and perfectly fluent in English and conversant with our culture, still had to sift his ideas through a sensibility spawned and bred in Moscow. His fine and elegant analysis was very far from Sevela's tumultuous style, but regarding substance he would probably always have more in common with Sevela and other émigrés than with Americans.

If one tried to place the third wave on a spectrum representing American political ideas, it would occupy one small corner. From Turchin on the left to Solzhenitsyn on the right, the third wave runs the ideological gamut — as the witticism goes — from A to B. Teddy Roosevelt's Big Stick policy would have appealed to them, but the mainstream of American politics today strikes them as a weak and unsavory trickle, best avoided.

Andrey Sedykh, the editor of *Novoe russkoe slovo*, told me a story to illustrate the quality of Russian émigré politics. The events took place in Paris in the 1930s. Two men began arguing about the prevailing political situation. One, showing calmness and detachment, took the long view, putting his faith in the future. The other, more nervous and aroused, at last exploded in exasperation, shouting, "Oh, its easy for you to talk, you Socialist Revolutionaries have a big party in Paris compared to ours. We Popular Socialists are only three, all told, whereas you already have eight members."

Politics among any émigré group often skirts farce, grandiose plans concocted in banal surroundings, fierce factional strife over paltry spoils, a bit like panhandlers fretting about the next corner's rival while the national economy speeds upward. Still, there's plenty of motivation to keep going; the ultimate prize is, to put it crudely, a whole country. And Russian émigrés are more nervously driven than most, since their tradition provides ready evidence that the most unpromising prospect may be deceptive — Lenin in 1916 hardly dreamed that he would be in the Winter Palace in 1917.

Coming out of the monolithic Soviet Union, the third wave is unfamiliar with the party politics that characterized Sedykh's generation, which had in its background the nascent parliamentarianism of turn-of-the-century Russia. But there are two distinct camps, and the arguments between them are not less bitter than between the splintered fragments of the first wave.

One of the disputing groups must be called the Solzhenitsyn camp, since he is by far its most prominent member, and the brooding edicts he issues from his Vermont retreat are welcomed by his followers like papal bulls by the faithful. The opposing camp has some fairly famous names, but no individual arrogates to himself the role of leader — a fitting state of affairs, since this camp subscribes to many of liberal democracy's tenets, including a suspicion of charismatic authority.

A main point of contention is the issue of Russian nationalism. Solzhenitsyn's camp endorses it; the opposing camp decries it. To Solzhenitsyn, nationalism implies a homogeneous society (which would mean, he readily admits, disaffiliating Russia from its Asiatic republics), one that is built on respect for native traditions, especially the Russian Orthodox religion. In such a society, laws and constitutions and governmental institutions would be of secondary importance — harmony would reign because everyone would believe in the same spiritual imperatives.

Indeed, though Solzhenitsyn has no love for the present regime, he sometimes suggests he would not mind if it remained in place as long as it confined itself to the administration of the country and did not meddle in moral matters: leach the communist ideology (which, Solzhenitsyn ominously notes, is an import from the West) and the Politburo may not be so bad. At least Soviet subways run on time.

Members of the opposing camp believe that Solzhenitsyn's form of nationalism raises the specter of racism: anyone not purely Russian might be deemed a pollutant of the desired national homogeneity. They also scoff at the idea of a society built on spiritual values instead of laws; they suspect that Solzhenitsyn's disregard for political institutions disguises a moral authoritariansim, perhaps a form of monarchy — and they think they know who Solzhenitsyn, with his grand pronouncements, has in mind for the top post. It all seems Utopian, with no precise explanations of how to reach the Promised Land nor much promise of satisfaction should one succeed.

Not that the more liberal camp has concrete plans of its own (though some among them refer vaguely to a "Danish model" of development). The ultimate evil of the Bolshevik Revolution seems to be to have crushed the political imagination: horrified by the results of 1917, dissidents of every stripe now shrink from contemplating any of the methods that succeeded then. Russian politics was stopped dead in its tracks; the only social instruments that remain are moral suasion or some sort of ethical exemplarism, which even some of the émigrés acknowledge implies a poverty of means. Asked to imagine what he would say if Brezhnev came to him and offered to institute any form of government he desired, Chalidze reportedly replied, "Leonid Borisovich, why don't you stay on yourself for five years — we are not ready yet, and anything else might be worse than what now exists." Indeed, recent history has so far given no reason to doubt the wisdom of this remark.

To the third wave's intramural squabbling, which causes problems enough, is added a new imperative, the need to impress America. Much more than was the case during the height of the earlier two emigrations, it is now obvious that Russia will be swayed, if at all, only through the efforts of the other superpower and not by a contingent of émigrés. Even as they wrangle among themselves, the third-wave émigrés keep looking nervously over their shoulders to see how their host country is reacting.

The Conference of Soviet and East European Dissidents, held at the New School on a pleasant May day, seemed like a good place to watch these complicated dynamics. It featured third-wave émigrés of various political belief and was sponsored by an American journal, *The Partisan Review*. There was even an American congressman, Bill Green of Manhattan, to get the proceedings underway by offering a welcoming speech.

In fact, the speech set an ambivalent tone that would hold throughout the conference. Beginning on a high historical note, the congressman remarked that the New School had a tradition as a haven for refugee scholars, authors, and thinkers, since many of the intellectuals driven from Nazi Germany had gathered here. "Now," he said, "the country forcing its intellectuals abroad is the Soviet Union."

After a few more remarks in this vein, the congressman abruptly shifted gears, bathetically downward. "I have many questions that I would have liked to put to the distinguished panelists assembled on this platform — they represent the conscience of the free world. Unfortunately, as you may know, today is Mother's Day, and my mother and wife await me, an engagement I cannot postpone."

It was not an auspicious beginning. In fact, the fourteen panelists had hardly bothered following the congressman's remarks and showed little interest in his hasty departure. Sprawled behind two long tables set end to end, in various attitudes of sullen weariness, they formed a tableau suggesting the Last Supper gone on several hours too long; the stand-in for Christ was the white-haired, patrician-looking moderator, *Partisan Review* editor William Phillips, who sat at the center of the company wearing an expression of distracted, almost otherworldly calm.

A case of intellectual hangover could not be discounted as the explanation for the panel's exhausted appearance. The day before, a similar assembly, with most of the same participants, had convened in Boston for morning and afternoon sessions. Like a band on tour, they had traveled through the night to the next gig.

But it was also likely that the panelists had more longstanding reasons for lethargy. Most of them had been in America for a while, long enough to have grown wary of America's public manner. A laudatory telegram from the Secretary of State had opened the proceedings, and in a few days several of the panelists would go to the White House for lunch with President Reagan; but though America seems concerned, the dissidents increasingly suspect it's all for show, part of a fatuous game of domestic politics. The moral passion they are prone to vent is now often held in check; they have learned to assume protective attitudes of irony and skepticism. (Right down to scrutinizing the smallest detail of America's welcome: the day after the White House lunch, the *Novy amerikanets* would report that one of the émigré guests found that the menu had been "modest as far as the number of courses went.")

The panelists suffered Phillips's mangled introductions, replete with mispronounced names and a slurring of achievements. From Sergei Dovlatev on the far left to the fiercely mustachioed novelist Vasily Aksyonov on the far right, it was a roll call of the Russian spirit in emigration, and incidentally, a study of Russian social types. Beside the brooding, proletarian presence of Dovlatev, Andrei Sinyavsky looked anachronistic, his flowing white beard, which virtually brushed the table, suggesting a holy man trapped in the wrong century. Valery Chalidze was natty in a dark suit and white shirt, like an efficient businessman, except that *his* business was the passionate defense of freedom. Viktor Nekrasov counterbalanced Vladimir Voinovich, both seeming slightly world-weary, which is the occupational hazard of acclaimed Russian authors. Down the line, Boris Shragin and Pavel Litvinov resembled two cheerful, overage cherubs, somehow managing to imply that the liberal wing of the emigration, at least, could form aggregates of goodwill. So it went — only Solzhenitsyn was missing, though his bumptious and uneasy spirit was at moments almost palpable.

In Boston, Phillips had incorrectly called the leading poet in the Soviet Union "Voznevsky" and had omitted the preposition of Sinyavsky's famous title "On Socialist Realism." In New York he began badly also, when in introducing Dovlatev he inadvertently substituted another panelist's biography. Dovlatev, not given to displays of feeling, sat impassively through this false version of his life, lifting his eyebrows inquisitively only when he heard that he had once been a visiting professor at Harvard.

Though unfortunate, Phillips's ineptitudes may have had some dramatic justification. In this company, he played the role of surrogate of American society, which is determined to honor Soviet dissidents at the same time that it fails to inquire very deeply into their careers. Indeed, the questions Phillips directed at the panel all seemed to have one overriding objective: to shake them loose from the obscure Slavic moorings and to fit them into more comprehensible Western categories.

For their part, the panelists appeared to have tacitly adopted a common strategy of response. Phillips's every effort to introduce an American perspective was met with jocular irrelevancies. Phillips asked, "Considering the renewed interest in Marxism in the West, especially in our universities, do you find that there is anything in the Marxist-Leninist corpus especially worth preserving?"

Yuz Aleshkovsky, a novelist, replied, "There are two things. Marx's grave and Lenin's mausoleum."

Phillips, trying another tack, asked, "What in American literature has influenced your thinking? Do you value the works of authors like Mailer, Styron, and Updike?"

Viktor Nekrasov, another novelist, said, "Recently I was lying on the beach in Honolulu, the most spectacular spot in the world. It was beautiful, warm, the waves lapped up on the shore, boys were jumping about on their surfboards — it was the rich, bourgeois world. And I, a Soviet émigré, was reading a book I couldn't put down: *Na krutoy marshrut* [*Into the Whirlwind*, by Evgenia Ginzburg]."

A brief silence followed, as if everyone were trying to assimilate the random images and discordant data which Nekrasov had compressed into his statement, as into a Haiku stanza. Somewhat testily, Phillips at last spoke up, saying, "I was asking about the influence of American writers."

To which Aleshkovsky responded, "Why sit here and discuss influence at all? I only know that if Russia ever becomes a normal society, we writers will be able to get together and drink three liters of vodka, knowing that we did something to bring the change about."

The audience of approximately two hundred people sat through these addled exchanges with good humor — perhaps they do things differently in Russia, perhaps their political discussions always have a balmy streak, who knows? seemed to be the prevailing view in the auditorium.

Only occasionally would quite a difficult spectacle unfold. A topic would arise which, like an electric current, galvanized the panelists, grounding their irony. Their unified front of slightly buffoonish good fellowship would decompose, to be replaced by anxiety about their history and that of their country. It was that way when the vexing question of Russian nationalism inevitably came round for discussion. The panelists became apprehensive, even irritable.

"All right, let's admit that nationalism is a vibrant movement in today's Russia, the best counter to communist ideology that exists," remarked one. "Nevertheless, it's dangerous to encourage such a form of thought among people who historically have been very aggressive."

"Pushkin was a nationalist; you can see that in his writings," responded another. "And it never harmed his moral vision."

"And what does that prove?" chimed in a third. "He lived a hundred and fifty years ago, don't forget."

The argument kept jumping the tracks of logic, in part because the disputants have covered this ground so often that they employ a shorthand that omits transitions, in part because they seemed wearily to foresee the deadlock that lay at the end of all their efforts. Like one of those plastic roly-poly dolls, the issue of Russian nationalism always reverts to its original, uncompromised position no matter how it is battered and tugged at.

A less recalcitrant topic was clearly welcome, and when someone in the audience asked about the status of the feminist movement in the Soviet Union, the panelists visibly relaxed, and some of their faces seemed instantly to begin to store up mirth in anticipation of witticisms they would offer.

Chalidze, who a few months earlier I had seen passionately discussing the Helsinki Pact, now rose to show the other aspect that dissidents present to American audiences. He said, "You know what Russian women say when they hear about American feminists burning their bras? 'Send the bras here instead, since we can never find anything as good in our stores.'" The other panelists laughed.

The conference lasted for several hours longer, and during that time there were a few stabs made at discussing serious topics, but Chalidze's remark reestablished the prevailing mood: good-natured mockery, like schoolboys playing a prank. Perhaps the émigrés wished to prove that, though politically dispossessed and enfeebled, they could still present a coherent public image, devoid of any mean squabbling such as might give an audience grounds for condescension. But the effect was unsettling.

In the lobby outside the auditorium, to which people began to gravitate to have a smoke and stretch their legs, a reporter from an American newspaper approached Aleshkovsky, mistaking him for another one of the panelists, the poet Naum Korzhavin.

"Yes, I am Naum Korzhavin," Aleshkovsky replied, straight-faced.

"I admire your work," the reporter said, "because you deal with important topics, and poetry should do that."

Still playing his role, Aleshkovsky replied, "I agree, but what, precisely, do you mean by important?"

As the reporter struggled with this problem, Aleshkovsky at

last relented, admitting his real identity. Everyone within hearing distance laughed in appreciation of Aleshkovsky's wit, including the reporter, and the episode did have the form of goodnatured bonhomie. Still, it was hard not to wonder precisely how much real cheer there was in an irony so extreme it caused one's personality to evaporate. Was Aleshkovsky's deeper motivation not annoyance that neither one of the third wave's leading novelists nor one of its leading poets was recognizable to America's distracted public eye?

Alexander Zinoviev was expelled from the Soviet Union after his book *The Yawning Heights* became a success abroad, which may or may not make him a dissident, depending on the criteria used. But in any case, his description of how he came to comprehend the essence of Western political life certainly reflects an attitude that is widespread among dissidents. The epiphanic moment, which he recalls in his book of autobiographical essays *We and the West*, occurred when he was shown an unfamiliar gadget.

"This — this is an appliance to puncture the shells of eggs," my acquaintance proclaimed with a note of triumph in his voice. . . . I thought, if a society begins to spend its intellectual and material resources on special gadgets to puncture eggshells, instead of on tanks, planes, and rockets, it is doomed.

Zinoviev's eager militarism is not atypical, but the crux of his remarks rests in his evocation of that gadget. To the dissidents, America is a spendthrift, frivolous society, lacking a moral core. Even those among them who favor political pluralism are shocked by our unbuttoned social life. A tolerance for different beliefs, they say, should not justify a circus of individual excesses. There are, of course, ready responses to the Russians' criticism, a whole constellation of historical circumstances waiting to be invoked and set into persuasive rebuttal; but there is also that gadget for puncturing eggshells. Once introduced into a serious argument (and Zinoviev, a philosopher of logic with a worldwide reputation, knows about arguments), how much countervailing proof, how much marshaling of evidence, would be needed to excuse it, and who would care to undertake the banal task? Let the eggshell puncturer remain, then, as Zinoviev intends it, a striking measure of the gap between American and émigré perceptions.

By the time I went to meet Boris Shragin, I had decided that the gap was unbridgeable. Shragin, who was active in *samizdat* circles in Moscow, belongs to the liberal wing of the emigration, but I now was resigned to the fact that such liberalism was a far cry from the familiar Western strain. A Russian may be able to quote Mill, but he grows testy when discussing labor unions or protest marches — to the émigrés, *any* reformist gesture seems a step onto a slippery incline that descends very quickly into the nightmare of left-wing totalitarianism. They know this with the same certainty that they know the sun rises each day: the knowledge is in their bones, they have lived it.

Reading Shragin's book, *The Challenge of the Spirit* (which was published in the United States in 1978), had only strengthened my opinion of émigré politics. Though much of the book is a polemic against Solzhenitsyn, it virtually repeats Solzhenitsyn's call for a purely spiritual transformation of Russia, as well as his warning to the West that a Soviet-style totalitarianism portends if we do not change our ways.

Shragin is in his mid-fifties, a bit stout, and with a wilderness of curly hair on his head which gives him a dashing look. I met him in his office at Columbia University, where he teaches a course at the Russian Institute. At first he was a bit distracted, perhaps because I had caught him just after a class, in that blank moment when every teacher occasionally questions the meaning of existence; but he soon enough became precise and direct. He was casually dressed in a sports jacket and jeans, the very picture of an American academic, but what he wore on his lapel surprised me. It was a *Solidarność* button. Third-wave émigrés cheer the Soviet Union's embarrassments wherever they occur, but they are too suspicious of workers' movements, so evocative of the grim days of 1917, to advertise their support of recent events in Poland.

When I remarked that I had lately concluded that émigré politics would always appear alien to Americans, I received my second surprise: Shragin forthrightly admitted the problem may lie with the émigrés. He said, "We Russians have no real political consciousness. We stress the moral element of public life, individual rights and so on, precisely because we have nothing else to set against the government's policy. Issues like taxation, the availability of social services, wages — everything that is a legitimate political issue in the West — do not exist among us. These are matters equivalent to the weather. It's raining? Workers get low wages? Very well, that's the way it is and nothing can be done about it."

I asked why he thought such an attitude prevailed.

"Partly, of course, it's the apparent power of the Soviet regime. Most citizens expect the regime will last a hundred, a thousand years, so what's the point of arguing with it. But it's also a result of a profound disenchantment with politics. After all, our Revolution promised so much: '*My starij mir razrushem do osnovy/ a zatem my novij mir postroem/chem byl nichem stanet vsem.*' [We'll raze the old world to its foundations/and then we'll build the new/And what once was nothing will be all]. Recognize it? 'The Internationale.' It offered quite a program to try and live up to."

Taken aback by his admission that the dissident movement had a weak political vision, I said that doubtless this was partly the result of the KGB oppression and persecution.

Shragin replied, "The Human Rights Movement in the Soviet Union is almost dead, and it's not because of the KGB but because the movement itself is exhausted, without a purpose. In general, the effect of the KGB is overestimated by foreigners. They think life in the USSR is absolutely horrible, whereas the KGB hardly bothers the ordinary citizen. There may be some unpleasant moments, but the idea that every step is terror-ridden, that your neighbor will report the slightest ideological lapse, that is fantasy. Nowadays everyone talks against the government. If a man were to say that the Politburo consisted of fools, do you think he'd be put in jail for that? Of course not."

Yes, the ordinary citizen, I said, but what about those in the dissident movement, thinking of the marks of persecution that many display upon arrival in America?

"Of course, it's different for them, but even so, very much depends on the individual. Fear is something inside of you, and once you come in contact with the KGB it can actually vanish. You see that it is an organization that doesn't work very well. You simply accommodate its presence. You are careful what you say on the phone, because its tapped. You are careful what you say in your home, because that's tapped. So you work around it. All our friends had those little plastic blackboards, children's toys, on which you can write and immediately erase. If we had an important idea to communicate, we simply used these boards. It's simply a matter of getting used to a certain way of behavior."

But still you left, I remarked.

"Well, yes, I had to. They were going to arrest me."

Would you go back if you could? I asked.

"In a flash. The West is a good place, with many advantages. You know, when our plane landed in Vienna I turned to my wife and said, 'At last we are alone, we will be able to talk freely to each other in our own home.' But still I'd go back if there were no threat of arrest. It's home."

Later, as I was leaving, I remarked to Shragin that he had broken down the stereotype of a dissident that I had carefully built up — where was the scorn of American politics, the invocation of the Soviet Union as an absolute evil?

"Well, I'm not typical, I think. Most émigrés do indeed believe that there is little to learn from the United States. They still see the world as they saw it in the Soviet Union. There the official line insists that everything communist is good, everything capitalist is bad. Those in opposition simply reverse the equation, which gives an equally distorted picture. Naturally they're bound to be disappointed when they come to America. They expected something like old-style Republicanism and they find the welfare state. Our emigration is infinitely conservative, well beyond

Reaganism, and much more interested in a moral vision than in politics. I am not typical, believe me."

He *was* atypical. "Oh, not Shragin," other émigrés would say, casting their eyes dramatically heavenward, whenever his name came up. And over ten months of looking, I never met another émigré as willing as he to concede that America might have political wisdom to impart, that our history showed lessons worth mastering. Indeed, a surprising number among the third wave believe that the Soviet Union may be more improvable than the United States: society here seems to them to have gone irretrievably round some corner toward terminal decay, whereas the rigidity there, while terrible, may through luck some day soften.

This may be based only on quack physics — the human tendency to think that hardness will more easily turn into softness than vice versa — but nevertheless the third wave's opinion has proven difficult to ignore. Much more than other new arrivals to our shores, they have a claim on America's attention. The Soviet Union and the United States have formulated their bitter ideological game in a way that whatever one side loses, the other automatically gains: the third-wave émigrés are one of the possible prizes. It would be good to have their approbation of our political and cultural systems. (We already know that they like our economy.) But till now very few have been willing to go as far as Shragin — and even he is nostalgic for Moscow.

Who are the dissidents? What have they done that makes what they say such compelling listening? In fact, they are themselves occasionally confused about the terms of a self-definition. One émigré has written, "We should put the word 'dissident' in quotation marks because it was invented abroad and signifies, in essence, no more than a group of people set apart by their thought from the basic mass of the population in the Soviet Union. Like other words of this type, it creates an illusion which does not exist in reality." For his part, Solzhenitsyn has tried to solve the difficulty by suggesting that instead of trying to distinguish between dissidents and nondissidents, it would make more sense to fix the percentage of dissident fervor in each individual. Other arguments, as bewilderingly scholastic, have also been invoked.

Serge Malchevsky, who now lives in New York City, has had his dissident status certified by Freedom House, the American organization that has long concerned itself with human rights questions in the USSR. He is included on the organization's list of available lecturers, along with such names as Alexander Ginzburg, Valentin Turchin, Pavel Litvinov, and others whose bona fides are beyond reproach. He did stand out in one respect, though; he appeared to be that rare creature, a dissident from proletarian ranks. The short biography beside Malchevsky's name rather startlingly implied a conjunction of manual labor and subversive energy: "Skilled laborer, pipe fitter, chauffeur, mechanic. Served seven years in prison, three years in exile for participating in informal political discussions and distributing *samizdat* and books published abroad." I was eager to talk to him and we arranged to meet late one afternoon — Malchevsky works a long morning shift as a cabbie, still trudging down the dreary proletarian path.

When I got to Malchevsky's home, a rented room in a small cottage on a quiet Queens side street, I learned he would be late for our appointment: he had gotten lost on his way back from a fare in Manhattan. It did not seem a good augury, to have a taxidriver befuddled by New York's geography. The elderly gentleman who owned the house received me graciously, leading me into the living room where I could await Malchevsky in comfort. The furniture was awkwardly arranged, so that when we seated ourselves on two adjoining couches it was more natural to look ahead, at the portrait of Tsar Nicholas II and Tsarina Alexandra that hung resplendently over the mantelpiece, than at each other. The effect was as at a shrine; and when my host — who turned out to be a former White Army officer — began to chatter on about his past, moving regressively from the Civil War against the hated Bolsheviks to his schoolboy battles with the old-style orthography (which was still the rule at the turn of the century), it seemed as if the spirit of the old Romanov days had been truly resurrected.

When Malchevsky finally arrived, he shook my hand, apologized for being late, and, perhaps noticing my glance, nodded briskly in the direction of the portraits. "My idols," he said. Clearly this was not a run-of-the-mill dissident. He was in his early fifties, with hair slicked back along the side of his head, which was bald on top; he had the energetic manner of a man used to physical work. It was warm that day and he was wearing shorts — if he hadn't yet mastered the techniques of a New York City taxi driver, he had at least learned the dress code.

After we settled back on the couches, a beer for each of us, I asked him to describe his dissident activities.

"It began in 1961," he said. "At the elections of local judges for my region, I wrote some anti-Soviet statements on my ballot before dropping it in the box. I can't remember the exact words, but I predicted the doom of the Soviet regime. In essence I said, 'Don't believe that you shall rule eternally in this land; there are forces that will overcome you. The hour will come when your barbaric dictatorship will fall.' I signed it 'A Student.'"

"How did they find out who had written it?" I asked.

"The KGB has its methods. For one thing, they have a huge dossier with handwriting samples. Everyone who applies for a job has to write an essay. 'I want this job for this or that reason. . . .' It all goes into the dossier.

"Also, they probably narrowed down the list of suspects to those who had disputes with the local judges. In fact, I must say that six months before I had been before one of the judges, and had been treated most unfairly. I had separated from my wife then, though I was still willing to pay child support, of course. She brought me to trial, even though I told her, that monster, 'They'll make up the most horrible charges once we get into the courtroom, say I'm a parasite, and so on.' That's the way lawyers are. But nothing doing, she went ahead — she had been a *Komsolmolka* (Young Communist) and did things by the book.

"And the court did treat me unfairly. They said I had been trying to disguise my income, hide my place of employment. I was made to feel like a common criminal. You have to understand how judges are in the Soviet Union — they are always the intelligentsia, the cross-eyed, the handicapped, all of them, the men anyway: it's almost a law. They are mean, envious, your ordinary bureaucratic rats, out to get the working man. Finally I said to the judge, 'Go to hell.' 'Quiet,' he shouts, 'or I'll have you sent away for contempt of court.'

"So a half year later when I saw this judge's name on the ballot, I just went into the voting booth and really let him have it, this rat who sits in judgment on other people's lives. And then, you know, as long as I was at it, I decided to add my general program, so to speak, condemning the whole regime. I wrote it all down."

So that was your dissident activity, I said, somewhat taken aback by its private nature.

"Wait a minute," Malchevsky said, settling into an experienced storyteller's rhythm. "They sent me away, of course, for a nice stretch, too. When I came back to Leningrad, I soon found that no one except my mother would have anything to do with me. The government had made me a nonperson. Friends turned away. When I went for a job, I was rejected as soon as they saw my papers — if I had been in jail for murder, that would have been all right, but when anyone saw 'Article 70, part one, anti-Soviet propaganda,' that was it. In my own country, I had become a nonperson, excluded from society."

And this, I said, trying to find a recognizable thread, this showed you the illegality of the regime and moved you toward the dissident movement?

"Wait a minute," Malchevsky responded, clearly satisfied that he had caught my interest. "At that time I had a good friend. I won't mention his name, but let's call him the gentleman with the last name beginning with B. Mr. B. was acquainted with a woman of fairly advanced age, an ex-ballerina down on her luck. In the 1940s, when we had an alliance with the West, she had many flirtations, affairs, romances with American diplomats and military attachés; then the Cold War came and she was convicted of espionage for things that previously had been allowed, just like that. In those days there were no discussions, no explanation — just take it, old girl, ten years' imprisonment.

"From 1947 to 1954 she was in the camps. If you've read Solzhenitsyn, you know what it means to be a woman in a camp. She suffered the greatest humiliations, a woman in the hands of a pack of animals. After Stalin's death, she was rehabilitated, etc., etc. — but of course that didn't give her back seven years or erase the degradation. At about this time, as luck would have it, she learned she had cancer, only about two more years to live. To make a long story short, she decided she would have her revenge, that since she had to go anyway, she would leave life giving the door a good slam, as they say. She decided to blow herself up in Lenin's mausoleum! She would die taking the most honored relic of communism with her, in one glorious explosion.

"She asked my friend, Mr. B., to supply her with explosives and a detonator. The mausoleum is very closely guarded, of course, policemen checking the queue for suspicious persons and more policemen at every corner inside. Her plan was to get herself a big fur coat and sew the explosive inside the lining.

"Mr. B. approached me. Since I had been in the military, I knew where to get explosives, on the side, so to speak, special channels. I began to ask around."

Amazing, I said, even to think of such a plan, foolhardy but brave, one had to admit.

"Yes, well," Malchevsky said, leaning back in a sudden access of introspection. "Fortunately or unfortunately, before things went much further the ex-ballerina died. Her cancer got her."

And the plan? I asked, let down by this anticlimax.

"Well there was none, with her dead. The only trouble is that my friend Mr. B. went around telling too many people of what we had intended, and the KGB got wind of it. The authorities claimed there was a whole group of conspirators, a veritable network of subversives, whereas it was just us two — they're terrified of the least hint of disorder. They gave me and my friend ten years each."

Probably not the stuff revolutions are made on. Nor, for that matter, did Malchevsky's actions even fit the description on the Freedom House flier I had seen ("participation in informal political discussions" seemed almost coy, considering his rambunctious history). Malchevsky's exploits seemed to hover somewhere between mere rowdyism and honorable derring-do, and altogether escaped the common Western notion of how a dissident behaves.

Afterward, conforming to the time-honored custom of the Russian host, Malchevsky escorted me out into the street and to my car. Slamming the door behind me and striking the confident pose of a second sending his boxer into the ring to defeat the favored champion, he urged me to take a recondite shortcut back to Manhattan. He made no allusion to his own recent misadventures in New York City traffic.

Trying to decide whether to follow his directions, I found myself weighing his dubious record as a taxi driver against his standing as a dissident. It may not be that unreasonable to follow a dissident's travel directions even if there is a risk of ending up at the wrong end of the Belt Parkway — it would be a sign of homage, a genial acknowledgment that their acts of courage in the Soviet Union inspire a general trust and that they are now welcome into American life. But Malchevsky seemed a tricky case, his history so full of holes that it would knock any scale of judgment off balance.

In the end, however, I did follow his suggestion, deciding that he deserved such a small gesture of good faith even if it did cost me some extra traveling time. Being a dissident in the Soviet Union, I decided, is only partly a matter of proper principles, of a coherent and impassioned resistance to oppression. Since petty anger gets punished exactly as if it were political rebellion, should we not honor it also? I made it back to Manhattan in fifteen minutes less than the outbound trip had taken.

SIX
❧ Religion

BEING a Jew in Russia has never been easy. The Tsarist regime feared that its Jewish subjects were too closely linked with world Jewry, that they had an overly autonomous communal system (religious and secular), and that in general they were an alien group adulterating the homogeneity of the empire's population. Beginning with Peter the Great, Russia's rulers promulgated laws restricting Jews. In 1786, Catherine the Great confined Jews to a Pale of Settlement (essentially in the southwestern provinces), and in 1835, Nicholas I brought official discrimination to a head with a series of edicts that forbade Jews from owning land or entering most professions, and that curtailed their opportunities for religious observance and teaching. Though there were intermittent improvements in the Jews' lot, anti-Semitic policy was the norm for the rest of the Romanov reign.

Moreover, Russia has always had a strong strain of popular anti-Semitism, including such vivid manifestations as the Black Hundreds movement that terrorized Jews at the turn of the century, wide circulation of the scurrilous forgery *Protocols of the Elders of Zion,* and pogroms so numerous they sometimes seemed the national pastime. Antipathy against the Jews was inflamed by the perception that they often executed the nation's money transactions, usually from an advantageous position — indeed, thanks to laws blocking their entry into other occupations, many Jews were merchants, moneylenders, and landlords' agents. The fact that the Russian Orthodox Church seemed to frown on the spirit of Judaism didn't help matters, either. By the time of the Revolution, fairly violent harassment of Jews was endemic.

Though a noteworthy segment of the Bolshevik cadre, from Trotsky on down, was Jewish, these men were hardly committed to Judaism. Socialism applied economic, not religious, standards in devising its blueprint for a new world, and indeed some early Russian socialist manifestos assigned Jews to the exploiting class. But once the Bolsheviks were in power, they became interested in policies that would prove the new order's break with the Tsarist past, including the treatment of minorities. In 1919 Lenin declared, "Hatred toward Jews persists only in those countries where slavery to the landowners and capitalists has created abysmal ignorance among the workers and peasants.... Shame on accursed Tsarism which tortured and persecuted the Jews." Even Stalin (in an uncharacteristic moment, to be sure) asserted that anti-Semitism "was a survival of the barbarous practices of the cannibalistic period."

But Soviet policy regarding the Jewish question, which was to subsume it to the general question of minorities, was prejudicial in its own way. Other minorities in the Soviet Union, whether Ukrainians or Uzbeks, can point to their own territory, a native language, and a flourishing sui generis culture. Jews have no territory — the attempt in the 1930s to get them to inhabit the desolate Asiatic province of Birobadzhan was a fiasco. And though Yiddish was at times endorsed by the regime as the language of a recognized national group, schools were generally forbidden to teach it. (Hebrew, which was construed as an aspect of Zionism, was totally suppressed.) Finally, Jewish culture, including a lively literary and theatrical tradition of long standing, expired from enforced neglect in the early 1940s. In other words, virtually all the appurtenances of Jewish life came under attack. A still more basic point, however, is that even if these appurtenances were permitted to exist, Soviet policy would still be inimical to Jews: in considering them as no more than a nationality, the policy pointedly ignores the view that they are the People of the Book.

Soviet officials respond that the West simply misunderstands the relationship between communism and Judaism, that the bourgeois frame of mind is not up to comprehending the categories of revolutionary thought. The communist ideal, they say, is always and consistently assimilatory: *all* the ethnic traditions that exist in today's Soviet Union must eventually vanish, absorbed by a culture that will obliterate the divisiveness of the capitalist past. Until communism achieves its full flowering, the vestiges of the old order, including religion, will be tolerated, though no more than that. In defending itself against the charge of bigotry, the regime can point to its Constitution, Article 52, which guarantees freedom of conscience, "the right to profess or not to profess any religion; and to conduct worship or atheistic propaganda."

In fact, it is reasonable to credit the Soviet argument up to a point. The behavior of the Soviet government in recent times shows that the country is not Nazi Germany, nor even contemporary Iran, where a bumptious theocracy can consign some citizens to second-rate status solely on the basis of religion. But if the Soviet regime is not a rapacious beast bent on stalking the Jews, it is just as obviously true that Jews suffer as a result of the system under which they live. The Soviet government sustains an environment where anti-Semitism flourishes. Thus, for example, though the use of *zhid* ("yid") is proscribed in official publications, it is a commonplace on the street, in the markets, in the offices of petty bureaucrats.

Several recent émigrés are now part of an Orthodox congregation that holds its services in a synagogue set up in a private home in Hoboken. The living room had a glass-front cabinet to house the Torah, and a table transplanted from the kitchen served the rabbi as a lectern. About twenty folding chairs were arrayed for the Sabbath worshippers, who, following Orthodox law, segregated themselves into male and female sections: a sheet suspended across the center of the room did the trick. In these makeshift circumstances, the enthusiasm of the congregation seemed even more pronounced, an unadorned spiritual passion. When they sang out the Sabbath hymns, there was an exultant boom.

Sophia Borkin, one of three female worshippers, emigrated

from Baku. She told me, "I had to come here because in the Soviet Union I could not live as a Jew. It's that simple. I had a good job, a good salary, a good apartment, but it wasn't enough. I wanted to live as a Jew and that was almost impossible. The government makes you work on Saturdays, and they won't accept religion as an excuse.

"In fact, for years my father did not practice Judaism. The Soviet system made him forget what it meant. He only came back to Judaism when my grandfather died and the funeral reminded him of all the rituals of his childhood. Then he taught me. I even began to wear a necklace with the Star of David on it. A man asked me, 'Why are you wearing that?' 'Why not?' I replied. But they don't understand. When I petitioned to emigrate, the factory managed called me in and told me he couldn't see how I could leave such a good job. Religion is completely alien to them.

"I think, in fact, that the people's attitudes are worse than the government's policies. For example, we had some non-Jewish neighbors with whom we got along very well in general. During Passover, however, the mother absolutely forbade her children to come to our apartment. She told them that Jews kill non-Jewish children and use their blood for baking. My father asked this woman, 'Do you really believe that?' She said to him, 'No, of course not.' But she still wouldn't let her children come to our apartment during Passover."

During the service, Sophia Borkin was raptly attentive to every word, and she sang the hymns so joyously that each note seemed to proclaim a dream realized.

The service was in the high Orthodox style, minutely in accord with every Talmudic injunction. The only deviations came when the rabbi intervened to explain the meaning of a particular passage — several individuals had only recently joined the small congregation and were not conversant with all the intricacies. Thus, near the end of the service, the rabbi momentarily halted the proceedings to explain that the "Sh'ma," the holiest of prayers, has 145 words, but since the Talmud holds that this prayer must correspond to the number of bones in the body, of which there are putatively 148, three words must be uttered twice each. Sophia Borkin took in even this esoterica without batting an eye, just one more element in the path of her spiritual renaissance.

But though the path arched toward the eternal verities of Judaism, it detoured through some local precincts. The rabbi, for example, periodically spoke in English, in that unique New York idiom that intimates an irony behind almost every statement. In explaining the intricacies of prayer and ritual, he maintained a seriousness that wavered only slightly, perhaps the verbal equivalent of a raised eyebrow; but he gave in to his impulses in the interval after the service. Rising to detail the congregation's straitened financial picture, and the unwillingness of the Jewish establishment to lend a hand, the rabbi became aggressively sarcastic, mockingly bitter. Remarkably, it was like nothing so much as watching a nightclub comedian with the mordant style of a Lennie Bruce.

For me the lesson of this Sabbath was clear, and not that surprising: religion, except in rare cases of ecstatic transport, is always culturally inflected. Sophia Borkin had escaped the oppression of the Soviet Union — but what she found was not the ideal form of Judaism of which she may have dreamed, not some eternal land populated by prophets and holy men conversing in God's tongue, but a place where religion achieved its pure form only occasionally, in the interval between secular intrusions. Of course, that's not so bad either.

In any case, Sophia Borkin's journey from Baku to Hoboken stands as one of the smoother transitions made by a Soviet émigré in the name of Judaism. Soviet ideology influenced many among the third wave, even those who thought they had turned a deaf ear. One result is that their concept of Judaism was distorted, pushed so far out of traditional shape that some American Jews claim they hardly recognize it. Not a few American organizations that shouted at the Soviet Union to "let my people go" have been left aghast at the sort of people who have come.

There are several agencies that are funded by national Jewish organizations which have as their purpose welcoming Soviet émigrés to this country. They provide a measure of material support, direct the émigrés through our bewildering bureaucracy, and generally help them to settle in. Religious sentiments often guide this beneficence; in return for the help they receive, the émigrés are expected to participate in Jewish life.

I visited one such agency in Queens, and Rabbi Bienstock, the director, sketched out for me the ideal balance between material support and religiosity, between aid and communality. But the reality, he quickly added, was all too different. Indeed, he seemed hardly able to get these perfunctory generalizations out of the way quickly enough, so eager was he to get on with an itemization of disappointments. He apparently was venting months of irritation. He said, "First of all we have to check that the émigrés who come to us are Jewish, as they claim. A lot of non-Jews have been let out by the Soviets, and they try to take advantage of our organization's benefits. It's hard to check with absolute certainty, of course, since many emigrated without identification papers, but we've developed some fairly sure-fire methods. We question them about who their friends were, where their relatives lived. It's not foolproof, but I think we do all right. I'd say that thirty percent of those who come to us are not Jewish."

I remarked that he had to become quite the detective in his dealings with the émigrés.

The rabbi eyed me coolly, perhaps appraising my own religious allegiances. Then he said, "What can you do; we have to protect ourselves. These émigrés are all — Jews and non-Jews — products of the Soviet system. They lie, they cheat, anything to get what they want, what they think they automatically deserve. They have no conception of the American system of voluntary charity. We bend over backward to help and we don't get a word of thanks. What's more, they don't believe a word of what I tell them, disregarding my religious instructions totally — though they're quite adept at making it appear they are listening up until the time they get some reward. Some go so far as to join a synagogue, hoping to get more support that way. Once they do get something, they leave immediately."

I said that he made them sound quite awful.

"Why not? After all, who has been permitted to come? Those who have been hand-picked by the Soviet government, which means we get the elderly, the psychologically handicapped, and the criminals. They are like animals, many of them, no soul at all. They drink terribly much, of course. On a holiday, no matter which one, it's the universal rule to get drunk. I tried to explain to some of them that New Year's Eve, for example, is a Christian holiday, having nothing to do with Jewish life. But it was as if I were talking to someone from another planet. They lack the basic concepts of humanity, let alone of Judasim. The Soviet system had done its work only too well."

I commiserated, saying his job indeed sounded difficult.

"Yes, it is, but you know," he said, "I would still rather be with one of these Soviet Jews than with an American gentile. A spark of Judaism always remains in them, and sometimes, with proper care, it can be made to flare up. Some émigrés even get circumcised, which is no joke when you are already an adult. I saw one *bris* of an eighteen-year-old that I'll never forget. When the young man awoke from the anesthetic, he looked around, then exclaimed, 'Now, at last I am a Jew.'"

The image of an adult male awakening from unconsciousness perfectly symbolizes the spiritual birth that American Jews hope to descry in the new arrivals: everything prior to that moment was mere preparation, a long journey through oblivion that culminates in a resplendent issue. But, in fact, "birth" fits the case of the third-wave émigrés rather poorly. Most are not at all eager to embrace the particular gift of life that the American Jewish community determinedly extends to them.

One émigré told me, sighing wearily, "In the Soviet Union we were despised for being too Jewish; here we are criticized for not being Jewish enough. *That's* the fate of a Soviet Jew, never to satisfy anyone."

The Soviet regime undercuts religion by subtle persuasion as well as by brute force. Its anti-religious policy depends in large measure on simply reminding men and women of the universal desire to be part of a friendly community. By insistently proclaiming Soviet society atheistic, the regime makes professing a religion equivalent to risking the displeasure of one's neighbors.

Judaism in the Soviet Union is seriously affected by this emphasis on civic conformity (much more, probably, than by overt persecution). Many Soviet Jews would not mind assimilating, if only to make daily life more bearable. But there is a Catch-22 in the Jews' predicament. The regime, though it despises religion as a divisive force, is too worried about the legendary trouble-making capacities of the Jews to let them melt into the population. Even those Jews who are most eager to assimilate are not allowed to shed all the distinguishing signs of their religion.

Even if an individual Russifies his or her name, sings the praises of atheism, and abjures Jewish practices, he or she is still technically a Jew. On the fifth line of the Soviet passport, in the space where citizens indicate their nationality, a Jew has no choice but to proclaim an affinity with the Seven Tribes of Israel. The only escape from this heritage is for children of intermarriage: at sixteen, they may enter into their passports the nationality of whichever parent they chose. All other Jews are fated to an ambiguous civic existence, simultaneously inside and outside Soviet society, their impulses toward assimilation held in check by a suspicious government, their dislike of communism mitigated by an allegiance to their native community.

The Jews' complicated sense of their place in Soviet society has its roots in the nineteenth century. When the socialist movement arose, many Jews were attracted. They believed that in transforming Russia, socialism would improve their lot also. Many other Jews, it is true, were less sure that their interests and those of socialism dovetailed quite so neatly. Given the choice, the preponderance of Jews would probably have emigrated rather than bet their future on the Revolution; but it would have been an agonizing decision. Russia was their home, despite all the injustice they had suffered there. In the event, most Russian Jews did not have the chance to leave, so they set their hopes on the Revolution perforce.

Obviously, that hope was largely disappointed, but that does not mean that all Jews in the Soviet period have lived as spiritual exiles, every moment at odds with the life that surrounds them. Soviet communism did great harm, but there have been successes also — the country was dragged kicking and screaming into the modern age, with its attendant material comforts. For those who remember a time when most homes had dirt floors, no electricity, and outhouses, such progress may weigh as heavily as religious tolerance. As important, Russians — including Russian Jews — are a fiercely patriotic people, and the twentieth century was filled with moments when defense of the nation overrode all other concerns. World War II was the critical test, and in fact that was an occasion when the reasons for the Russian Jews' allegiance to Russia were multiplied. Nazi Germany was the enemy of both their country and of Judaism.

The *Assotsiiatsia veteranov i invalidov* (The Association of Veterans and Invalids) is composed mainly of third-wave Jewish émigrés who served in the Red Army, and who thus must grapple daily with the consequences of their decision to support Stalin in his hour of need. The association now fights on two fronts. On one flank, it skirmishes with the United States Congress, demanding to know why service in the Red Army does not qualify the veterans for GI benefits: weren't they fighting in alliance with American soldiers, exposing themselves to equal danger for the common cause? On another flank, the association is in pitched battle with the many members of the second-wave emigration who had joined with General Vlasov to form a division to fight on the German side against Stalin — and the dispute about principles is made more galling by the association's perception that many Vlasovites have attained respectability and comfort in America, while many men of the third wave, who fought as America's allies, must endure close to poverty.

The association quarters itself in two tiny rooms of an upstairs wing of the American Veterans of Foreign Wars building in Brighton Beach. The floorboards creak, the desks and chairs are blanched from age, and the paint on the walls is peeling; but the office bubbles with activity, as if important work were afoot. When I arrived, a middle-aged secretary was in a heated telephone conversation about pension rights, and she merely nodded me in.

The four men in the main room were absorbed in their typing chores and in shuffling papers, and did not look up. But as soon as I identified myself as an American — a native speaker of English! — they gave me their full attention.

One man, the director, said, "You could perhaps help us with the VFW downstairs. We could use their assistance in pressing our claim with the US Congress, but there is such a language barrier that we can never explain our problem."

The man had the bluff appearance of an old soldier, hair combed straight back from a high forehead, chest thrust forward, a slight bounce to his gait, as if still on parade; but his tone when he spoke of the American VFW was plaintive as a child's — if only he possessed the simplest of human gifts, he said, the ability to make himself understood, the association's righteous cause would prevail.

He said, "How can such a thing be? We fought for the Allies, but America prefers not to recognize us. It pays more respect to traitors, anti-Semites. While the Vlasovites were scheming with Hitler, the Nazis were killing thousands of Jews. Was it wrong to fight for one's country against such evil?"

I had no answer to this, and in the pause the secretary's shouted phone conversation, which she had shifted into a still shriller gear, filled the room. Throughout our talk, it provided a jangly counterpoint, but no one else seemed to pay it any attention, as if in this office frustrated shouting was the most appropriate background music.

When I asked more specifically about the association's relationship with the second-wave emigration, the director beckoned one of the other men to come over, introducing him as Aron Abramovich, an authority on Jews in the Red Army.

Aron Abramovich said, "Why bother with the second wave? I've met some of them and tried to discuss matters. They say I see everything from the parochial point of view of a Jew. Well, from what point of view should I look at things? A Nazi one, as they do?"

Everyone in the office — except the secretary, who was now launched on a no-holds-barred tirade — nodded approvingly at this statement. But even within the association there can be disagreements about the role of Soviet Jews. Every attempt to detail a position seemed to release a welter of cross-purposes.

Aron Abramovich declared, "There were many Red Army generals in World War II, and many more colonels. Some Russified their names to avoid friction, but still it is possible to pick out hundreds of Jews who were crucial to the defense of the motherland. Jews made a difference."

But the director objected to this. "No, no, that is not true. Some Jews did get to the top of the army, but very few. The anti-Semitism was too great. Jews wanted to contribute to the war effort, but they were kept on a tight rein, as they always have been."

The director's comment is the footnote many Soviet Jews wish to add to a discussion of their history. After itemizing the reasons for trying to fit into Soviet society — self-preservation, a natural allegiance to one's homeland — there remains an undissolved impulse to prove they were dissociated, out of the mainstream. After all, in accepting Soviet citizenship, they were abiding communism; by their zealous participation in the war effort, they were promoting a system that was hostile to an integral aspect of their being.

Always close to the consciousness of many Soviet Jews, the issue of complicity has lately flamed anew thanks to Solzhenitsyn. Driven by a dream of an ideal Slavdom, he has denounced everything corrupting the purity of the community. The worst evil, for Solzhenitsyn, is communist ideology; even more than its substance, he seems to detest its Western provenance, likening it to a foreign disease infecting the Russian body politic. He can be vicious in attacking any group that he believes has promoted the spread of communism. His critics, noting the great number of Jewish names on his list of offenders, call him anti-Semitic; Solzhenitsyn grandly retorts he is a historian objectively recording the facts.

In the face of such ex cathedra pronouncements, men of lesser reputation are likely to lose the thread of their own arguments, and Aron Abramovich seemed to be revising some of his earlier opinions as he denounced Solzhenitsyn's. He said, "Solzhenitsyn distorts and lies. When he speaks of the labor camps, for example, he says that some woman prisoner managed to get preferential treatment by insinuating herself into the good graces of the labor leader who was a *zhirny evrey* [a greasy Jew]. Well, of course if the man was a Jew perhaps the fact should be mentioned, just as saying someone was a Ukrainian. But Solzhenitsyn does it too often, and with malice.

"And anyway, it's simply wrong to imply, as he does, that Jews were disproportionately represented in the top cadres. They weren't. Solzhenitsyn never even mentions the top men — Yezhov, Beria — who of course weren't Jewish. Its a new kind of writing, lying by implication."

Aron Abramovich paused in his outburst, obviously looking for the phrase to clinch his argument. He said, "At best, Jews were on the second level of command of the Soviet establishment, not the top."

It seems an impoverished form of pride, to claim that evildoing was limited to a secondary degree of complicity, but that statement symbolizes the dilemma of Russian Jewry in general. Caught up in an ambiguous history, they must continually sort out the meager possibilities that destiny offers, constantly choose from among the grayish shades of moral behavior. Pure and simple principles, such as one likes to believe are inherent in questions of religious affiliation, tend to corrode in the swampy grounds of Soviet society.

Just as I left the association, the secretary brought her tirade to an end by slamming the receiver back into its cradle with a force that seemed intended to cause physical harm to the person at the other end of the wire. Exhausted by her extended outburst, as if she had been performing manual labor, she leaned back in her chair and lit up a cigarette. The men in the office at last turned their attention to her, regarding her with genial approbation — the explosiveness of her final gesture must have been appreciated, a relief from the customary fog of ambiguity that surrounded their efforts to define the Soviet Jew's moral position.

The Brighton Beach YM/YWHA, like other branches of the organization, provides its community with various social and cultural services, upon which it sprinkles quantities of religiosity in doses ranging from heavy to minuscule. I observed two instances.

The youth group that meets two nights a week in the second floor game room gets a virtually imperceptible dose of religion, but still the Soviet teenagers who show up to play Ping-Pong or pool, or simply to hang out, know that they come under Jewish auspices. I wanted to learn what, if anything, this meant to them.

On the telephone, the youth group counselor had told me to expect tough, street-wise kids, not too eager to talk to an outsider. They lived in a rowdy neighborhood, and as the last ethnic minority to arrive, had to fight for a piece of turf. It sometimes caused a wagon-train mentality, the counselor said, an urge to form into a tight circle of only émigrés.

Hanging up, she had said, "When you get beaten up in the schoolyard several times because you're Russian, you think of yourself as Russian."

Though I knew the Y was somewhere near the boardwalk, I had neglected to learn the exact location. Passing two teenagers who were conversing in Russian, I stopped to inquire, also in Russian. The taller of the two, his sullen features half hidden by the peak of a leather cap, appraised me coolly, then briefly ejaculated, "*Khuy ego znaet*" ("Who the fuck knows"), and turned back to his friend.

The casualness of the obscenity was startling, but it was salutory at that moment to be reminded that the Russian teenagers of Brighton Beach do not speak in the well-modulated tones of characters in Pushkin. In fact, as I learned upstairs in the Y game room, their way with language is highly varied, a polyglot tour de force. Thus, though most have quickly mastered colloquial English, they prefer Russian for transacting their games of Ping-Pong and billiards; speaking to an outsider, even to the group counselor, who had a serviceable Russian, required a switch back to English; while expletives come in both languages, and require an analysis of tone and volume before their full meaning is clear.

The elaborateness of their speech patterns should not be surprising. Even more than their elders, these Russian teenagers lack a sense of where they belong. They did not ask to leave their old world (their parents decided for them), but they have been hustled headlong into the new one (while their parents often hang back in the safety of émigré enclaves). Though they may look, in their skin-tight jeans and leather jackets, to be well enmeshed in American life, their psychological state still floats erratically. Their complicated use of language is a necessary semaphoring system, signaling degrees of intimacy, establishing areas of trust and suspicion.

The game room was a cauldron of adolescent exuberance, each teenager rebounding like a random atom from one passing fancy to another. No one seemed ever to play a Ping-Pong match all the way through before dashing on to some rambunctious flirtation that had caught his or her eye; if a young man momentarily subsided next to the video-game console, it was only till he saw a good-natured brawl in another corner of the room that he could clamber into. Used to subjects who sat still for my questions, I felt totally at sea, uncertain how to make this whirlygig slow down so I could scrutinize it. Finally I decided athletic prowess might claim their attention: I challenged the reigning Ping-Pong champ to a game — victory would lead to the rapport that I sought. But I had forgotten that Ping-Pong is virtually a national passion, played endlessly from an early age in the Soviet Union, and I went down to ignominious defeat before the young man's expert spins and slices.

Afterward, perhaps moved by pity for my poor showing, one of the spectators of the game did stop and talk to me. He turned aside my effort to insinuate the intimacy of a Russian conversation, but we had a nice chat nonetheless. Igor was sixteen, but built like a professional football player. He told me he'd dropped out of school to work as a loader and truck driver, but he intended to go back to finish his studies eventually: education was clearly the way to get ahead in America — his father kept telling him so, and he was probably right.

The family had first lived for a while in Los Angeles, but his parents were happier in Brooklyn, in the tight émigré enclave where they could go days without speaking a word of English. Igor said, "Sometimes at home my father tries to speak English, saying I should help him learn by correcting his mistakes. But his English is so bad that my brother and I just laugh. Then my father gets angry and tries to give us both a beating, and English lessons are over for the day."

I asked if he had any American friends.

"My best friends are other Soviet émigrés. Still I know one or two Americans pretty well. They're OK."

Tell me, I said cannily, if you went to a soccer match between a New York team and a visiting Soviet one, who would you root for?

Igor hesitated only an instant. "The Russians," he said. "For sure."

So you'd call yourself a Russian still? I said.

"No, I wouldn't. That's a different question. I wasn't called a Russian when I was there, so I won't call myself a Russian now."

Would you call yourself a Jew, then, like there? I asked.

"No, not that either," Igor replied, more emphatically.

Others I spoke to that evening also had trouble finding precise descriptions of themselves. Among those I heard were Russian-American Jew, Soviet-emigrant Jew, and Soviet-American who was forced to emigrate, as well as several complex efforts that petered out in confusion. In fact, the problem baffles the third wave in general, and though not being able to define oneself in a phrase sounds like a minor social embarassment, it points to profounder issues. Virtually every other group that has come to America has been able to describe itself easily enough, perhaps resorting to a hyphen now and then to encompass an additional allegiance. The third-wave émigrés require a whole contraption of hyphens and parenthetical clauses, and even then it is uncertain that they have trapped their elusive historical identities.

The teenage émigrés are deployed on the front lines of the third wave's struggle to find its way in America. They get into American life most quickly, and often into the least hospitable environs; they need all the support the Brighton Beach Y can give. But the Y also seeks to extend its protective auspices to the elderly generation of the third wave. On another floor, on another day, I observed what I can only call a Jewish education-class-cum-concert, attended by about one hundred older émigrés.

Even the dress of the audience announced the hesitant, shambling progress that the older arrivals make toward Americanization. Fancy apparel purchased since coming to America was worn in slapdash combination with items from Moscow's GUM store. Over flared American corduroy slacks, men retained their old squarish jackets of iridescent gabardine, and stout women with peasant kerchiefs and shapeless skirts walked about in modish knee-high boots. They seemed engaged in some sort of good-natured dismantling of American style, reducing it to just those items considered suitable. The same off-handedness was visible in the émigrés' physical appearance: after a certain age, Soviets care nothing for cosmetics — take us as we are, warts (virtually a national affliction, in fact) and all. Looking like a Gogolian tableau, the audience sat waiting for the program to begin.

The dress of the woman conducting the program would alone have established her preeminence. She wore a severe black suit with a contrasting white ruffled blouse, smart in any circumstances, high finery in these. But she also had a peremptory tone, as if addressing a class of unruly schoolchildren, which showed she was in charge. "Remember that we must make a good impression on America," she said, though America was hardly manifest anywhere in that room. "No talking, no getting up during the performance. *Ditsiplina, ditsiplina!* [Discipline, discipline!]"

When the audience quieted down, she continued, "Tomorrow is Purim. I remind you that the synagogues in our neighborhood welcome you. You should take advantage of the opportunities that America offers you, and tell your friends to do so also. I am disappointed more people did not attend today's event. We all know that in the Soviet Union not everyone knew what it meant to be Jewish, but now there is a chance to learn."

When she proceeded to a short lesson on Jewish tradition, telling the Purim tale, her brisk manner suggested an anthropologist trying to explain electricity to a long-lost tribe of aborigines. The audience, however, listened attentively, though given the recent emphasis on the virtue of discipline, it was hard to gauge the genuineness of their interest. Certainly, they were happier when the pedagogy ceased and the entertainment began.

A poet arose and read his works. He read in the customary Soviet style, theatrically and with broad gesticulations. When he likened Brighton Beach to Odessa, he motioned out the window and toward the beach and Sheepshead Bay: the wintry vista of desolate stretches of sand and water (with one oil tanker plying its dreary route) did have intimations of a Soviet scene, but the poet's point was that it was better here, and the audience, applauding, enthusiastically agreed.

The woman in charge reappeared to introduce the musical segment of the program. Lest anyone had not taken her earlier point, she said, "Purim is a holiday of happiness and joy. I wish you success in your new homeland. Remember — Purim is celebrated in all *free* countries of the world."

An elderly violinist played Strauss's "Blue Danube Waltz." He didn't play very well, torturing the tremolos and exaggerating each sentimental passage. But the audience was transfixed, and the woman in charge seemed to relax a bit. The event was going to be a success, a small extension of Jewish culture — even if it was effected through the unexpected agency of an Austrian from La Belle Epoque.

As I rose to leave, I glanced out the window again to confirm the poet's metaphor of Odessa. I noticed two men, their clothes and manner marking them as émigrés. They were trying to start a fire on the deserted and windswept beach, using some discarded planks and newspapers. It didn't appear that they were very comfortable, but apparently they preferred their occupation to submitting to the Y program for spreading Jewish culture. Like many émigrés, they had probably led the vagabondish spiritual life in the Soviet Union, and would continue to do so here. It would take more than Strauss to domesticate them.

The erratic relationship of the third wave to Judaism manifests itself in various ways, and one of the more curious is in Jewish émigré attitudes toward Russian Orthodoxy. The Orthodox Church in America is sometimes excoriated, occasionally praised (and embraced, through religious conversion), but rarely merely abided as a religion having little bearing on Russian Jews. Scandal, real and imagined, keeps the pot of emotions at a boil.

The *Novy amerikanets*, temporarily taking on itself the role of representative of émigré Judaism, recently published an article, entitled "Save My Son," which accused the Russian Orthodox Church in New York City of luring a young Jewish émigré away from his mother's influence and into the "net" of Russian Orthodoxy. It was a clear case of kidnapping, the *Novy amerikanets* averred, coolly adding that "a man who renounced his religion is not worthy of being called a man." The article took pains to note that the priest who had purportedly engineered the plot was himself a *vykrest*, which is a derogatory term for a convert.

The priest in question is Michael Meerson-Aksyonov (the name added after the hyphen denotes his evolving religious persona), who converted in the late 1960s after being attracted to the Russian Orthodox revival that was just beginning in the Soviet Union. He became deeply involved in the movement, working in the underground circles that were devised to elude the regime's bullying attentions. Russian Orthodoxy is often as much nationalistic ideology as religion, an evocation of love for the Russian land and tradition as well as a Christian creed, and its current revival has struck a sympathetic chord among a population that is disenchanted with communism's abstract promises. Such a fervent movement can get out of control, and is certainly more likely to spark unrest among Russia's chauvinistic and mystically minded masses than are the political dissidents, who depend on logic and invoke a doctrine of universal human rights. The regime is therefore especially wary of religious activists, and when Meerson-Aksyonov's activities finally came to light, he was forced to emigrate. (Technically he still fell under the Jewish quota, and, in fact, the Soviet bureaucracy relaxed its rules in quite a few similar cases, so eager to be rid of troublemakers that it hardly bothered with precise definitions of Jewishness.)

Meerson-Aksyonov is now the priest of the Church of Christ the Savior, whose congregation includes a number of third-wave émigrés, some who were Orthodox in Russia, some who converted after arrival. The church stands on Seventy-first Street off Second Avenue — though *stands* may be the wrong word, conjuring up a stately architecture, whereas this shabby two-story brownstone seems to require support from the buildings crowding in on either side. The church's ecclesiastical status, by contrast, is independent. During the nineteenth and early twentieth centuries, the Russian Orthodox Bishop of America was appointed by the Metropolitan of Moscow; but after the Revolution, when the Church in Russia became fully subservient to the state, the American branch declared itself "autocephalous," self-headed.

Nevertheless, the Church retains all the essences of Orthodoxy, which means it remains unmistakably Russian. The iconostasis behind the altar depicts events that occurred on Russian soil, and the liturgy has always been in Old Church Slavonic, which is close enough to Russian for a worshipper to believe that God is a countryman. Indeed, the birth of Russian Orthodoxy and of the Russian nation were virtually contemporaneous, making participation in that religion seem like an aspect of citizenship.

The Mass that I attended at the Church of Christ the Savior was served in an airy, high-ceilinged room that was a bit of a surprise after the narrow doorway and cramped corridor of the entryway. In fact, much of the scene was composed of incongruous elements, simultaneously makeshift and inspirational. Behind the ornate altar, the multileveled iconostasis seemed especially bedraggled, with several spots in need of new paint. The choir section was tiny, a mere jumble of five stools, but the bass and his four colleagues exalted as if for the ages. And in a niche in the back of the room, the sexton sat grumbling over his accounts and invoices, providing a mundane counterpoint to the murmured liturgy. It all seemed appropriate, however: Russian Orthodoxy has long advertised its unprepossessing manner, a certain slapdash quality that balances the mystery. Worshippers should be made to feel at home.

At the climax of the service, when the priest vanished behind the iconostasis, the mass reached a noteworthy level of informality and conviviality. A young mother in jeans and clogs set her infant daughter on the red rug leading to the altar, and since the child had only one gear — forward, energetically — it took the combined efforts of various members of the congregation to keep her out of harm's way. As she continued crawling about, the infant became the focus of a common task, everyone cooing soft Russian endearments at the same time that they continued the religious ceremony. If an émigré longed for intimations of home, if he felt nostalgic for the Russian spirit, attendance at a Russian Orthodox service might be the perfect balm — and that, indeed, appears to be one reason why some third-wave Jewish émigrés convert.

When I met with Meerson-Aksyonov in his office, he was as informal and congenial as the ceremony had been. He still wore his gray tunic, but he had transferred the white plastic collar to his breast pocket and donned sandals. Behind his glasses, his eyes flashed amiably each time he smiled, which was often. He is in his late thirties, dark-haired and bearded, and speaks English fluently. In general he has the air of someone at ease — New York City can hold no worse than what he has already endured. When he discusses the dangers of his life in the Soviet Union, he is equable, as if describing no more than a fairly strenuous camping trip: perhaps there were rough terrain and some wild beasts, but nothing an experienced woodsman couldn't handle.

I asked him about his activities as a dissident.

He said, "A lot of it was educational. Russians hardly have a sense of their own history. So we organized seminars, solicited papers, obtained historical material. We also published books and newspapers, illegally of course, and this meant we used a lot of material that had to be translated."

"Sounds as if being a dissident was a full-time occupation," I said.

"There are people who devote their whole life to advancing the *samizdat* movement, working at a regular job during the day and at illegal activity at night. I was a bit luckier, as far as free time went. I worked at the Academy of Sciences, at the Institute of History — a research institute, if you know what that is. You don't have to show up there except maybe twice a month to collect your salary."

In Meerson-Aksyonov's amiable retrospective, jokes are not out of place. He said, "You shouldn't think that a job at a research institute is paradise. Have you heard this one? A man who works at an institute is asked, 'What do you do at your job?' He replies, 'I pretend to work, and the government pretends to pay me.' The salary was truly minuscule, but at least I had time for my dissident activities."

I remarked that with so much going on — seminars, meetings, publications — it was surprising that the authorities did not realize who was involved and arrest them.

"Moscow is a big city and the KGB isn't all that efficient. It's possible to get lost if one tries. During the last five years I was in Moscow, I changed my apartment every six months." He laughed heartily. "I was younger then, I had more energy. I don't know what I would do if I had to live that way now. My wife wants to move to a larger apartment here in New York, and I'm too lazy to even think about it."

To me this sounds like an overly modest account of a dissident's life in Moscow, and I ask Meerson-Aksyonov to explain more particularly how he managed to avoid the authorities.

"Well," he said, "you have to realize that Russians have been managing this sort of thing for decades, for centuries. We work our politics by means of intimate circles, because it's pretty hard for the government to distinguish between individuals meeting just for tea and those meeting to discuss human rights. Especially in the early days of dissent, in the 1960s, the movement was a very tight circle. In those days, everyone would come to my house, and we'd sit around one table. We were all from the same part of Moscow society, anyway, and most of us had known each other for years. There weren't even factions then — we all just knew that Soviet society had to be changed. Only later did we split up into those who stressed civil rights, those who spoke of Zionism, those interested in a religious revival within the Soviet Union."

I asked his opinion of the current situation in the Soviet Union.

"I am most interested in the new religious spirit that seems to be spreading among people in the Soviet Union, and I try to keep in touch with events there, but it's not easy." Meerson-Aksyonov suddenly became pensive, his spirits seeming to sag for the only time during our conversation. "Also, I hate to say, we have to spend some energy defending our flanks, from attacks from fellow émigrés. There we could all feel united, perhaps because our common enemy was so near. Over here, we've taken to squabbling among ourselves. Most surprising, some émigrés now even use the style that only party hacks used in the Soviet Union."

I assumed that this was an allusion to the *Novy amerikanets* attack on him, and my hunch was confirmed a few weeks later. In one of the other Russian-language newspapers, I noticed a rebuttal Meerson-Aksyonov had composed. Referring to the epithet that the *Novy amerikanets* had affixed to him, he wrote, "I must note that in the Russian language, the word *vykrest* is never published, just like the word *zhid* [yid]. The article 'Save My Son' cannot be called anything else but a provocation. We would not have been surprised to find something similar in *The Moscow Komsomol*."

It was, obviously, a far cry from the days when everyone would sit around one table of a Moscow apartment, as Meerson-Aksyonov had put it in his conversation with me. Then, Orthodoxy had been part of a passionate underground alliance; but with the Soviet regime thousands of miles away, actions that once would have been accepted as part of the common cause are being examined for the slightest taint of self-interest. When the Orthodox Church in America raises its banner to summon the faithful, many third-wave Jewish émigrés see only a devious attempt to proselytize. Even those who went for years without giving the slightest thought to the meaning of Judaism may react with a zealot's anger. Say this for pluralistic America, with its free give-and-take among the various religions — it makes one think, more excitedly if not necessarily more profoundly, about one's affiliations.

In fact, when they were in the Soviet Union, many third-wave émigrés never stopped to consider the extent of their commitment to Judaism. It seemed unnecessary; society did it for them. "Jewishness" was a characteristic so tenaciously ascribed to them by others that spiritual introspection appeared redundant.

The example of Soviet society's insidious influence on religious consciousness might incline us toward favoring the opposite extreme, an ideal place where men and women would be allowed to define their religious beliefs without any influence from society. But even if that were desirable (and the notion is moot), it is hardly attainable. What one thinks of being a Jew — or a Catholic or Muslim — is rarely the simple result of communion with eternal values; the heritage of relatives, the views of friends and colleagues, the gossip of the neighbors, in fact all the complex activities of a society at work also exert an influence.

The case of the third-wave Bukharan Jews, from the Soviet

republic of Tadzhikistan in Central Asia, helps to show how closely religion is tied to culture. They were among the least alienated of Soviet Jews, for a number of reasons. One, though they no more than other Soviet Jews could call a territory uniquely their own, the Bukharan Jews were so concentrated within a small area that they developed strong regional allegiances. Two, though their language has a strong Jewish component, it is quite similar to that of their gentile neighbors (and much more so than the European Jew's Yiddish or Hebrew is to his neighbor's Russian). Three, the population of Tadzhikistan is little given to anti-Semitism (perhaps because Oriental regions have historically accommodated diverse groups). In all, it may be true to say that the Bukharan Jews (who are Sephardic, from the Eastern and Mediterranean branch of Judaism) feel closer to their non-Jewish Tadzhek neighbors than to the Ashkenazic Jews of European Russia.

A number of Bukharan Jews now live in the Borough Park section of Brooklyn. They have formed a small congregation headed by a rabbi from Jerusalem, no Bukharan rabbi being available. Borough Park is virtually an enclave of Jews, a neighborhood bounded by the crumbling slums of the inner city ghettoes; but it is an enclave of Ashkenazic Jews, which means that the Bukharans, who keep to themselves, constitute an enclave within an enclave.

On the phone, the rabbi told me, "They don't mix much with the Ashkenazim, who have altogether different habits, who are not really as passionately Jewish as the Sephardim."

He invited me to come and meet them, but it could not be for a Sabbath service as I suggested — the rabbi had no intention of implicating himself in my sin of driving on a holy day. I went to Borough Park on a Wednesday evening instead, to visit a family and their friends who were sitting *shiva*, the week-long commemoration of a deceased relative. These can be grim affairs, bereavement stretched to a painful tightness; this *shiva* wouldn't be like that, the rabbi had asserted, Sephardic Jews make even grief show its joyous aspect.

When I entered the neat two-family home, I quickly noticed other signs that I was not among European Jews. Seven men were sitting around the dining room table. Several wore embroidered and sequined squarish caps instead of yarmulkes, and one had disdained a chair in favor of a stack of pillows that barely brought his chin to table level. All with fierce mustaches, with swarthy skin and dark eyes, the men seemed not too far removed from their ancestors' life of feats of horsemanship and hunting. One offered me a cup of tea with a gesture of elaborate hospitality: the traditional gesture of welcome to a traveler.

One wall was covered with pictures and momentos of Bukhara, and instead of a door, a beaded curtain partitioned the room from the corridor. I had just successfully negotiated the Battery Tunnel, the curves of the Brooklyn Expressway, yet some unexpected detour apparently had deposited me in the Orient. When, after a few minutes of silent prayer, it was time to rise, turn in the direction of Jerusalem, and sing the "Sh'ma," I found myself confronting a glass-front cabinet displaying a trove of wealth — plates with solid gold trim, enameled miniature mosaics, sparkling silver — which even more than by its look of luxury astounded me with an air of an exotic, Eastern way of life.

The reading of the prayers was in Hebrew, but during the numerous interruptions for drinking bitter Tadzhek tea, the table talk was in Tadzhi (with a few digressions into Russian for my benefit). Indeed, when the strictly ceremonial part of the evening was over and the rabbi left, Tadzhi took over completely: with the official representative of Judaism gone, sitting *shiva* became a Bukharan affair.

Bukharan culture is strictly patriarchal, and the women who had been preparing dinner in the kitchen did not join us in eating it. They did not even enter the room to serve it. Two of the younger men set out the bowls of chicken and rice and lettuce, and one also circulated a small silver bowl for everyone to wash his hands.

The young man with the bowl attracted my attention. Though it was warm in the room, he wore a thick sweater under his suit jacket, and his hawkish features were half masked by a fedora.

He had a fastidious, almost prophylactic, manner of carrying the bowl.

The man on my right, noticing my curiosity, said, "He's our *mohel*, does all the circumcisions for our community. He was the mohel in Samarkand too, though one had to be careful how and where one performed a *bris*. Some Jews who were members of the Party even tried to make out they didn't know what was happening with their own sons. They would arrange to go out of town on the day the *bris* was to occur, and when they came home they'd act surprised their sons were circumcised."

The chicken, divided into several outsized pieces, was piled on two platters at either end of the table. Tearing and cutting it into edible portions was an occasion for amiable jokes and laughter, and each diner accepted his meal with a gracious nod, as if for a gift bestowed. A spirit of hearty communality prevailed.

"Good Samarkand *plov*," my neighbor said, giving me my portion of chicken and rice. "Something Americans can hardly recognize, let alone cook."

The table talk, my neighbor whispered to me, was also of Samarkand, of the good old days when these men were still in their natural element. They laugh as they recall old events in distant places.

I asked them to tell me how it was to be Jewish under Soviet rule.

An elderly man replied, "Things were not perfect, of course. They tried to make us work on Saturdays. Still, we managed, and it was infinitely better than it had been under Stalin."

"Still, we managed" — coming from a Soviet Jew, that's tantamount to a song of praise. Presumably, the affinities between their religion and the Tadzhek culture had shielded the Bukharan Jews from the harsher forms of prejudice; indeed (to judge from my evening with them), their Judaism was *sustained* by their sense of being Tadzhek. If the ultimate attributes of their God were universal and transcendent, His trappings seemed derived from Central Asia. Sadly, the meshing of religion and nationality was finally unsatisfactory; the two ideals slipped their gears and grated often enough to make emigration necessary.

After we consumed the *plov* and drank some more tea, one of the men invited me to accompany him to a party. To celebrate his grandson's birthday, a hall had been rented, a caterer hired, and more than one hundred guests invited.

"No, of course you won't be in the way," he said, waving aside my protestations. "We're not like Americans, we like guests."

I asked if that meant he was not happy in his new country.

A big, barrel-chested man, he shrugged his shoulders with a motion that suggested a boxer's defensive crouch. "What can one like here except the opportunity to make money? It's chaotic, no culture, no traditions."

During our two-block walk, he explained to me that the party would be very unlike the *shiva* I had just witnessed. His daughter had married an Ashkenzic Jew. "She is happy. They say Askenazim make better family men than Sephardim," he said, but still he looked dubious, as if describing an extreme form of intermarriage.

The party was an extravagant affair — exuberant good cheer lubricated by plenty of vodka. A singer wailed a sad song in an exotic Azerbaijani dialect, accompanying himself with a tambourine. As if struck by some mysterious impulse, a woman in her fifties rose from her seat and performed an intricate, sexy dance, happily oblivious to the proprieties of her age. A number of tambourines appeared among the guests, exciting those who gained possession. Soon many people were dancing, and the members of the small band were perspiring freely as they tried to keep up with the festive air.

Still, whenever I spied my host during the evening, he looked a bit ill at ease — not unhappy, but the bonhomie I had noticed when he was with his Bukharan comrades had drained away. He no longer looked as if at home, and I wondered if his discomfort could not be taken as exemplary of the Bukharan Jews' spiritual odyssey. In Tadzhikistan, they had a homeland which sustained their daily habits and attitudes, but they left in order to express their religious urges fully. Now they are in a country where religious freedom prevails, but where the surrounding culture cramps their own, driving them into the narrow refuge of their apartments. Every step into the world, even into the environs of their fellow Soviet émigrés, requires compromise.

The senses of religion and of nationality seem always to seep into each other. Indeed, for all of the third wave, excepting only a handful of religious purists, the journey to America has underscored the cruelty of emigration as a therapy for the soul: in stretching to comprehend one part of their identity, the émigrés almost invariably damage some other.

SEVEN
❧ *Literary Circles*

In any history of Russian literature, Alexander Pushkin would be the hero. His reputation rests not only on the merits of his literary corpus but on his role as codifier of culture. After him, Russian writers confronted the West knowing they had a powerful native tradition behind them; when they borrowed, or even imitated, they confidently assumed that no alien elements could seriously attenuate the Slavic essence of their works.

For third-wave writers that sense of detachment is in jeopardy. They find themselves in the midst of America's booming and buzzing cultural life, having to notice all of its products instead of only the easily exportable variety that they had remarked on when in the Soviet Union. A sea change of attitude is required — the extent of which might be grasped by trying to imagine Pushkin creating his elegant hymns while living in Manhattan.

If that seems far-fetched, it's worth noting that Pushkin's desk, the one from his familial estate, Mikhailovskoe, *has* floated over to New York's West Side on the tide of the third wave. It stands in the apartment of his great-granddaughter Natalia Pushkin, who emigrated in 1975 and now works as a makeup artist for the New York City Opera Company. Soviet customs regulations forced her to leave much behind, but there are still many items in her living room which evoke her unique heritage: some books from the poet's library, a brooch that had been passed down through several generations, a portrait of Pushkin's wife (an evil figure in most literary histories, since she drove her husband to engage in a fatal duel, but in this setting just another ancestor).

I asked how it felt to live with such an ancestry.

She said, "When I was in grade school and we had lessons in memorizing poetry, I was always a bit uncomfortable when it was time to do Alexander's. During the recitations, everyone would turn in their seats to see how I was reacting. But that was the only time it was awkward. He is the nation's poet, true, but he is also a relative."

It was astonishing to hear Russia's greatest literary genius referred to by his first name. The author of *Eugene Onegin* just another member of the family! The mementos in the room seemed to lose their hallowed air and become artifacts expressing the common wish to keep in touch with one's ancestors — all except the desk, which, I found, still had an unmistakable aura. Literary genius is purely verbal, we are told, not reducible to the black markings on a page and still less to the tools of the writing trade; nevertheless it was unnerving to think that the great poet had sat at this very desk, rested his elbows on its edges while waiting for his muse, then pressed upon its broad surface as he transferred to paper the limpid phrase born in his excited imagination. And now the desk stood on West Eighty-sixth Street, a few houses up from Ray's Luncheonette. It was as if some bit of Hawthorne or Melville (though we have no true equivalent to Pushkin in the American tradition) had turned up on Gorky Street, to be bombarded by the influences of an alien culture.

Literature has always been the flagship of Russian culture. It is the esthetic form that first made Europe sit up and take notice of its northern neighbor, and it is the esthetic form that best expresses the nation's continuing obsession with moral issues. Russians, émigrés included, are enormously proud of their literary tradition, and will not suffer much fiddling with it.

Even the first-wave emigration, which was cosmopolitan in most matters, zealously insisted on a quality of Russianness in its literature. Thus, though the first wave stayed in Europe for almost twenty years, its authors continued to write almost exclusively of Russia, whether in the elegiac style of Nobel Prize winner Ivan Bunin or in the weepy variations of his many imitators.

Literary Circles 179

Trying something different was to risk anathematization. Vladimir Nabokov was practically drummed out of the émigré community for the crimes of being too French, too flippant, not sufficiently nostalgic.

The matter of literature's Russianness agitates the third wave also, in forums ranging from fiery journalistic polemics to the Brighton Beach clubhouses where elderly émigrés congregate. I decided to sample an event that seemed likely to fall in the middle range of intensity, passionate beliefs tempered by professional decorum: I went to the annual convention of AATSEEL (American Association of Teachers of Slavic and East European Literature) in Philadelphia.

The corridors of the Sheridan Hotel were filled with Slavists from all over the country. They came in typical academic sizes and shapes, but there were two features that hinted at an émigré influx into the field. First, in the sea of tweed and sensible suits, there were flashes of garish pink and plush velveteen — fortified by their new American salaries, émigrés often seek some decisive relief from years of boring Soviet fashions. Second, a surprising amount of Russian was being spoken. It is an awesomely difficult language for a foreigner to master, and many American Slavists are unwilling to commit a complex Russian sentence in public; the émigrés roamed the corridors, wielding their native language as if it were a weapon proving their superiority.

The titles of the papers scheduled for the morning session did not strike me as promising — a typical example was "The Curious Concept of Unity in *Notes from the Underground*," which evoked the dreary prospect of a man arguing with himself about issues no one thought of contesting — and I decided to wait until the afternoon, when the panels devoted to émigré literature were to convene. The main event, the showpiece of the convention, came last. Nebulously entitled "The Spirit of Emigration," this panel needed all the space of the hotel's gaudy central auditorium. Every seat was filled, a notable proportion by Russian émigrés. Indeed, though there were no Russians on the panel, there was a general expectation that the critical issues of the third wave would be explored. The panel comprised two Czechs, one Hungarian, and a short, nondescript man whose name I did not catch, from some outlying region where the native language (perhaps Macedonian) is fast becoming extinct. This man gave a talk too elliptical for the audience to follow, about the meaning of the novel in his native land and in America, and then descended from the dais, not to be seen again. Everyone was waiting for the Czechs, and they got what they hoped for. Though the speakers' comments were addressed primarily to the condition of Czech literature, it was easy to extrapolate and to apply the conclusions to the crisis facing third-wave literature.

Milan Kundera, whose novel *The Book of Laughter and Forgetting* had recently received rapturous reviews in the press, looked every inch the successful author. His gray hair, cut modishly short, his steely blue eyes, and the pallor of his gaunt face were all accentuated by the dark turtleneck sweater that he wore. He read his comments in accented but fluent English.

Czechoslovakian literature, he said, had been the conscience of his country since communism took over, and it might be the conscience of the world as well. Czechoslovakia's political and social institutions had succumbed to the encroaching forces, but its literature survives abroad, thus proving a culture's power to endure even in the worst of times. In fact, the uncertainty of life in exile, when all the odds are against cultural survival, simply represents in emphatic form the eternal condition of great literature, constantly threatened, constantly struggling. Czech writers in exile should take up the challenge willingly, never despairing. They must show the Czechs in Czechoslovakia, and oppressors everywhere, the meaning of freedom.

The novelist Joseph Skvorecky, a man with a sort of rumpled and modest manner, presented a quiet rebuttal to Kundera. The first job of an émigré writer, he said, was to write about life in emigration. Not nostalgia nor angry regrets about what has happened in one's homeland, but an imaginative description of one's present life had to be the goal. Skvorecky ran through a list of Slavic émigré writers, noting that almost none of them wrote what was happening to them in their new countries, only about what once was or what they hoped soon would be. One exception to the rule was the Russian novelist Edward Limonov, Skvorecky remarked, adding that the vicious critical reception that Limonov had provoked showed how unwelcome his sort of approach was.

As the crowd milled around after the close of the day's proceedings, it was clear that the majority supported Kundera's position. Skvorecky, moreover, had hurt his case by invoking Limonov's name. Limonov's novel *Eto Ya, Edichka (It's Me, Eddie)*, which is a picaresque account of misadventures in the shadier and more offbeat realms of émigré life, is generally mentioned only in angry, disdainful tones. Anyone who treats it respectfully is either a fool or at odds with the principles of the third-wave emigration.

As I headed for the exit, an émigré friend cornered me. "Limonov," he declared, "is not an author to be mentioned in a serious discussion of émigré literature. He writes in Russian, it is true, but he is not a Russian writer."

I asked if it were not true that Limonov's novel had style and energy.

"Granted, all that is granted. But he has no sensibility. Even if one admits that émigré writers should pay more attention to America in their works, *he* does it all wrong. Limonov describes émigré life as if it were a cesspool, and having done that, he happily dives in.

"Read Lvov," my friend told me. "Read Lvov. If you want to read an émigré writer who writes about America correctly, read Arkady Lvov."

Lvov's work does indeed form a remarkable contrast to Limonov's easy acceptance of America; and Lvov's tentative, nervous appraisal of his new home is doubtless more congenial to the majority of third-wave émigrés. One story in particular, "The Hotel Astoria," exemplifies Lvov's attitude, and many of his compatriots' also.

A Russian family deplanes late at night at Kennedy Airport. Since they have no relatives or friends in America, they are taken by a social agency to a hotel near Times Square. Repelled by their squalid room, they rush out into the street, there to suffer a series of indignities peculiar to American urban life. First, they are almost crushed by a mob trying to obtain the autograph of a fatuous celebrity; then, the father intercedes in a fight between two men which everyone else ignores, and for his trouble is abused by a policeman; finally, an icy wind, made more piercing by the canyonlike avenues, attacks them until they cry. They retreat to the hotel, and at this point the story acquires a truly nightmarish air. Instead of the private refuge that the family sought, the hotel room proves to be an instrument of cruel restraint, merely making them more convenient targets for the assaults of the city. In a room directly across the hotel's narrow shaftway, too close to ignore but too distant to allow any interference, horrible acts of homosexuality, bloodletting, and bestiality are taking place. In America, Lvov's story suggests, the dominant culture can pervade everything, prevailing practices may intrude into every private retreat. If Russians expect their way of life to survive, they must have the cunning and strength to make their way in an uncongenial climate.

Never trust a novelist. I had arranged to meet Edward Limonov in a bar on upper Broadway, assuming that my reading of his autobiographical novel would allow me to pick him out in a crowd: a nonstop sexual dynamo, the narrator is constantly disheveled and unbuttoned, with a rollicking, buccaneer's style you don't often find even in the West Eighties.

On the phone, Limonov had told me, "Don't worry, unlike other Russians I don't have the habit of always being late." But nothing resembling my expectations appeared. If he hadn't finally walked up to me and shaken hands, we never would have connected. He had on a white suit, white shoes, and a black turtleneck — in general, a fastidious young European gentleman out for an evening's stroll, and with courteous manners to match. Emphatically, not the Edichka of his novel.

After we settled down at a table, I asked him why he thought his book had upset so many third-wave émigrés.

"A few people were offended because they claimed I had created characters similar to them," Limonov said. "But who would have recognized them? Perhaps their three closest friends. I changed all the names. In five years these same people will doubtlessly be angry that I didn't use their correct names, so that they could go down in history for something, at least."

But, I said, what about all the other readers who were annoyed, the ones not in the book?

"What can you expect? They come from a society that is completely backward regarding the methods of literature. When a Russian writer decides he is going to write something daring, in the modern style, he usually falls somewhere short of James Joyce — in other words, approximately fifty years behind practices in the West. My book is more than modern, it's postmodern, so it's hardly surprising the émigré public doesn't know what to make of it."

I asked if the scandal surrounding the book disturbed him at all.

"In some ways, yes. I have a few friends who have become very careful in my presence, because they are afraid I will put them into my next book. Misha Baryshnikov avoids me altogether. But in general people reacted out of jealousy, unhappy to see that someone who wasn't part of the leading intellectual circles in Moscow might become famous in America. Those people I don't care about at all."

I remarked that perhaps all the anger directed at him could be taken as evidence of Russians' well-known deep concern for literature, so that a book could still evoke the most ardent feelings, pro *and* con.

"Yes, perhaps, but finally all this emotion is tedious. I'd like to get beyond émigré circles, with their petty quarrels. Nabokov never succeeded till he left his émigré sensibility behind. All those early works of his, any émigré author could have written them.

Lolita is his masterpiece, and it has nothing Russian about it. I'd like to be an American author also, like he was," he said with a note of real desperation creeping into his voice. "I really would."

I knew that Limonov had spoken frequently of leaving Russian culture behind, but hadn't realized he felt his dilemma so acutely, as if spreadeagled painfully across two cultures. I asked him to explain the reasons for his dissatisfaction with the role of Russian writer.

"One is in a completely distorted situation. In the Soviet Union, you are required to write about factory workers or about miners, and when you emigrate to the West you are expected to expose the terrors of the labor camps, of the Soviet system. Both topics do not interest me. I want to write about myself."

And you did, I said, in your novel.

"It's not that easy to escape the vicious circle. Someone will always find a way to exploit a Russian writer. When they published *It's Me, Eddie* in Germany, for example, they gave it the title of *Fuck Off, America*. In some places, anti-Americanism sells. Perhaps someday my books will be judged on their merits and I'll find my real audience. As it is, my American readers seem to be confined to University Slavic departments, and I've seen what they are like when I go on a lecture tour. Dry old professors and unattractive female graduate students — a real cottage industry."

I mentioned that I had heard that his book had been picked up for American translation.

"Yes, after thirty or so rejections, one publisher finally accepted it. If you don't write political tracts like Solzhenitsyn, an American publisher doesn't know what to make of a Russian writer. Our approach to literature is alien to them. Russian writers are not so good at structure, at careful organization, but I think we go deeper than American writers."

Later we took a stroll on Broadway, chatting randomly. There had been a rain shower that had given the streets a glistening polish, prompting Limonov to remark that the neighborhood looked greatly improved recently, better stores, cleaner sidewalks. I said that was a surprisingly knowing appraisal for an émigré. But, he responded, he was something of a connoisseur of urban life, having been forced to traverse broad reaches of New York. How much could an émigré see, I wondered. Plenty, and very quickly, he said, since the third wave's path often went through slums and a string of SRO hotels.

"I finally got into a hotel on the West Side which wasn't too bad," he said. "The Hotel Embassy on Sixty-ninth Street."

That was a name with special resonance for me, since my family had put up there upon first arriving in New York (after a twenty-year detour through Europe) in the early 1940s. Family legend suggested a cozy, quasi-Edwardian establishment; but now, Limonov reported, drug dealers roamed the corridors, displaying their wares.

"America has changed almost as much as the Russian émigrés who come here," Limonov remarked, courteously.

We ambled farther uptown, Limonov brushing aside panhandlers with a native's aplomb. He liked New York, he said, though he now lived much of the year in Paris. I offered that I had been born in Paris, though I had left while still an infant, and wondered how he liked my birthplace. For an answer I had to be satisfied with his rueful remark that it was in Paris that he had come to feel himself a true citizen of the Western world, in that instant when he was practically caught in a crossfire of Arab terrorists attacking a Jewish restaurant across from his apartment: a quintessential moment of life in a twentieth-century democracy.

At Ninetieth Street, we realized we had a few acquaintances in common, and we stood for a while on the corner casually itemizing their virtues and flaws as if we had deep reservoir of agreed-upon standards. We mildly differed on several individuals, struck an accord on most, and found ourselves in emphatic harmony on the value of Vladimir Nabokov's works — sharing a chuckle over Humbert Humbert's puns is not high criticism, but it's a reliable indicator of common tastes.

As we got ready to part, Limonov said, "You know, I realized it would be hard to make it in America as a writer, but then it hadn't been easy in the Soviet Union either. I wasn't a member of the Writers' Union, so there was no way to have a steady income from my writings. I supported myself by working as a tailor, taking orders from people who wanted better clothes than the crap the state-owned stores offered. I was a good tailor, too."

That last detail disarmed me. I had met Limonov only several hours before, yet was confident that I already knew him. His character was open and guileless, and besides there was his confessional novel to draw upon for information. His conversation, his judgments, and the history he had briefly sketched, all seemed to fit into a familiar pattern. My own experience, while not identical, seemed to me close enough to allow me to comprehend the key moments of his life. But the image of him as a tailor dissolved my easy assumptions.

It wasn't that I was astonished to learn that in the Soviet Union some men of talent survive only by doing manual labor — there are similar instances in this country, after all. Rather it was his description of his work, his offhand comments about cuffing pants and hemming skirts, that disconcerted me. Limonov's life in the Soviet Union took on the heft of reality. Before, I had thought, yes, his life must have been hard, trying to write must have taken a lot of energy; now I saw more exactly the weight and density of his efforts. Sympathy was possible, true comprehension, never. It was a good lesson. Third-wave writers, just like third-wave émigrés in general, may seem fully understandable because they talk an idiom not unlike our own, pursue dreams much like those we dream. But their past is sui generis. Finally, they are aliens to anyone who has come of age in America.

A successful writer in the Soviet Union, one the regime at least countenances, can live in a grand style. He may not accumulate the wealth of his Western counterpart (though he doesn't do badly, either) but he enjoys public adulation in high degree. If he is a poet, his verses are memorized by thousands; if a novelist, editions of his latest effort sell out within a day. Like our rock stars, the successful Soviet writer is recognized and cosseted wherever he goes — though instead of being greeted by the squeals of adolescent groupies, he's more likely to have to accept solemn thanks for illuminating life's deepest questions. Russians can be brought to fever pitch by intimations of moral profundity.

Emigré authors are shocked to discover the placid nature of American readers, and their disappointment is compounded by blows to their amour-propre. While they were in the Soviet Union, many of them were pleased by the rumblings their work caused abroad; if the sound was faint, they assumed this was because they were distant from the source, and they expected the volume to intensify as they traveled westward. They thought they were eagerly awaited, whereas it now appears they were awaited with a mild curiosity that only intermittently flickers into sustained attention. Solzhenitsyn's mighty welcome has proven to be an isolated case.

Vasily Aksyonov, a writer who emigrated to America in 1974, has described the prevailing mood among his émigré colleagues.

"After years in the Soviet Union, these people decided on a 'feat,' a breaking away, and now naturally they expect their reward. They come, our geniuses, for recognition, for Nobel Prizes. They come to enlighten and astonish the West," but, Aksyonov wryly notes, "the West stubbornly refuses to be enlightened or astonished."

Aksyonov's remarks are in the third person, but he has elsewhere expressed his discontent with his own reception. He had been the reigning prince of progressive Soviet prose from the late 1960s forward, receiving homage from a large segment of the public (especially the young) and from his fellow writers. His tales, with hippielike heroes and in a jazzy idiom that borrowed from American slang, suggested that his was a sensibility that would travel well. He's had several novels published since he has emigrated, and *Time* even ran a piece welcoming him into American culture, but it cannot be said he has in general made anything like the impression he did in the Soviet Union.

I caught up with Aksyonov at a ceremony for the Literary Fund of Russian Writers, which convened on the Columbia University campus. He was to be one of the main speakers, but he was not present during the early part of the proceedings. After the opening speeches, the audience, which filled the auditorium, was treated to the readings of some works-in-progress. These were delivered in styles ranging from passionate to high rhetorical, by men who seemed determined not to let the opportunity of a public hearing slip by without squeezing it for all it was worth. But the audience, though respectful, behaved as if a mild anesthetic had been released in its midst. The purpose of the occasion, to raise money for indigent Russian authors in America, apparently cast a pall.

Then, during a brief interval in the readings, Aksyonov appeared, moving discreetly toward a seat in the front row. He never got there. The calm demeanor of the audience snapped, people rushed to intercept Aksyonov. He was surrounded by autograph seekers, by editors trying to enlist him into literary projects, by well-wishers simply eager to shake the hand of the man who had given them such pleasure over the years. To Aksyonov it must have seemed like Russia all over again, at least as long as he did not leave the tight émigré circle that cosseted and acclaimed him.

Aksyonov at last extricated himself from his fans and led me to a quiet hallway off the auditorium for a few words. I thought I noticed a slight sagging of his energy as he left the sustaining atmosphere of the émigrés and prepared to deal with an American; and, indeed, his words sounded a bit overly processed, material cut to fit the bland contours of America's curiosity, and nothing like the give-and-take style Aksyonov had shown among the émigrés.

He said, "The freedom of the West is wonderful but disturbing for a writer. It's as if you've suddenly broken through the sound barrier. A deafening silence descends after emigration. At first you think that nobody needs you, and you even miss the Soviet Union. Working there was hard, censorship tough, but all the difficulties were like the handicap an acrobat sets up just to overcome. It gave you a style."

Aksyonov paused, seeming to reflect on the startling spiritual journey he was describing. Then he said, "But eventually you get used to freedom. You begin to realize that this is what you always dreamed of. Perhaps a writer needs a different muse in the West than in the Soviet Union, but if he's good, in time he'll find his way. I'm glad I emigrated."

It was time for Aksyonov to give his reading of a work-in-progress, and I returned to my seat to listen. The audience quieted, ready for the day's highlight. With a sly grin, the woman making the introductions mentioned the piece on Aksyonov in *Time*, noting that in it he had not only discussed Russian émigré literature but the joys of American society, including, wonder of wonders, the pleasures he had discovered by taking up jogging. The implication of this introduction was clear: while *Time* honored Aksyonov for his standing as a Russian writer, he reciprocated by showing he had become Americanized.

Aksyonov accepted the introduction with good grace — indeed, he approached the lectern with what seemed a pronouncedly athletic gait, as if to say that jogging, at least, was an aspect of Americanization which did no harm. But he must have also sensed the need to solidify his standing with his first constituency, the émigré audience, for he began his reading with a bit of chauvinistic foolery. "My work," he said, "is about a photographer. Its title is *Skazhi izum!* [*Say 'Raisin'!*]. The English equivalent, what photographers in America say to their subjects, is *Say 'Cheese'!*, which of course requires a speaker to open his mouth much wider. We know that Americans put great emphasis on their extravagant smiles, that their wide grins advertise their happiness."

Thereafter the reading was straightforward, but Aksyonov's opening aside struck me as significant. It suggested how far he was from solving the problem of satisfying two audiences, of finding some congenial American path down which his Russian muse could comfortably stroll.

Aksyonov, in fact, may in time find his way. He's been published here, our journals pay attention to him: he's a working writer, which means he daily acquires new knowledge about how literature is practiced in his adopted country. For the majority of émigré writers, the outlook is less promising. What they planned —

indeed, all they could reasonably achieve — was not to merge with our native culture but to set up a little shop of Russian literature amidst the great bazaar of American products. It hasn't worked, and isn't likely to.

"But who in America needs our Russian literature, our truth, our soul? Who here will be interested in our problems concerning totalitarianism, our drama and our humor? And which Russian writers live on in America? Pushkin? Forget it! Platonov? Babel? Zoschenko? They have all been buried by their translators. No one knows of them.... Why is the West not interested in us, who are the heralds of the coming clash, fugitives from yesterday come to today? Why did we read ourselves silly with *their* writers, from Kafka to Lorca, and why did we imitate the heroes of Hemingway and Remarque?"

These words, by the émigré writer Ilya Suslov, sum up the feelings of the third-wave literary community.

As if matters weren't bad enough, an emigre writer's difficulties are compounded by the West's peculiar conception of Russian culture. Russia captures our attention because it is outside the familiar European tradition, but not yet so alien as Oriental or African culture. Russian writers depict an exotic terrain, but one with vaguely familiar landmarks: the effect on a Western reader can be the flattering idea that he actually understood more of the world than he had previously thought.

When I mentioned my interest in the question of Russia's mediate position between East and West, several émigrés told me, "Go see Kuzminsky, go see Konstantine Kuzminsky," and finally I went.

There are good reasons for Konstantine Kuzminsky's reputation in the émigré community. He not only writes poetry, he is also the rallying point for a movement. He goads other poets to keep working, promotes their careers through a network of connections, collects and publishes their efforts. He told me, "At critical moments in a country's literary history, individuals come forward who can attract and hold together a literary movement, instead of only pursuing their personal careers. Apollinaire, for example. I am something like that."

Kuzminsky assumed this role while still in Leningrad, when he was at the center of the group of young writers who reached maturity in the late 1960s, the second generation of "the thaw." At the time he held a job as a blue-collar worker at the Hermitage Museum, shoveling snow, carrying crates. (It was dull work, though Kuzminsky asserts it at least provided him with the opportunity to sharpen his appreciation of painting.) Off the job, he organized poetry readings, collected Joseph Brodsky's poetry and published it in a *samizdat* edition, and — what he considers most important — culled the countryside for poets whose work was not generally known. He is now publishing a collection of these lesser lights. He told me, "When some émigré writer comes to me and begins to weep about a manuscript that he was unable to smuggle out when he left, I say to him, 'Forget about it, you can in time reconstruct it — the real tragedy is that you didn't bring out the manuscripts of the hundreds of others, who are still trapped in the Soviet Union.'"

It is said that Kuzminsky was so immersed in Russian poetry that if at a public reading a poet stumbled or misread a line, Kusminsky would jump up to supply the missing metaphor, and with a passion equivalent to that of the author. At night, he reputedly wandered through the Leningrad streets, declaiming poetry at startled cabbies and suspicious policemen. Indeed, to hear him talk on the subject is less to see a man discoursing *about* Russian poetry than to see Russian poetry itself talking, through a corporeal vehicle.

This vehicle, it must be said, has a distinctly odd manner. I had been warned to expect idiosyncrasy, so I didn't blink at the hooded and belted monk's robe which Kuzminsky wore when he opened the door of his basement flat. I was only slightly startled by the bedroom into which he led me, a veritable chamber of esoterica, one wall completely festooned with paintings, icons, and, over the carved wooden headboard of the bed, a long, breech-loading rifle. ("An antique," Kuzminsky said, "though the Russian army fought its last four wars with it — and won three of them.") What finally unsettled me, however, was that Kuzminsky elected to conduct our interview in a supine position, reclining grandly on his rumpled and book-bestrewn bed. Since I could not join him there, I took the only other available seat, a small stool at the foot of the bed, feeling like the court jester before his lord.

Kuzminsky said, gravely, "Excuse me, my bed is my office. I haven't been outside this flat more than ten times in ten months. I'm working on the second volume of my contemporary poetry collection."

But Kuzminsky is no dyed-in-the-wool Slavophile, so fervently attendant to the needs of the Russian national soul that he ignores the passing scene outside his window. He has seen much of the United States, more than most émigrés, more than most Americans. Upon first arriving in this country, he told me, he lived in Austin. "Right in the center of the country, the bellybutton of America," he said, reaching easily for the metaphor. Indeed, he speaks English fluently and enthusiastically, with a touch of the poet, so that even his occasional missteps have a certain gracefulness.

I said that I would begin our talk with a general question.

"Shoot it," he exclaimed jovially.

I asked him to comment on the condition of Russian poetry today.

"When you speak of Russian poetry," he answered, "you of course have to discount the official Soviet brand, along with certain of its fellow travelers. People like Evtushenko and Voznesensky have talent, but they are sluts." He rendered the last word with just enough of an accent to make it starkly emphatic, more a capital condemnation than just a slur.

He leaned back against the headboard, savoring his venom, then addressed my question again. "You have to understand about Russia. Kipling wrote that 'East is East and West is West, and never the twain shall meet!' — but they did meet once, in Russia. Russia has a Western consciousness and Western religion, but an Eastern way of life. Its head is in Europe, its body in Asia."

After a short pause, he added, "Unfortunately Americans know only the head. So, as far as poetry goes, they know only the classical tendency, which is based on Western forms. They know nothing of the Eastern tendency, which comes out of Asiatic Russia. Who is the most famous Russian poet in Americans' eyes? Joseph Brodsky, who is completely Western in outlook. As it happens, he's traveled to Asiatic Russia, to Siberia, several times, but he learned nothing, not a word of the local language — he prefers translating Blake and Donne.

"I belong to the opposite tendency, and I'll tell you why. When I was growing up I dreamed of Africa, South America, the South Pacific, all that stuff. I read a damn lot of books by explorers, like Stanley and Livingston. I wanted to be an explorer. As soon as I got to university, I saw that someone like me would never be allowed to go abroad. So I turned eastward, to explore Russia. And I learned that's not so bad, either, since Russia is one-sixth of the world. I've been to Siberia five times, hunted there, fished, Jack London–style. And I've put it all into poetry.

"That's the real Russia, not the depraved Russia one sees in parts of Leningrad, in the cities. At Komsomol dances in Viborgsky [a Leningrad neighborhood], I can tell you, it's complete decadence. The young guys at the door check the girls who want to enter for underpants — those with are turned away, those without can pass."

I asked how he liked America, considering his deep commitment to Asiatic Russia.

He said, "First of all, I like it better than Europe, which is smothered by bureaucracies run by old farters. Europe is too small for someone used to Russia. I once went from Moscow to Siberia by train, seven days and nights without a stop, drinking vodka all the way. When I went from Vienna to Paris by train I was awakened three or four times during the night, each time we crossed a damn border and they wanted to check my passport.

"I was lucky, when I came to America, to go to Texas first, which gives the same sense of space as Russia. Its wonderful lakes and rivers, where I fished with my Texas pals, are like Russia too. I enjoyed myself there, in the good parts anyway, just as I like the good parts of Russia. As for the other things, shit smells the same everywhere; it's an international product."

I asked what he thought of American poetry.

"I've read Merwin, Auden, a lot of others — and, no, they are just too different from Russian poets. Poetically our countries have nothing in common, nothing except some abstract ideas perhaps. On the page, nothing. Russian poetry is young, and the Russian language still very flexible, so that we have at least another century of exploring our rhymes, while in America, that sort of thing is already exhausted. As a result American poetry strikes me as boring stuff. I do not judge only with my ears or my eyes — I'm like an animal: my nostrils tell me, no, that's not poetry."

He didn't much care for much of the country, he didn't like the poetry — well, then, I asked, how did he manage to survive in this alien culture?

Rising at last from his bed, as if better to deliver a concluding homily, Kuzminsky said, "No culture is alien to a true artist. He can digest everything, no matter how hostile it may seem, let it be New Guinean war chants or American poetry."

I remarked that not many of his compatriots had his confidence and equanimity.

"Well, it's the effects of capitalism on them, I think. Public attention suddenly appears to be a commodity, a limited commodity. So if someone else gets it, you think you are being deprived. That's what accounts for all these disputes within the émigré community, which I usually stay out of. But I did sign one letter of protest, because it gave me a chance to announce my credo."

I was heading toward the door, but Kuzminsky caught my elbow to make his final statement. "The letter was to the *Village Voice* and I signed it, 'Konstantine Kuzminsky, anarchist and monarchist.' I like anarchy for its freedom, monarchy for its glory. Neither exists in this damn world. I know some Russian monarchists in New York and I admire them, as I would have admired Bonapartists *after* Waterloo. To be a monarchist during the king's reign is one thing, to be a monarchist after he has been deposed — that is true glory."

> *In the autumnal blue*
> *of your church-hooded New*
> *England, the porcupine*
> *sharpens its golden needles*
> *against Bostonian bricks*
> *to a point of needless*
> *blinding shine.*

In a sense, we owe the existence of these lines to the Soviet regime. Though they suggest the sort of familiarity with Boston vistas that we might expect only of a deep-dyed New Englander, they were written by a recent émigré, deposited on our shores by the consequences of Soviet policy. Joseph Brodsky's knowledge of English has now become so refined that occasionally he allows himself a quick, agile dash through our native idiom.

He's had a headstart, to be sure, since when he was in the Soviet Union he was already proficient enough to have made an excellent translation of John Donne. Much of his life there had a Kafkaesque turn — because his poetry was deemed to have no social usefulness, he was convicted of "parasitism" — and his acquisition of English fits that pattern. He perfected his knowledge even as he was suffering through the bleakness of his imprisonment in northern Russia; he had in his possession an English-Russian dictionary and an old anthology of English and American verse, and he relieved the drudgery of prison life by puzzling out the exotic and arcane lexicon.

He now holds professorships in several American universities. One of the places at which he teaches is Columbia, and it was in New York that I called him to make arrangements to meet.

Brodsky has a famously mercurial temperament, swinging from good-fellowship to misanthropy black as night, so I was a bit anxious when I dialed his number. When he picked up the phone, I immediately launched into an explanation of my project, hoping to drown any negative reaction on his part in a torrent of words. He was having none of that, however. "Get to the point," he interjected abruptly, making me wonder just how far the privileges of genius extend.

The next time I called, however, he was a paragon of graciousness. Accommodating himself to my schedule, he genially suggested that we meet at Cafe Reggio in Greenwich Village, where he usually took his coffee. He was indeed a habitué: when he came in he shook hands with some cronies, redirected me from the seat I had taken to a better one, and simply nodded at the waiter by way of placing his order for some coffee.

At forty-four, Brodsky's red hair is thinning and graying, and his extremely fair complexion makes this an especially emphatic transformation. It was as if he had taken some sort of vow to use only wan colors in person, thus husbanding a robust palette for poetry. His glance darted about continually, only occasionally coming to rest on me as I posed my questions — he seemed to want to take in *all* of his surroundings, all of the world, instead of just the phenomenon that happened to be most proximate.

I felt uneasy as our conversation began. I knew that Brodsky, much more than other émigrés I'd met, is canny about American ways, about our urge to sum up experience in a few well-chosen words. I said, "Excuse me if some of the questions I ask sound foolish. It's the occupational hazard of interviewers."

"Excuse me," he said, "if some of my answers sound foolish; it's the occupational hazard of those who are interviewed."

I asked about his affinity for the English language and American culture, which is much in evidence in the poem about Boston.

"In one sense, mine is a typical Russian response. We've always been attracted to Anglo-Saxon phenomena. Do you know that the English are the only European nation for which the Russians have never had a pejorative nickname? The English temperament, that air of reserve, has always been admired by Russians, perhaps because it is the opposite of our own manner. And the American style of cool, of irony, that gets our attention in much the same way.

"For me that style is epitomized in two phrases that I heard long ago and which have stayed in my mind. The first is from Robert Frost. 'The way out is through.' The second is a bit of folk wisdom. 'Don't get mad, get even.' That's the sort of psychology I admire."

So you were ready for our Western ways even before you arrived, I said.

"One is never quite ready for something which hasn't been experienced. You have to live through it. When I first came out to the West, I remember, I was sort of dazzled, but I soon got a more realistic perspective. Once I wanted to travel from Paris to London, and since up to then Western life had seemed so free, so generous, I forgot that such a thing as a passport might be necessary. I still remember how the English girl behind the counter listened to my explanations, then coolly turned me down with one sentence. 'I'm truly sorry, but you know the world is far from perfect.' That's very good advice for life in the West."

What is especially surprising here? I asked.

"Oh, small things, just the details of life. Every Russian writer, for example, is taken aback by the absence of an intellectual class. In the Soviet Union, belonging to such a class was a part of our way of life. Here if I do find myself among a group of American writers, do you think I hear a discussion of ideas or literary technique? Not a bit of it. The main topic is royalties."

Still, I said, it must be better to listen to discussion of royalties than waste time trying to figure out some means not to offend the Party line, as had been the case in the Soviet Union.

"Of course. No one would dispute that. But in my case I can't say I felt that sort of ideological pressure on my work. The Soviet state may have arrested my body; they didn't get my mind."

Was that really possible, I wondered, to remain completely

above the demands of Soviet society? I mentioned his poem "To Zhukov," seemingly a hymn to the Red Army hero of World War II.

Brodsky laughed. "Oh yes, that certainly looks as if it could have been printed in *Pravda*. But really I think one might better explain it by looking at the work of the poet I most admire, Auden. He had a way of *feeling* his way into a poem, and many of the ideas and concepts which he invokes are really there for the sake of the structure of the poem. Bad poets do it the other way around."

You make yourself out as apolitical, I remarked.

"Yes, especially now, here in the West. If I had stayed on in the Soviet Union, who knows how I would have behaved."

I remarked that his approach struck me as very different from the majority of third-wave writers, who seemed obsessed with conveying to America the precise nature of the political evil they had escaped.

"I steer clear of that sort of thing. It's a useless endeavor in any case. Even the structure of the language forbids it. English is fine for making absolute statements, but it's not a good tool for trying to comprehend the sort of evil that exists in the Soviet Union. For that you need Russian, in which every sentence comes equipped with its own qualification, reservation, addition. Think of it like the water that comes into a washbasin. English has two faucets, two spigots. Russian has two faucets but one spigot, in which all the fine distinctions get nicely mixed."

But, I protested, thinking of the Boston poem, your English is more than adequate to get your point across. Why, come to that, you probably could continue your career writing in English.

He paused, brought up a little short for the first time in our conversation. "You know, sometimes I think I could, especially when I see what gets published. Oh, there are American poets who make me turn green with envy, but the majority — they sound like they are writing bad prose."

"You'd be an American poet," I ventured, "or at least a Russian-American poet."

But Brodsky had apparently already come down to earth from

his brief reverie. "No," he said simply. "A poet is defined by the language he writes best in. I am a Russian poet."

Indeed, he is still immersed in Russian history — not the politics, which he says he has left behind, but that historical tide that was released by Pushkin and brought to a flood stage by Akhmatova. The rapids and whirlpools of the Russian literary tradition are his most animating ideas, even here in America. America is good not because it feeds his poetry directly — there is not, he noted, all that much Americana in his work — but because it does not intrude overly, leaving him free to negotiate the intricate itinerary of a brilliantly imagined voyage through Russian literature. (Indeed, he explores some very local areas: he only recently made the critical discovery that iambs just won't work in Russian poetry for passages of dramatic narration.)

I said that he seemed to feel quite comfortable in America.

"Yes," he said, breaking into a happy grin. "Though, all things considered, I'd prefer Boston to New York."

I left my meeting with Brodsky thinking, well, yes, perhaps Boston would be marginally more suitable, and then the world might get a few more poems magically evoking New England vistas; but no matter where he settled in America, the deepest feeling, the heart's blood of his poetry, would always come from a different source. As he has written (in his magnificent, native Russian):

> *The North buckles metal, glass it won't harm;*
> *teaches the throat to say, "Let me in."*
> *I was raised by the cold that, to warm my palm,*
> *gathered my fingers around a pen.*

It's the foot soldiers of culture, those artists in the second rank of talent's armies, who must worry most about the effects of emigration. Men like Joseph Brodsky are members of a transcendent club of geniuses who in their work can disdain any acknowledgment of the longitude and latitude of their earthly homes; while others, like Konstantin Kuzminsky, are driven by a sense of mission so obsessive that they continue to do precisely the same work they would have done had they remained in the Soviet Union. For the rest, which means the vast majority of émigré artists, making a career requires them to persuade America of their significance. They dream up artistic schemes with which to storm our cultural fortresses, altering their weapons several times over and with impunity, according to which ramparts look most likely to give way.

One émigré I met exemplified this uncertain condition. As the former director of a small theater in Moscow, he was indisputably in culture's infantry, albeit perhaps an NCO. The audiences for his productions, he told me, were enthusiastic but small, and his troupe sustained itself on the profits of tours away from the capital. In the provinces, people hungered for sophisticated drama, and the functionaries of regional arts councils were often ready to add a bit to the official rate of payment. It wasn't spectacular, but it was a living.

Upon coming to this country, the director formed a company to perform for Russian émigré audiences. He calculated that there were enough émigrés in New York City to support fifty performances a year. New Jersey and Boston would support fifty more. San Francisco was not out of the question, nor, in time, Israel.

We spoke in the spacious Washington Heights apartment that the director occupies with his wife and daughter. It was virtually empty of furniture. He told me, "There will be time enough for a table and some chairs. Now I devote everything to the theater."

A man of strong opinions, the director explained to me his philosophy of performing Chekhov in the Soviet Union. It's a matter of playing it straight, letting the fact that Chekhov's criticism of the status quo might apply as well today as in the 1900s speak for itself. He showed me a scrapbook of laudatory reviews from the official press, proof that he had hoodwinked the authorities.

I asked him why he left Russia.

"You can accomplish only so much there," he said with a shrug, as if the topic were not worth discussing.

As we drank tea from glasses placed in the ornate metal holders that the director had managed to get by the grasping Soviet customs officials, he again became animated. "Listen, I must say something. I do not want to be discourteous, I know I am just a guest in this country. But I must say that America is a desert as far as the theater is concerned. I've been to Broadway, off-Broadway, off-off-Broadway. It's trash, off-trash, off-off-trash. The problem is that there is simply no tradition here, no theatrical school. I think that in time my company will put on plays not only for émigrés but for the American public. I don't want to sound egotistical, but I believe Americans have much to learn from us." He considered his fingers. Perhaps he was calculating how many dates would be available for this part of his schedule.

The man's enthusiasm whetted my interest, and I resolved to go and see his company in action. The week after our talk, I drove up to the YMHA in Washington Heights, where the large auditorium was already filled, even at five dollars a head. As a gesture of Anglo-Russian cooperation, he had decided to open the season with *A Streetcar Named Desire* in Russian translation. He took the role of Stanley Kowalski for himself, though he is far from resembling a young Marlon Brando.

The production was decidedly threadbare, the costumes distinguished from the actors' mufti only by the addition of some trinket or scarf, while the set was furnished only with two chairs and a gimcrack sofa. It was a world pauperized even beyond Tennessee Williams's intentions, though it was impossible to say if this circumstance derived from the company's meager budget or the Russian émigré's adamant refusal to glamorize proletarian life.

The single opulent feature of the Kowalskis' New Orleans apartment was a large portrait of a bewhiskered and muttonchopped man with the dour look of a displeased patriarch. The characters assiduously disregarded it, but its mystery shadowed their every word. Finally Stella pointed to the wall and asked Blanche DuBois to consider the wonderful likeness of her husband, and with that information in hand it was indeed possible to distinguish my new acquaintance's thick features behind the figure's facial hair.

He soon appeared in the flesh, wearing a bright polo shirt and jeans that had been gaudily cuffed: all in all, a dandy as conceived on Gorky Street in Moscow. Stanley crossed to stage left, threw himself into one of the chairs and, with an ostentatious flourish, poked a deodorant dispenser underneath his shirt. He did *not* however, strip to his undershirt, as has every Stanley since the play first opened. I registered this difference as a sign of the famous Russian public modesty; but, then, as if intentionally to rebut my conclusion, Stanley suddenly began to fondle his crotch with gusto. Throughout the play, in fact, he suggested man just past the Neanderthal stage of evolution.

As the drama unfolded, I began to perceive the director's intention. The play had been given a slightly askew focus, which was most evident in the one departure from the literal translation that had been employed throughout: describing her ancestry, Blanche claimed not only the French forebears that Tennessee Williams had provided her, but Russian grandparents as well. Her revelation brought applause from the audience; they seemed relieved to have sighted a familiar landmark amidst the curious behavior of New Orleans low life. Thereafter, Blanche got an especially sympathetic hearing, and the play suddenly took on the aspect of a cautionary tale of the émigré experience. When at the climax of the play, Stanley violates Blanche, it seemed that America's crass materialism had mangled the Slavic soul.

A few weeks after the performance, I visited the director again and asked him about his interpretation of the play. He said, "I am a man of the theater. I leave meanings to the sociologist. But I will say this — Blanche's path in the play is not unrelated to the path of the third wave. She came to the Kowalski apartment filled with hope, with ideals, with dreams, and none of these things survived in her new environment. Russian émigrés have also been disappointed in their dreams."

I asked if he meant Stanley to represent America?

Smiling slyly, he said, "As I said, I make art, not sociology, where every event has a defined meaning. Anyway, why exaggerate? We émigrés have gotten much from America, at least materially. Spiritually there have been problems; we are losing our souls here."

Our conversation was interrupted by a phone call. The director took the call in the adjoining room, and I could hear him arguing angrily about some theatrical matter, finally slamming down the receiver in exasperation. When he returned, he said, "If you want to know the truth, the spiritual life of the émigré community has fallen so low that many have altogether lost touch with art, certainly with drama. I tried to present good theater to them, but they gave me no support. Well, all right, enough of them. Now instead of trying to show Russian émigrés the meaning of their lives in America, I'll show America the spiritual life of Russia.

"Right now I have rehearsals going for one well-known Russian play, which I have translated into English. It's about the love affair between a Party functionary and an idealistic woman. An American who saw one of the rehearsals asked me, 'Why don't they simply spend the night together; that will solve their problem.' How could I explain that communism does things to the spirit that can't be resolved by a night of love? The play will be able to show what I mean. Perhaps we émigrés still have a role to play, showing the world that we managed to escape."

When I spoke to the director, he had hopes of mounting his production on Broadway, but when it finally opened it was in a small theater near the garment center. It ran, somewhat staggeringly, for several weeks, then expired. Rousing American audiences, even when it's for their own good, is no easy trick.

EIGHT

❧ The Life of Art

THE third-wave émigrés sometimes give to their art the aspect of a trophy. Though they have been deprived of Russian citizenship, they claim they are the custodians of the only contemporary Russian art that has any merit, and that this proves the superiority of the life they have chosen. As it happens, America is quite eager to support this interpretation of third-wave culture — every tremor of talent by a third-wave artist helps to prove that this country nurtures the creative freedom that the Soviet Union stifles.

This mixture of esthetics and politics is volatile, and occasionally explodes in the émigré artist's face. Painting (and the happenings/performances/conceptualizations that are painting's contemporary cousins) is the most troubled of émigré high culture, because politics flows most facilely through it. Painting can evoke recognizably Russian themes (much more easily than music, for example), but is not so trapped in Russianness (as literature often is) as to be inaccessible to a foreigner. Painters may stamp some symbol of communism's evil onto their canvases and know it will be appreciated. At the same time, however, they run the risk of appearing to trade on the emotions that politics arouses.

The misadventures of Mikhail Chemiakin are a case in point. Shortly after arriving in Paris in 1972, he published the album *Appollon*, including along with his own works a selection by artists still active in unofficial circles in the Soviet Union. He was bitterly attacked in sections of the French press for trying to acquire an aura of political rebelliousness by association. Chemiakin sued the harshest critic for libel and won the case. But the affair showed how easily a Russian émigré artist slips into an ambiguous position: every friendly wave in the direction of one's homeland may in today's excited political situation get interpreted as a self-serving flourish.

Experience had taught me that many émigrés answer the phone sullenly — perhaps a vestigial reflex from the days when most unexpected calls brought bad news. Even by this glum standard, however, Chemiakin's greeting, a shallow grunt, sounded uncongenial. But another of the émigrés' vestigial reflexes is hospitality to strangers. Chemiakin suggested I come round for a visit, and I accepted the invitation.

His studio was a splended two-story affair in fashionable SoHo, and his attire, when he opened the door, was equally eye-catching. He wore cruel-looking boots over tight jeans, a sleeveless tank-top that revealed a lacework of scars on his shoulders, and, around his neck, a thick metal chain of vaguely religious denotation. His glasses were constructed of a dark horn that was so heavy it suggested an item of a knight's armor — indeed, he in general trailed an aura of bold anachronicity, the intimation that contemporary life was too narrow to hold his restless spirit.

I found myself retreating to the security of a formal interview very quickly. Could he, I asked after we settled ourselves (I in a chair, he leaning magisterially against the wall), could he describe anything in his Russian past that beneficially affected his esthetic development.

"I *have* seen Russia. My father and mother were both officers in the Red Army. I grew up in the Soviet provinces, wherever they happened to be stationed. My father wanted me to go to officers' school, to make a military career. Instead, I found myself in the Pskov Monastery for a while, which was even more primitive than any godforsaken provincial barracks town. That kind of background lets one see the real Russia, the way all of the country used to be before the current regime took over. And I've had more than a taste of the modern style, too, thank you. Later, after I had become an artist, the authorities put me into a psychiatric ward to try and break my spirit. Yes, I know Russia."

Looking about, it seemed to me that Chemiakin had brought with him to SoHo a chunk of his native land — not, to be sure, the Soviet Union or even the Russia of the nineteenth century, but some more elemental *Rus*. The studio was filled with icons and other medieval artifacts. The high-backed chair I sat on, with its elaborately carved arms, would have befitted an early Muscovy prince, and an oak table, heavy enough to knock down a rampart, evoked images of feasts and wassail. Beneath the table lay a bulldog whose creased head folded directly into a creased body without any pause for a neck, some strange sort of brute that had slipped off the evolutionary ladder.

Motioning at this panorama of bygone Russia, I said that modern Soviet life might indeed seem dreary by comparison, but didn't it at least provide a working artist with a sense of limits to transcend?

"Oh, that argument!" Chemiakin exclaimed, without much pleasure. "Of course it's true that an artist has to have a sense of limits. In America where everything is permitted, most artists have taken advantage of the freedom by 'expressing themselves,' as they put it. They have no idea if these 'selves' are part of anything larger or, indeed, worth expressing at all. In that sense, yes, the Soviet Union can help some artists, by imposing limits against which to struggle. But a truly great artist doesn't need limits imposed from outside. He sets his own limits, finds his own traditions."

Could he be more explicit, I asked, by showing how the issue affected his own work?

"Certainly," he said, clearly awaiting just this question. "You know certain forms are eternally present in human culture. It's the job of a true artist to seek them out. The sculpture of Egypt and the painting of medieval Europe are similar, if approached correctly. I work within these eternal limits."

He showed me a series of sketches that he had lately done. He said, "These look like contemporary figures, but look closely and you will see the statues of Easter Island, those most primitive shapes." As in a child's puzzle book, hidden forms did indeed lurk in an innocent landscape, bodying forth only under close scrutiny. "Man throughout the centuries has always responded to these shapes," Chemiakin stated.

Had he, then, I wanted to know, left his native tradition behind, dissociated himself from the émigré school?

"There is no émigré school," Chemikain said in a tone of such emphatic disdain that he startled even the sleepy bulldog into rearranging its corrugated body. "There was once something of an artists' community in Moscow and Leningrad, before everyone emigrated, but even that was a strange business. Artistic talent hardly mattered. If an artist was antigovernment, that was considered sufficient credentials. For that matter, the *degree* to which an artist was antigovernment also was hardly noticed. My activity landed me in a psychiatric hospital, courtesy of the regime, while so-called conceptual artists put a pickle into some flour and called it political art. All right, perhaps the important thing was to have an artistic community united against the government, and so every little action was worth something. Now that we have emigrated, however, all sorts of squabbles have arisen, and some people go around claiming a bravery they never exhibited while in the Soviet Union, and even attack those who were truly courageous."

I was to learn that Chemiakin's appraisal of the émigré artists' disputes was too bland by half. An urge for judgment prevails that is religious in its scrupulosity. If in the Soviet Union an unquestioning camaraderie bound the artists, now every velleity of their past motives comes under analysis. History is no longer divided merely into categories of good and bad, a division that served adequately in the Soviet Union, but into the finest ethical fragments.

It matters greatly if one signed petitions supporting unofficial exhibitions, or attended these exhibitions, or participated in them — or, a not uncommon alternative, only told friends of plans to do one of the above. The most privileged moment from the past is doubtlessly the famous 1972 open-air exhibition in the Moscow suburb of Belyaevo, mounted by a group of unofficial artists. It led to one of those rare times when the regime was forced to back down, to a degree. (The local police had reacted to the exhibition by bulldozing the paintings and beating up the participants, but public outcry, at home and abroad, moved the higher-ups to grant permission for several comparable exhibitions at later dates.) So many émigré artists have insinuated a connection with the Belyaevo exhibition that it now suggests that circus trick where innumerable clowns tumble out of one tiny car.

The eagerness of émigré artists to prove their participation in the unofficial art movement is the natural desire to show a connection with the forces of good, but the nature of America's attention is also a spur. We have indicated that we will pay the most attention — and often hard cash — to those artists who resisted the regime. Esthetic judgment may go by the board if an artist can show he tried to take the Soviet government down a peg.

With commercial success at stake, there was bound to be some intramural squabbling in the émigré artist community, and it is intensified by the fact that the moments in dispute lay irretrievably in the past. The curriculum vita listing political activity against the Soviet regime is, for all émigré artists, largely a completed record, not open to further entries. All that remains is the interpretation and appraisal of actions committed long ago.

That can be a nasty business, and some disputes have taken on a mythic dimension. In fact, those artists, like Chemiakin, who have decided to leap into the crystalline spheres of eternal art may well be motivated less by the prospect of pure estheticism than by the desire to escape the intractable arguments of the émigré artist community.

Vagrich Bakhchanyan is forty-four, a fact that has circulated more widely than most such mundane data because one of his recent artistic efforts was a book of three hundred sixty-five full-face photographs of himself, commemorating every day of his forty-third year of life. He has the large and swarthy features of his Armenian heritage, and a subdued manner curiously at odds with the rambunctious tenor of his work. (One example: he has designated himself "Advisor on Mail Art to President Reagan," and he stamps this information on all his outgoing envelopes, including those heading for the Soviet Union — it gives him pleasure, he says, to imagine the confusion of Soviet postal clerks as they scrutinize these unusual items.) No matter how exhilarating the events he describes, he remains dourly deadpan; when discussing the sad situation of émigré art in America, he appears positively despondent.

"We've been thrust into a completely new environment, we make our way uncertainly at best. Sometimes it seems that the Russian artists who succeed in America are simply those with a talent for self-promotion. Well, that's the American way, so why criticize? In fact there do seem to be great opportunities near at hand, the sort we all dreamed of when we were in the Soviet Union. But unfortunately life in the Soviet Union did not train most of us to know how to take advantage of such opportunities.

"I've had my own experiences with the American art establishment, thank you. I wanted to do some performance art, a type of happening. I went to the Museum of Modern Art, to the section where Malevich's paintings hang, just to feel at home. There my wife started to paste cards with communist political cliches, like 'All power to the Soviets,' to various parts of my clothing. On my forehead I put a big label reading 'Agit-prop center.' I was going to stand there, a living art object.

"But before we could finish the job, a big black security guard came over and stopped us. I was led to the office of a young administrator who talked to me very pleasantly for a while, though when I asked him what rules I was breaking, he was a little vague. I could sympathize with him — who knows what to expect from these crazy Russians! Finally he decided I should be allowed to finish my performance. I was so pasted up with placards that I could hardly walk, so the guard had almost to carry me back to my place near Malevich. Now when I go to the museum, he always recognizes me and gives me a smile. That, however, is about all the acknowledgment my effort received."

Habitually mordant, the tone of President Reagan's Advisor on Mail Art turned still blacker. "With all these problems that we have adjusting to America, you would think that Russian émigré artists would at least support one another. In the Soviet Union, where we had a common enemy, there was a sense of community, of purpose. But that has changed. Some of us finally managed to mount our own show at the Franklin Furnace Gallery in SoHo. It was called 'Russian Samizdat Art,' and for once the American critics took notice. The show was reviewed in *ArtNews;* the *Village Voice* sent a critic, as did other American publications — and yet there wasn't one word in the Russian émigré press. Jealousy is now the watchword among émigrés. As if silence weren't bad enough, one émigré critic — Margarita Tupitsyn — took the time to write a letter to the *Village Voice* attacking the politics of the participating artists. Really, it was like something you might find in the Soviet newspapers, a real *donos.*"

Donos translates as "denunciation," but it has peculiarly Soviet overtones that cannot be rendered into English. The word evokes the worst of Stalinist times, when colleagues were afraid to mention the slightest disapproval of the regime to each other, and even offhand remarks in intimate circles got reported to the authorities. The memory of Osip Mandelshtam's betrayal and arrest after his reading of an anti-Stalin poem at a gathering of supposed friends can still chill the blood of a Russian artist. The power of the *donos* has weakened, but even today a letter to the local newspaper complaining of an individual's politics will cause difficulties.

To characterize Margarita Tupitsyn's letter by the same term is fatuous. Her criticism in the *Village Voice* of the Franklin Furnace show would, of course, never provoke a ripple of reaction from our authorities, assuming they even bother to read that self-styled broadsheet of New York's avant-garde. But Bakhchanyan's comment did have a polemical point: it was a reminder to the world, and perhaps to himself, that Soviet émigré artists had once braved bureaucratic repression, and deserved a measure of homage for that.

Tupitsyn's letter called precisely this view into question. In one easy gesture she destroyed the image of the émigré artists as freedom fighters, and for good measure subverted the much-favored esthetic theory that an oppressive political climate fostered the spurt of creative energy in the Soviet Union during the 1970s. The catalog of the Franklin Furnace show said, "The negative environment for modern art [in the Soviet Union] has its sad but positive side — the forbidden fruit is sweet," but Tupitsyn called this "inaccurate." In general, her letter questioned the main tenet of the Franklin Furnace show, and of many other émigré artists besides: that in invoking their history of being at odds with the Soviet regime, they were putting forward political credentials that deserved continuing respect.

Seated amidst paintings and sculptures in the Center for Contemporary Russian Art, where she works as curator, Margarita Tupitsyn seemed almost a work of art in her own right. A far-flung ancestry has donated genes that have created strikingly contrastive features, dark Slavic eyes set off by high Armenian cheekbones; and she was attired in the fashionable regalia of the season, mannish sport jacket and leather trousers.

She speaks English fluently, and generally keeps to an ironic manner. By way of introduction she told this anecdote. "My maiden name is Masterkova. Once when I was in high school in Moscow, I went to the local library and requested Bulgakov's *The Master and Margarita*. The book wasn't well known then, and my friends were sure I was only mocking the librarian by playing word games with my name and surname. That's probably the closest I'll ever come to being famous."

When our conversation turned toward the controversy in émigré art circles, her tone remained lighthearted, but a note of intensity was added. "What can one say? It's reached the level of the ridiculous." She shrugged, a gesture connoting something halfway between resignation and scorn. "Recently there was a ball on Long Island, commemorating David Burlyuk, the artist and friend of Mayakovsky who settled in America at the beginning of the twentieth century. Everyone from émigré art circles was there. It turned into a fiasco.

"Two of the organizers of the Franklin Furnace show were the most to blame. They came armed with slingshots and started to shoot things across the room at my husband and me. The invitation to the ball had stated that there would be happenings and performances during the evening, and as these two had a reputation as performance artists everyone assumed their behavior was something along that line. For a while so did I, and I played along—but whenever I got hit, it was quite painful. You are supposed to suffer for art, but not *that* much, I decided. It ended with quite a brawl, one of our great artists lying on the floor unconscious. That's the level of intellectual argument which we have reached, slingshots and fists."

Looking at Tupitsyn, I found it hard to picture the events she described—she had the air, not uncommon among Soviet women, of being far above anything coarse, an inherited aristocratic bearing that had perversely grown more refined under the dictatorship of the proletarian. I shifted our conversation to a focus that seemed more suitable, and asked about her intellectual differences with the organizers of the Franklin Furnace show.

"Their main error is that they fail to see that it's a question of context. It's foolish for them to talk of their exhibition as politically significant, to speak in their catalog of 'forbidden fruit,' as if they were doing something politically daring. The gallery is in the United States, right here in SoHo, not in the Soviet Union. In fact many of the works in the exhibition were created *in* the United States. Where is the politics in that?"

She allowed that she was relatively young, still in her twenties, and hence not expert in all aspects of art history—but about the meaning of the Franklin Furnace exhibition she was adamant. "It's not so easy as one may think to make political art in America. It's an altogether different story from the Soviet Union. Recently an artist was arrested for walking around Red Square with a placard extolling Solzhenitsyn. What would happen if an artist did something comparable here, say displayed a sign honoring Andropov? Nothing, of course. An artist can say he is doing political art in America, but that doesn't mean he succeeds. Everything here is too fragmented, dispersed in a way it was not in Russia. It's just an entirely different context."

As the afternoon wore on, we talked of other things — of what it meant to grow up in the Soviet Union, of Tupitsyn's aunt, the painter Lydia Masterkova (an actual participant at the Belyaevo open-air exhibition), of the beauty of Moscow. But the matter of the dispute in the émigré art community seemed to linger, a shadow on an otherwise bright field. When she escorted me to the exit, Tupitsyn returned to the topic one last time. "I don't think any Russian émigré artist in America really does political art, but of course I'm not saying one shouldn't use political imagery. It's what we émigrés know best, after all, having grown up in the Soviet Union. You should come and watch a performance that my husband and I and some colleagues are putting on next month. You will see what I mean. The imagery will be political, but there will be no political point."

I did go and watch the Tupitsyns and four or five of their colleagues (I'm not sure how many, the proceedings were fairly frenetic) perform at the Kitchen Theater in SoHo; but what I saw was how tricky it was for third-wave émigrés to take a firm grip on their artistic identities. "Context" trips up even those who are most aware of its dangers.

The announcement I had gotten in the mail depicted Lenin in heroic profile against brilliant red backdrop, and straight-facedly invited attendance at "The 28th Party Congress." It would take place on November 7, the anniversary of the day the Bolsheviks had stormed the Winter Palace.

At the appointed time everyone at the Kitchen appeared to be in high communistic feather. Upon entering, the audience was first greeted by ushers dressed in authentic Red Army uniforms and then blasted by a recording, played at top volume, of the Russian Red Army Chorus singing of the Motherland's martial triumphs. The lobby was festooned with posters of the glorious NEP period of the 1920s, urging the citizenry to study, labor, and reproduce more zestfully for the good of the Party. At the back of the stage hung stately portraits of Stalin and Lenin, their faces set in expressions of aloof kindness. Not a hint of irony was evident in the dispositions of any of these props — but the whole point, of course, was that the audience would be capable of its own ironic interpretation.

The deadpan style carried over to the performance. There was a film in which actors struck dramatic poses in counterpoint to passages from the *Communist Manifesto*. The words "Workers of the world unite, you have nothing to lose but your chains!" flashed on the screen, prompting a shot of a man in overalls struggling with manacles and leg-irons, with the World Trade Center looming formidably in the background. And so on. Communism's holy writ juxtaposed with capitalism's monuments to man's exploitation of man — there was no need for commentary: the audience could draw its own inferences about the intellectual merit of the sort of Soviet propaganda that this film duplicated.

After the film, two actors delivered, absolutely verbatim, excerpts from an actual Party Congress. A sound track had been set up to explode into applause at appropriate intervals, and it did so with an alacrity that exaggerated even an *apparatchik* enthusiasm. But otherwise there were no unrealistic inflections. The humor depended on context. Transplanting the iconography of Soviet politics to SoHo was in itself enough to make it an object of fun.

Lenin's famous phrase "Under Communism, all are artists in life, not merely in dreams" was drained of all high idealism and became an occasion for a jape. How? Surely not because the idea itself, the esthetic transformation of daily life, is fatuous. Rather it must have been that we in the audience knew how woefully short of the goal the heirs of Lenin had fallen — and also, most significantly as we sat in that comfortable SoHo theater, how much closer to success was America's effort. Our laughter had an element of smugness, a sense that America, for all its flaws, has achieved more than other countries we could name. For this purpose alone, it would seem, if Russia did not exist, America would have to invent it.

In general, the evening's performance seemed to draw on our readiness to believe that America is a place devoid of ideological pressures, an immaculate context in which the ideological absurdities of other countries can be vividly displayed precisely because the native landscape has nothing comparable to distract an audience's attention. But is that really true?

The fact that the context of art should prove so troubling to the émigré artists is ironic, since it was a particular irritant when they were in the Soviet Union. In that country the most basic physical circumstances in which art is exhibited, the museums or halls or private apartments, help to convey a message. The art hangs as within an active cathode-ray tube, subject to continual ideological pulsations from the environment.

The museums housing the official monuments of communism, for example, are hardly neutral repositories of culture. They have the aura of a temple, and the capacity to inspire awe even in a nonbeliever. In these grand and stately halls, the most far-fetched examples of Socialist Realism — peasants astride gleaming tractors or brawny laborers exhorting their turbines — can appear impressive. What seems risible when looked at in reproductions while sitting in an American living room has the force of a tightly coherent world view when looked at en masse in a Moscow museum. Indeed, to walk through one of these museums is to feel the disturbing intimacy of power, as if some angry god had temporarily arranged himself into an accessible posture. Many museums require a visitor to don *tapichki* (felt overshoes) — the aim is to safeguard the luxurious parquetry, but as one shuffles along, cumbrously shod, it's easy to feel part of some vaguely religious ceremony requiring special vestments. The first time I was handed *tapichki*, I was so sure a worshipful attitude was expected that I started to remove my shoes, which set the grandmotherly attendant off into gales of laughter.

The aura of the Soviet state in the field of art is so strong that it influences even dissident artists. Indeed, one salient aspect of the unofficial art movement, which arose in the 1960s, is its links to the dominant ethos: because the primary aim of these dissident artists was subversion of the regime's artistic ideology, it was essential to pay attention to the enemy — a backhanded compliment, to be sure, but a compliment all the same.

Thus an artist like Oskar Rabin, one of the guiding spirits of the unofficial art movement, edged only very tentatively toward the abstractionism of Western art; it was necessary to stay close enough to Socialist Realism to be able to criticize and transcend it. (One of Rabin's most famous paintings depicts the regime's sacred text, the newspaper *Pravda*, as a wrapper for a dead fish.) Though some unofficial artists began to explore nonrepresentational and conceptual modes in the 1970s, the main thrust of the movement was a mocking variation of the hegemonic tradition.

It goes without saying that in contemporary America no comparable relation between an official and unofficial line of art is conceivable. Our central tradition has taken to wobbling all over the place, hardly standing upright long enough to serve as a target; and works of art that might once have qualified as rebellious avant-gardism now appear as shocking as applesauce. And our showplaces reflect this fluid cultural moment as fully as the showplaces in the Soviet Union reflect its cultural rigidity. The difference represents a sea change of attitude, and Russian émigrés are often flabbergasted by American museums' policies of democratic porosity, such as allow the values of high art to seep out into the mundane world while hoi polloi's preferences are absorbed in return. One émigré told me, perspicaciously, "At the Museum of Modern Art, where I went to see the Picasso show, Americans clearly wanted a T shirt with Picasso's picture on it as much as they wanted to look at the paintings."

Not surprisingly, unofficial Soviet art that travels from its native locale to America may suffer a great change of meaning. I had first seen Evgeny Rukhin's paintings in his studio in Leningrad. One day Rukhin simply appeared at the dormitory way out on Vasilevsky Island where most foreigners are housed as if in quarantine. Any Soviet citizen seeking admission had his identity papers scrutinized by the hard-eyed *kommandant* guarding the door, and few were willing to risk the official displeasure that could ensue. But Rukhin, a giant of a man with laughing eyes that peered out between a mop of hair and an unkempt beard — giving his visage the look of a helmet with a slightly open visor — seemed hardly to care about official displeasure. He had already been expelled from the Artists' Union, which left him without any authorized means of selling his work; selling to foreigners aroused suspicions, but it wasn't strictly illegal, so he decided to give it a shot.

When I visited his studio, the place seemed to reflect its owner's easygoing manner. Consisting of two small, low-ceiling rooms (so low that Rukhin had almost continually to stoop), it was strewn with paint cans, rags, old icons awaiting restoration, and empty bottles of vodka. Altogether, it was like a jagged shard of Bohemia stuck amidst the dreary uniformity of Soviet life. In that studio, the words *opasno dlya zhizni!* (Caution! Life-threatening!), which Rukhin had painted across the bottom of one of his canvases, slipped their commonplace association with the signs placed near high-voltage wires and became, instead, an announcement of the subversive power of art.

I saw that Rukhin painting once again when it was part of an exhibition mounted in the Johnson Museum in Ithaca, New York. (Rukhin himself was dead by this time, killed in a suspicious fire that destroyed his studio.) All of its crabbed and explosive energy had drained and dissipated, thanks to the new setting. The Johnson Museum is all airy spaces and glass walls, an architecture that successfully suggests a reciprocity between the inside of the museum and surrounding life. As a theory this may be nobly democratic, but it was fatal to the Rukhin. There was nothing in the Ithaca landscape, redolent with the lush pleasures of capitalism and democracy, that could obviously provoke Rukhin's cry for humanity.

Choosing the right place in America to exhibit émigré art can, therefore, be a weighty decision. The Center for Contemporary Russian Art, whose curator, Margarita Tupitsyn, welcomes America's attention unequivocally, has taken up residence in the heart of SoHo. The Museum of Unofficial Soviet Art, by contrast, has settled in Jersey City, about a forty-five-minute trip. The Manhattan skyline is spectacularly visible, but as part of a distant vista: the location might imply that émigré art is happiest at the periphery of American culture, cognizant of the mainstream but content to live off its own native energies. There was, however, also a banal economic reason for the site, the opportunity to buy cheaply the squat, red-brick building that once housed the local fire department headquarters.

Alexander Glezer, the director, does not shy away from the more symbolic interpretation of his museum's location. He told me, "Here in America, art is very much a commodity. Anything that sells is fine, even if it is art that destroys the values of culture. An émigré artist can easily be seduced into painting that way also, but he would be losing touch with his true talent, his Russian perspective."

Glezer, a short dapper man in his middle forties, speaks with some authority about contemporary Russian art. Before he left the Soviet Union in 1976, he was the majordomo of Moscow unofficial art circles. He encouraged artists who were at odds with the official Artists' Union, he displayed and sold unofficial art to foreigners, and he organized illegal exhibitions. He finally ran afoul of the KGB when he resisted its suggestions that he exploit his foreign connections to provide information. He was given the choice of emigration or jail. Ten days in a Lubyanka cell convinced him to choose the former, but he managed to negotiate the right to take about fifty of his favorite canvases with him, and arranged for many more to be smuggled abroad by friends.

These paintings, which now form the mainstay of the museum's collection, are in the more conservative line of the unofficial tradition — Rabin, Rukhin, Masterkova — with a few more abstract efforts added. As he showed me around the exhibition, he said, "Some Americans who have gotten to know Russian culture through its literature are disappointed with our painting. But painting cannot be as politically explicit as Solzhenitsyn. It's impossible to circulate canvases covertly, like *samizdat* manuscripts. A Russian artist must tread a thin line between legality and illegality, and Americans should understand that."

As yet, not many have. The museum attracts few visitors, and walking through the two floors of paintings can be as forlorn as strolling through an unkempt cemetery.

Glezer said, "In the Soviet Union our fight was not only about what was *on* the canvases but where we could *put* them. The authorities tried to break the unofficial movement by blocking all means of exhibiting. We had to strike back by insisting on our right to show our work. That's when we organized the Belyaevo open-air exhibition. I was at the center of the organizing effort, along with Oskar Rabin."

While he spoke, Glezer smoked incessantly. He had the Russian habit of treating a cigarette as if it were a small but potentially vicious enemy, continually catching it in different grips, sucking it quickly, almost as if in ambush, finally stabbing it to death in an ashtray. Sometimes his sentences seemed no more than hurried interruptions between puffs. He said, "Now of course we are finally free to exhibit as we like."

Of one painting by Lydia Masterkova, an expressionist composition of wavy lines and a burst of light in one corner, Glezer remarked, "From elements that are basically abstract, a good Russian painter can still make a fairly realistic painting, a painting that is recognizably Russian. Masterkova's lines, her use of light, reminds me of the sun behind Russian birch trees. I will always maintain that there is such a thing as specifically Russian art — art that shows the Russian spirit's courage."

I drove back from Jersey City to New York with a Russian émigré artist who had been at the exhibition that day. He told me, "Glezer is a bit of an unfortunate case. From all the attention he got from the KGB and the noise the West made about unofficial art while he was in the Soviet Union, he expected he would make quite a splash when he arrived here. There were a few shows in Europe, but no one is really excited. The flavor of his collection doesn't seem to come through in America. I told him he would do better, instead of hanging the canvases in a museum, to reconstruct a facsimile of a Moscow apartment. A dirty sofa, some empty vodka bottles, the smell of stale cigarettes like one gets after an all-night discussion about the meaning of art. That would bring out the real power of the paintings."

The artist's name was Vitaly Komar, and he is one half of the young team (he is thirty-nine; Alexander Melamid, his partner, is thirty-seven) that has achieved the greatest reputation of any of the third-wave émigré artists. In 1975, while they were still in Moscow, the team's exhibition at a SoHo gallery won excellent reviews, stirred the American public's enthusiasm, and — most welcome — persuaded the Soviet authorities to furnish visas posthaste. After a brief detour to Israel (Melamid is Jewish), they came to America, finding further success. They are the first émigré artists to win a grant from the National Endowment for the Arts, an honor Komar whimsically compares to getting the Prize of the Soviet Ministry of Culture.

The binational perspective of this joke is also apparent in much of the team's artistic efforts. They are obsessed with bridging the two cultures, conflating their past in the Soviet Union with their American present. Komar's and Melamid's credentials for such a mediating role are in good order, since they were as eminent in unofficial circles in Moscow as they are successful here. Their conceptual art was highly regarded, they spoke out against the persecution of fellow artists, they participated in the Belyaevo exhibition, the famous "bulldozer" exhibition.

Significantly, however, they seem to regard that last event — which other émigrés usually consider the unofficial art movement's Calvary — with some irony. The way that Komar described the Belyaevo exhibit to me on the trip back from Jersey City made it sound like a great adventure, a moment of historical importance, but not a sacrosanct memory.

"When the police attacked, I saw that they threw the 'Double Self Portrait' done by Alex and me onto the back of a dump truck. I ran over to it, with a couple of thugs at my heels. I started to run faster — art has to be saved at all costs, after all," he said with a grin.

"As I got hold of the canvas, the thugs caught up with me. 'It's mine,' I shouted, pulling at it. 'Give it here!' they screamed. 'No, it's mine!' And so on for a minute or so. Finally, they pulled it away, but when they tried to destroy it, to snap it in two, it wouldn't break. Our art is well constructed, no matter what some critics say."

Though Komar treated Belyaevo ironically, he did not ignore the brutality that took place. "Three policemen chased down Victor Tupitsyn and tripped him to the ground. Two of them held him while the third clubbed him, aiming the blows between his legs. They didn't stop for at least three minutes. It took courage to be present at Belyaevo. It's a different question, though, what it all means now, here in America."

Subsequently I visited Komar in his apartment in Manhattan, hoping to learn more of his views on émigré art. He welcomed me with almost extravagant solicitude, steering me to the most comfortable chair and presenting me with coffee of his own concoction. His face is thickish and his glasses have heavy lenses, but his features are remarkably expressive: he's capable, when animated, of showing self-deprecation and pride simultaneously, assigning each emotion to a prescribed area. In our conversation he was continually animated.

In answer to my question, he said, "In Moscow we worked in many styles. We were as eclectic as possible. One year we did three different series, and each in a totally different style — pop art, conceptualism, expressionism. The very idea of pluralism, in and of itself, was attractive. Living in the Soviet Union, with its dogmatic Party line, we came to believe that freedom meant the absence of the uniform and expected. We made our art *kak ugodna* (every which way)."

He gave me a sly look over his thick horn-rimmed glasses. "But we've changed a bit since coming to America. Our next show, in fact, is very much in one style. When we arrived here we saw pluralism at first hand, and it stopped being an ideal. Every day when I go to the supermarket, I see pluralism. That's enough; I don't have to put it in my art also."

No doubt, I remarked, with pluralism rampant in this country, it's harder for an artist to take a stand.

"Hard but not impossible. An American friend of ours was invited to have a show at a famous American museum. He let the curator know that he intended to include one exhibit suggesting that some of the museum's wealthy patrons had taken part in some not very pretty real estate speculation. The invitation was withdrawn. He's a dissident, same as Alec and I were in the Soviet Union when we got kicked out of the Union of Artists. What does a dissident artist do in the Soviet Union to support himself? Alec and I gave private lessons. What does our friend whose show was canceled do to support himself? He teaches. Our countries have more in common than one might imagine. It's only necessary to look from the right perspective."

With so much in common, I said, it does seem likely that your art will be understood by the American public.

"I'm only afraid they will understand it *too* easily," Komar said. "It's not easy art, but Americans have the habit of assimilating everything instantaneously. They look at Andy Warhol's soup can and think they grasp all of the irony at once. Art is not taken seriously enough. Some of the canvases of our new show look simple, all elements very recognizable, but it's not so. Alec and I aim for something deeper, mysterious."

Pressed to explain what he and Melamid were aiming for, Komar said, "We want to bring together Russian and American perspectives, our past and present. Perhaps that is why Alec and I admire Marc Chagall so much, though his style is not at all like ours. In his work one sees nostalgic elements in juxtaposition with images of his new life in Paris. It's the harmony of two worlds, of who he was and who he became."

Komar's comments made me eager to attend the opening of

his and Melamid's new show. There was an intimation in his words of a sensibility that felt at home in America, with no need to advert continually to images of an evil Soviet Union in order to gain attention. Perhaps he and Melamid had found a way to finesse the difficulties that seem to stymie so many third-wave émigré artists.

But when I arrived at the Ronald Feldman Gallery a few weeks later, my first look around left me disappointed. There were works with an American motif, but these did not suggest that the artists had effectively married the two cultures. Indeed, these works were relegated to a smaller room off the main hall, like guests who had been invited to fulfill a social obligation and then are coolly ignored. A series of parodies of WPA art, cutout posters blaring the platitudes of our Depression years, occupied one wall; while off by itself was a painting of a centaur rampant, draped in red velvet and hooves flailing, and with the features of a smiling Ronald Reagan. The humor was thin, the artistic tone uncertain. In one corner was even more emphatic proof that the artists had managed less to explore American culture from inside than to heckle from a distance: on a large banner, a sentence in Cyrillic letters was inscribed so elegantly that an American viewer might naturally assume a sentiment of exotic grandeur — but in fact it spelled out Russia's favorite obscene injunction.

Nor did the heart of the exhibition, in the gallery's main hall, immediately suggest a breakthrough in the third wave's esthetic vision. True, the artists' style was remarkable, a monumentalizing, neoclassical mode with allusions to David, Caravaggio, and Tiepolo, all done up with layers of pigmentation and a glossy varnish that created dramatic highlights. But what was the substance thus highlighted? Each of the twenty 72 × 55 paintings portrayed a hagiographic moment out of the communist tradition. One called "Lenin Lived, Lenin Lives, Lenin Shall Live" depicted Lenin on his bier, majestically draped in a red banner, while a vaguely allegorical maiden weeps at his feet; another depicted the Kremlin as an aspect of an inspirational vista, surrounded by ruins and visible through a bosky bower, with shafts of light reflecting off its towers as off a hallowed relic. Were Melamid and Komar only playing that old émigré trick, simply transplanting Party iconography from Moscow to SoHo, to see how it stood up in its new context?

The public reaction suggested this was indeed the point. At the opening, spectators laughed and joked about the musty hyperbole of Soviet ideology, and critics in reviewing the show pointedly remarked on Komar's and Melamid's talent for exposing the foolishness of the Kremlin's view of the world.

Yet, though the work of Komar and Melamid sustains such a reaction, it was probably not their goal. At the opening, I ran into Mikhail Werboff, the elderly portraitist I had met months previously at the Meeting of Russian Writers, at Columbia University. He looked a bit bewildered.

"It's all parody, you see," he said of the paintings, but then added quickly, "It is parody, isn't it?" There was a moment of ambiguity in the paintings. They were too reverent to be mere mockery, too passionate to be only scorn.

Between accepting congratulations from well-wishers, Komar told me, "Some people laugh, thinking we mean only satire. Others take it absolutely seriously. One émigré accused me of disseminating Soviet propaganda, adding that it might be a good idea for Alec and me to return to where we came from. The reason the paintings can seem both one thing and the other is because our feelings are mixed in. There is great nostalgia in them. After all, these are scenes from our childhood, our life, what we grew up with."

"I Saw Stalin Once When I Was a Child" is the painting that makes Komar's point best. Half drawing aside the red velvet curtain of a car's rear window, Stalin peers out into the dark night, at the unseen child of the title. The canvas is gloomy, with only Stalin's face illuminated, presumably by a streetlight: he appears remarkably amiable, even kind. The implied drama of the scene, with the car about to drive off and thus dispel the magic of a chance encounter, evokes the full power of a child's wonderment.

As we stood in front of this painting, I asked Alexander Melamid how he and Komar had achieved the complex mood, showing Stalin's benign side along with his hauteur.

He said, "Maybe it helped that I posed for it. We painted from a photograph of me costumed as Stalin. It was a bit of a job getting ready for the role. It took weeks to get my mustache to proper length. Then we had to find a greatcoat such as a Red Army generalissimo might wear. We had to settle for a World War I French officer's coat that we found in an Army-Navy store. Finally I was Stalin."

Did it make him feel odd, I asked, being in the shoes of that legendary tyrant?

"Why tyrant? I was eight when Stalin died, Vitaly ten. For children Stalin was a figure of love and protection. For our parents he was terrifying, not for us."

To filter a tyrant's history through the rosy haze of childhood is disingenuous, and neither Melamid nor Komar is that. Rather, their position appears to be to allow the past its proper scope, including their mundane feelings, the day-to-day sense of life. They were, after all, a part of Soviet history as well as its victims, and they don't hide this fact behind the rhetorical flourishes that other émigrés have resorted to.

Off the evidence of their show, Komar and Melamid have not managed as effectively to size up their place in American history. But they may yet prove up to the task. They are both eager to study their new home and are suspicious of received ideas about it, which may be the sine qua non for a successful emigration.

Melamid told me, "I like to walk up and down New York, just to walk and to look. Especially in the poorer neighborhoods, like the Lower East Side and Spanish Harlem, where people sit on their front steps and play in the street. I had exactly the wrong idea when I was in Moscow about what I would enjoy in America. Now I see it's the wealthy neighborhoods that are monotonous and uninteresting, hardly the real America that I want to know."

Neither Melamid nor Komar is populist in their politics (like the rest of the third wave, they lean to the right), but they are fascinated with the details of American life. They regard the grander myths of our republic with a grain of salt, but they seem ready to honor the common facts of our everyday life. That is a promising perspective for a Soviet émigré artist, much more likely to yield understanding, and good art, than is one more rehearsal of the Armageddon that portends between the forces of West and East.

NINE

❧ The Structure of Everyday Life

IN the Soviet Union, if you are walking down a street and notice a queue in front of a kiosk, you immediately join it. There is no point in asking what item has gone on sale; since it has attracted a queue it must be worth acquiring. If you have no need for it, some relative or friend certainly will. To pull out the string bag that every adult always carries, to ask "Who is farthest? [*kto krainyi?*] (since "*kto poslednyi?* [Who is last?]" sounds derogatory to the sensitive socialist ear), and to set one's jaw for a half-hour wait till the queue gets moving — this is a complex act that every Soviet citizen has reduced to a reflex.

The Soviet Union is still fighting the economic backwardness that history bequeathed. As recently as the 1930s, the economy was no more than equal to that of today's Egypt; pulling the country into the modern era (while taking time off to fight a devastating war) required sacrifices, most of them exacted from the consumer goods industry. But the Soviet citizen's desperate hunger for goods has a psychological as well as a material cause — his *expectations* about his standard of living are seriously at odds with his actual circumstances. The Soviet Union's international power, loudly broadcast by the nation's propaganda machine, implies a system that should be able to sustain domestic comfort also. It doesn't, and the discrepancy between economic expectations and economic reality has, as one wit put it, made the Soviet Union a consumer society without consumer goods.

Soviet citizens especially envy Americans, since they can see that the United States has turned the trick of adding domestic comforts to international power. When a third-wave émigré arrives in this country, he is confronting his dream. Vladimir Bukovsky has described that vertiginous moment in his book *Letters of a Russian Traveler* (1981):

> Upon seeing the piles of shoes, the heaps of clothing, the different sorts of salamis, all types of meat in unlimited quantity, and besides a multitude of all sorts of products, goods and items the purpose of which we don't understand — then Soviet man is simply thunderstruck, and for many, especially women, real psychosis sets in.

(Indeed, Bukovsky's breathless syntax and excited references to indiscriminate "heaps" and "piles" suggests he himself may have a touch of the malady he describes.)

The émigrés' acquisitive fever is fueled by the habits they developed in the Soviet Union. Goods must be purchased immediately, since they may not be available tomorrow; cost is not very important, since money is less scarce than goods, which in any case can always be bartered. Purchasing an American car is perhaps the clearest symptom of their condition: realistically, it does not fit into the budget of most new arrivals, but many émigrés nevertheless buy one very soon, delighted to possess such blazing evidence that they have escaped the dreary Soviet economy. (Since many émigrés can afford only the older models, their enclave of Brighton Beach is beginning to resemble those old South American republics that ran entirely on reconstructed antique Fords and Chevrolets.)

An American friend of mine, a college professor who is married to a recent émigré, told me how he had been taken, at a forced-march pace, through four of the more elegant Fifth Avenue stores by his wife and mother-in-law. They were on the track of an evening gown, despite his expostulations that the wife of a college professor rarely had the occasion to display such finery. Seemingly obsessed, his wife had finally settled on an opulent creation costing about a month's salary.

"When Tanya tried the dress on before a mirror, what I can only call a strange look came into her eyes," my friend told me. "She said it was the first time she regretted not being born during the Tsarist era; her gown would have been just right for a ball at the Winter Palace. It's like that with most émigré purchases, more fantasy than reality."

My friend's tone wavered between amused condescension and anxiety — after all, his financial future was at stake. "Their background makes them like children. All impulse, no thought of tomorrow. They very soon learn how to use a checkbook, but they refuse to learn about balance statements."

But eventually he reverted to a more academic style for his analysis. "Sociologists have pointed out that living in an underdeveloped country can dull the capacity to plan for the future. You live for the moment, buy on an ad hoc basis, take advantage of opportunity when you can. That describes the third-wave sensibility fairly accurately, but I think that Soviet life also affected their psychology in another important way. They had the continual sense while they were there that day-to-day life was not simply impoverished but outside their control, that goods were available if only the authorities would relent. Now suddenly, in America, life seems in their control. Their buying habits are a form of aggression, compensation for years of passivity."

Indeed, the émigrés accumulate goods with stunning zest, but if they are passionate in this pursuit, they are not careless. During their years in the Soviet Union they were taught to view the products of America's marketplace with a certain skepticism — which was just as well, since this balanced the envy. A common reference in Russia is to *vtorostepnie kapitalicheskie produkty* (second-rate capitalist goods): the phrase is in the bumptiously chauvinistic style of *Pravda,* but everyone uses it, and without irony. Soviet citizens are aware that the West's fancy clothing can split at the seams and that chemicals give the food its appetizing color. Whatever psychological or propagandistic function this belief served in the Soviet Union, it inclines the émigrés who come to America to buy judiciously. They make distinctions, they compare prices, and they routinely scorn those "impulse" items enticingly stacked near supermarket checkout counters. As for our national addiction to junk food, that leaves them aghast.

"*Otrava* [poison]," Tanya said succinctly when I offered her a Twinkie.

What seems to bewitch the third wave is not mere abundance but the possibility of choice. Whereas before they had to buy every valuable item that came their way, now they can discriminate. Though they are often extravagant, they still hew to a strict line of selectivity, as if checking off a shopping list they had dreamed up while in the Soviet Union. This makes sense. The Soviet economy did not simply deny them goods (they got some of what they wanted occasionally); it kept them from creating a personal style, which depends on the capacity to pick between alternatives. In the land of the turbine and tractor, all flights of fancy were grounded. In America, the third-wave émigrés see the chance finally to parade the personae they previously could only imagine in their mind's eye.

Russians have historically had a different relationship to money than we have had. Throughout the Tsarist period, status depended less on wealth than on social position. (Peter the Great's "Table of Ranks," which assigned every citizen of the empire a place in the social hierarchy, remained influential into the twentieth century.) At the time of the Revolution, indeed, much of the economy was still on a feudal footing, consisting of an intricate web of obligation and largesse instead of straight money transactions. Though the Revolution altered the role that money played, it of course did not do so in the direction of Western practices. Bolshevik doctrine stigmatized money as a means of oppression, an adulteration of normal human contact; financial accumulation was frowned upon, and was in some cases judged a capital crime.

In today's Soviet Union, the doctrinaire zeal of early communism has yielded to a more pragmatic style, but money still occupies a shadowy place in the social scheme. Money is not the high road to social status (though social status may confer money as one of its rewards). Everyone understands that an impressive position in the Party is a better means of securing goods and services than is a wad of rubles. Significantly, though savings banks exist, they are notoriously underused. Why save when having a lot of money guarantees neither social status nor (given impoverished consumer goods economy) the ability to make expensive purchases? It makes perfect economic sense for a Soviet citizen to spend money as soon as it is acquired — an inclination that is strengthened by a native tradition that esteems the extravagant gesture and derides meanness and thrift.

Among the third-wave émigrés, attitudes toward money are changing. Our capitalist ethic is persuasive, and our capitalist economy can be unforgiving toward instances of excess. Still, for the moment at least, the old views persist, and many émigrés look with astonishment and a little disgust at Americans' way with the dollar. I heard the epithets "cheap" and "tight-fisted" applied to my countrymen often and with considerable passion. Open-handed spending may have evolved in Russia as an aspect of its economic and social history, but it is now a point of personal honor, almost a mark of one's essential humanity.

I once witnessed an episode that reflected in virtually purest form the émigré attitude toward money. It took place in the National, one of several new nightclubs in Brighton Beach which cater to the third wave. Its style is high rambunctiousness, bordering on chaos. The band's percussive beat bounces jarringly against walls of oversized mirrors and chrome fixtures, but that hardly interrupts the clientele's conversation, which is carried on at a raucous decibel level that overrides all interference. The club has a mezzanine level in addition to the main floor, vastly increasing the confusion since there is a lot of commerce between tables in the form of ceremonial toasts. Probably not surprisingly, given the hectic atmosphere, the matter of food is treated offhandedly — the waiters seem to lack the enthusiasm that would be needed to negotiate a path through the crowd to the kitchen, and indeed the patrons seem hardly to notice that their food orders are filled so erratically. (When that evening I got my veal cutlets after our dessert, my complaint was brushed aside as trivial, a misplaced desire to adhere to solemn convention in the midst of jovial chaos.) The reasons to go to the National are to drink vodka, to dance, and to watch the floor show.

The entertainment on the evening I was present was an exhibition of belly dancing, not a strictly Russian custom but apparently Eastern enough to qualify. As the dancer moved around the spotlighted area on the lower level, she occasionally paused in her serpentine movements long enough to allow members of the audience to express their gratitude by stuffing dollar bills into the halter of her costume. Some adolescents smiled broadly as they did this, but for the most part there was nothing indecent in the proceedings. The audience respected and admired the dancer's performance; they began to clap rhythmically, in time with her dance.

Upstairs on the mezzanine level, most of the diners left their table and crowded around the railing in order to look at the spectacle below. They also cheered and clapped. And there, off to the side, was the detail that riveted my attention. It was a brawny man, in his late twenties or early thirties, dressed in an ill-fitting blue suit and with blond hair slicked straight back. He was probably a taxi driver or a laborer, in any case someone who had come to find his pleasure after a hard week's work. He stood slightly behind the crowd of people at the balcony and a bit off to the side, so no one — absolutely no one but me — noticed the way he calmly took a roll of bills from his pocket and, peeling them off one by one as if they were petals on a delicate flower, slowly wafted them down toward the belly dancer below. It was done solely for his own pleasure. He separated himself from his hard-earned money in a sort of private exultation.

Soviet cities give off a sense of stability and order, in large part, perhaps, because they seem so consciously to celebrate history. Virtually every plaza has a statue, usually of someone in an inspirational posture that summons up a crucial moment of the nation's past. Numerous buildings bear plaques attesting that some personage once resided within. Even the streets themselves may signify, as in the Barrikady district in Moscow, where one treads on cobblestones like those torn up by workers looking for handy weapons during the 1905 disturbances. All these mementos are stressed by the regime: the hope seems to be that a display of Russian history will prove the inevitability of the present.

Russians love to stroll through their cities. It is the typical pastime on any holiday in Moscow or Leningrad or Odessa when frostbite isn't a danger. But because of the special, monumentalized nature of the cities, many promenaders assume a peculiar perspective. They've learned the trick of pushing the urban landscape to the far periphery of consciousness, a stable background whose lessons they've already learned and see no need to study again.

Since window-shopping is out of the question (those few store windows meant to attract a buyer's attention will be cluttered with pots found to be in overstock or items equally uninspiring), watching the passing parade is the only activity that is left. At first this may seem a singularly unrewarding way to spend a day, since every passerby looks more or less like every other. Where the egalitarian ethic has not taken its toll, the tight domestic economy has done the trick. To the knowing eye, however, the prevailing grayness can reveal unexpected variety. The stitching on a pair of jeans can suggest connections in high places, while the buckle of a belt may strongly imply a trip taken abroad. Soviet urban dwellers are masters of exegesis, sensitive to any unusual sign.

When Russians come to America, they continue to indulge their passion for strolling. They walk up and down our city streets, covering distances that can amaze and exhaust any native who tries to keep up. But their gait and endurance are all that remain constant. American cities are so little like Russian ones that they deserve another category altogether.

To learn of the émigré reaction first hand, I took my friend Zhenya Novokovsky, the computer programmer from Leningrad, on a walking tour of various sections of Manhattan. Always given to exclamation, to little shrieks and whoops of emotion, Zhenya became on this trip a finely tuned seismograph, registering every murmur of joy and displeasure — with the needle hovering, as it turned out, mostly in the area of acute dismay. Times Square was, quite simply, an abomination. Cavernous and glass-walled Sixth Avenue only made her dizzy, she said. She refused outright to go to the top of the Empire State Building. Even the tranquil and quiet Cloisters, which I thought would make for a calming interlude, made her nervous. It was only a cunning facsimile of tranquillity, she opined, not the real thing.

She did not relax until we found ourselves walking down a nondescript stretch of Columbus Avenue. Pointing to the squat brownstones with small, slovenly stores on their ground floors and rusted fire escapes creeping up their facades, she said, "Well, here at last is a neighborhood for human beings."

I realized that her reaction might be only a Soviet émigré's attempt to find some still point in the midst of the New York whirligig (uninteresting neighborhoods, untouched by renewal or gentrification, may be all we have that give the sense of stability which devolves on Russian cities as a result of their complex histories), but still I was piqued by her casual dismissal of so much of my hometown.

At least New York is interesting, I said, something is always happening.

"As something is always happening in some regions of hell," she replied.

You mean the crime rate, of course, I said. But that's the price of democracy.

We walked for a few moments in silence, as if we could think of no way out of our deadlocked conversation. But then Zhenya relented — trust a Russian woman to value congeniality over the satisfaction of holding her own in an argument. "It's not as if Moscow streets are so safe," she conceded. "There are *stukachy* [informers] and KGB everywhere. In the subway, at a football match, everywhere. If you go to watch a parade, the people marching *and* those watching are *stukachy*. It's just that there you know who is friend and who is foe."

How, I wanted to know.

"You learn. When I walked down a Moscow street, I could tell instantly if a passerby was KGB. You develop a pretty good instinct. And if all else fails, you can fall back on physiognomy. A person's character always is revealed in his or her face."

I had, in fact, heard many émigrés make similar statements. "He has an honest face" — this sort of judgment, which to us sounds merely quaint, is an article of faith among many Russians. In a country where everyone dresses and behaves more or less like everyone else, it's obviously comforting to believe in the power to extrapolate morality from facial structure.

Can't you use your instincts here, as well? I asked.

Zhenya looked dubious. "Somehow it's harder here. And it's not only that I'm new to this country. The problem is that it's hard to concentrate; there are too many distractions."

A museum endows all the exhibits within its walls with meaning — a viewer can interpret every item with confidence, knowing that its presence in this location means it is part of a familiar tradition. That's the way it is in a Russian city, where the landscape, full of monuments to the Soviet system, is a constant reminder that every passerby is somehow part of a closed society. An agent of the state or a dissident, someone with connections or someone trapped on the dreary level of the average citizen — there are not that many variations.

American cities are more like carnivals than museums. There is no discernible pattern to the street life, just as there are no compelling norms to our society as a whole. Each new meeting is an adventure, and an individual's identity is most often not knowable until the encounter is at an end.

Zhenya is not much given to introspection, but by the end of our tour she had turned moody and querulous. When we parted she told me with some anger, as if I were responsible for the state of affairs, "An annoying paradox seems to exist. Though the

Soviet Union is supposedly the more secretive and more dangerous society, walking the streets there is less of a mystery, with fewer unknowns, than walking the streets here."

This is how the writer Serge Dovlatev has described one of the quintessential experiences of New York City life: "A friend and I were riding on the subway. Next to us was standing a young woman. Suddenly she turned pale. She didn't feel well, she was nauseated. All the seated passengers turned their eyes away.
"My friend said, 'Give up your seat to this woman.'
"There was no reaction.
"My friend had practically to shout into the face of a broad-shouldered, bearded Yankee, 'Hey you, you cattle, get up!' "

Dovlatev concludes that something is out of joint in this country, the moral fiber has frayed. Drawing such portentous conclusions from experiences on the transportation system may at first glance seem excessive, but perhaps it's a wise approach. Doesn't the way the English decorously queue up at bus stops or the Frenchmen's hauteur toward taxi drivers reveal something significant about those societies?

During the year I spent in Leningrad, I got to know the Soviet transportation system quite well. Every weekday I'd traveled into the city center from Vasilevsky Island on the dilapidated No. 49 bus, which looked like one of those vehicles in animated cartoons, turning corners virtually section by section, fenders askance and headlights jiggling. The driver manipulated the floor shift with such a show of vigor that it was a reasonable assumption that the bus was propelled forward solely on the power of his right arm.

But it was less the physical than the moral circumstances of the ride that made it memorable. There was an honor system of payment. A passenger drops three kopecks into a cashbox located in the center of the bus and tears off a ticket for himself. The system has several flaws, two of which regularly came into play on the No. 49. First, if a bus is crowded, as the No. 49 always was in the morning, a passenger may find himself crushed into a place distant from the cashbox, necessitating an elaborate hand-to-hand relay. (Sending my fare off down the line on the No. 49, where many, many hands were involved, I felt as much confidence in getting a return on it as if I had thrown it down an echoless well.) Second, lacking the correct change, passengers have to enter into negotiations with each other to come up with the proper fare to deposit, a dreary activity the first thing in the morning.

The fare system has another, more dire, flaw also. It's not that hard to avoid paying altogether. It can be exhilarating to beat the government out of three kopecks and ride for free, "to play the rabbit," as the saying goes. Only rarely does an inspector board a bus to demand a show of tickets and to exact fines from offenders.

I was on the No. 49 fairly late one night. I was going, after much vacillation, to meet a fellow who wanted to buy dollars at black-market rates. He needed dollars urgently, I wanted extra rubles to buy a collection of Pushkin which I coveted — the mixture of altruism and greed proved too much to resist. In any case, I told myself, though selling dollars is technically illegal, it is a practice so widespread as to be considered an integral part of the Soviet economy.

Because it was late, the bus was nearly empty. One woman sat toward the back studying *Pravda* with an intensity that suggested she was trying to decipher a code hidden in the exhorting headlines. I paid little attention to her, I was absorbed in thoughts of my impending transaction. Absentmindedly, I fumbled in my pocket for some change, and finding only a single kopeck and a half-ruble piece, dropped the former into the cashbox and detached a ticket.

The woman slapped the newspaper to her lap ostentatiously and glared at me, obviously offended that I had paid too little. I briefly glared back at this self-appointed guardian of the common weal, then sat down and directed my glance out the window. We turned off the bright and wide Bolshoy Prospekt and headed for the murk around the Lieutenant Schmidt Bridge. The redeployment of light must have triggered a sixth sense, for I felt the woman's glance on my neck. I turned to see her staring at me, her features contorted by an emotion just short of a shriek.

Suddenly the unease I felt about the black-market deal welled up and overflowed, seeping into the little moral vacuum created by having "played the rabbit." I dropped the half-ruble piece, all the change I had, into the cashbox, then went back to my seat, a respectable citizen once again. The woman returned to her *Pravda*.

Hypothesis A: if a society imposes so many rules that individuals are always breaking one or another, the citizenry is likely to feel an urge to conform to most rules as a form of compensation.

Hypothesis B: when individuals from such a society are transplanted to another one where public morality is lax, they will react ambivalently — they will enjoy the freedom, but they will also feel nostalgia for the old way, the rules that structured their lives. If a fellow passenger on a subway refuses to give up his seat to a lady who has fallen ill, they may well see this as a subversion of the social order, demanding outraged action.

Of all the third-wave émigrés I know, I guessed that Pavel Tseitlin would be the one who would make the smoothest transition to his new culture. When still in Moscow he had seemed thoroughly Americanized, right down to the ironic style and sardonic jokes of a New York City intellectual. After he signed a letter protesting the political persecution of a colleague at Moscow University, Tseitlin had been dismissed from his position as mathematics professor, and it had been made clear to him that an application for a visa would receive favorable action — an ominous suggestion, tantamount to an order to emigrate or take the consquences. Since his standing with the authorities was as low as it was likely to get, Tseitlin saw little risk in openly cultivating Americans who were passing through Moscow.

Such meetings seemed to him a reasonable way to prepare himself and his wife for their new life abroad. The Tseitlin apartment on Vladimir Street became a way-station for scholars on US-USSR exchanges: in return for one of Masha's marvelous home-cooked meals, they were quizzed on the salary scale and tenure rules of American universities, and were subjected to bad jokes, odd colloquialisms, and luckluster limericks, created by Tseitlin in an effort to bring his English to native fluency. By the time he was ready to emigrate, he was as Americanized as most Russians can get.

They settled in a small New England town, where Pavel got a professorship, and that is where I visited them, seeing them for the first time since those Moscow days. They had made a smooth transition. Pavel had a good post, Masha had gone back to school to get her doctorate in medieval history, and they had already acquired a reasonable fraction of America's bounty — a car, a color TV, a dozen electrical appliances and, for Masha, who is a real Slavic beauty, a closetful of fancy clothes. Indeed, when we talked about the book I was writing, Pavel seemed to intimate that he was now quite removed from the rest of the third-wave émigrés, that they were as much an object of curiosity for him as for me.

"Most of them will never fit into American society. At the deepest level they are different. In the terms of your sociologists, Russians are basically 'other-directed,' concerned first of all with the good opinion of others, whereas Americans are individuals, 'inner-directed.' That is why Russians have a sense of shame, but no guilt, and Americans are just the opposite. You can never mix two such different sorts of ingredients."

He *was* Americanized, having even mastered our sociological lingo. But as I sat in their small apartment, waiting for Masha to finish preparing dinner, I was surprised to find how strongly intimations of their former Moscow lives persisted. Partly, no doubt, Russia was in the air because I had that day helped them unpack their steamer trunks that had finally arrived after a nine-month voyage, and the contents — items carefully selected to evoke an irretrievable past — were still scattered about. But it was more than that also. All the newly bought American goods, all Pavel's analyses, remained somehow contingent, merely adorning a Russian essence that would not fade.

And Russia was pungently present in the meal Masha set on the table. Though she had relied on ingredients purchased at the flashy supermarket down the road, she had magically recreated the domestic cuisine of her native land — even altering the commercial yoghurt to make it resemble tangy and milky *prostakvasha*. Our meal, in fact, more than anything else I saw that day, reminded me that I was with people from a society so harsh that there's no avoiding its indelible imprint.

In the Soviet Union, a meal may be a crucial event, ritualistic as well as nutritional. The public side of life there, the Soviet workaday world, is sterile and dreary, burdened by the oppressive attention of the government: many citizens can get through it only with a strategy of detachment, performing assigned tasks but expending no emotion. They reserve feelings for domestic circles, for family, friends, lovers, and it is the dinner meal that often is the locus of this intimacy. The food is not sumptuous and the setting is often ramshackle: the glory of the meal is that emphatically shoddy materials have been mixed to create a joyous product. The food one sees in Soviet markets is an assault on the senses: slabs of dank and discolored beef, vegetables so wizened they seem to have just emerged from a sentence at hard labor, cheeses of various names but equivalently bland taste, all served up grudgingly by rude clerks. The successful meal in a private home is thus a victory cry, a sign that the hostess has, through bribes, promises, or black-market deals, snatched pleasure from a world designed to deny it.

Though there may be only a few formally invited guests at the start, visitors continue to drop in at erratic intervals. The meal is usually served in the kitchen, the only room large enough to accommodate everyone. Once seated, no one rises — there would be little practical point since the rest of the house has been cannibalized of its parts to furnish the kitchen for the occasion —

but the effect is to heighten the impression of the table of food as a vivid circle of congeniality, holding people together.

The conversation stretches endlessly. I have heard brave political plans, also utter claptrap in a philosophical vein and salacious anecdotes of abysmal taste. It's talk for talk's sake, an attempt to protract the pleasant moment. Not surprisingly, jokes are an important part of every Russian's style; they are required to help stuff the evening, make it expand at its seams — indeed, one of the few ways an honored Western guest can give offense is by failing to match these jokes with a native repertoire. Jokes about homosexual Armenians, about the prototypical Jew Rabinovich, and about sly Georgian businessmen fill the air. Lenin, who appears frequently as the main actor of a joke, transubstantiates from a tyrant into a mild bungler, cuckold, and all-around ignoramus, which is more fitting for this homey atmosphere.

The meal inevitably goes on past one o'clock, the hour when public transport slams shut. But though privately owned cars are rare and taxis skittish when approached at this time of night, no suggestion that the guests will be stranded miles from home is allowed to mar the festivities. Even later, when the host according to custom escorts his guests out into the deserted streets, the jovial mood does not flag. Questions about Life and Love and Art are blithely resolved; the sidewalk is abandoned for the middle of the street, where one can bellow and sing with more freedom; the occasional passerby is treated not as a rival for the rare taxi that does appear but as a fellow actor in a good-natured farce. Everyone is extravagantly content, happy that they have managed to subdue at least for a while the dreary oppression of Soviet reality.

In the morning the streets of Russian cities are reclaimed by the official forms of life. Intimacy recedes so abruptly you doubt it was ever present. The men in their standard dark suits and white shirts without neckties, each toting an outsized, fake-leather briefcase, hardly look around as they hurry to their jobs; the shopgirls are nonchalantly rude; the older women, seated on park benches, scrutinize each passerby for some sign of nonconformity. And overseeing the grim scene, on almost every corner, are gray- and red-uniformed policemen. The only relief is the knowledge that come evening, one can again return home for dinner with family and friends. Masha was famous in Moscow for the feasts she concocted, creating an atmosphere of congeniality even in the worst of times. It was surprising to see her working her old magic in that New England town, in the midst of democratic and bountiful America.

After the marvelous dinner was over, I asked Pavel how he liked his new country.

"I like it very much, and not least because I can still get a bit of Russian-tasting food, as you can see. Not only that, I still have my Russian books, my Russian friends who visit me, and of course my Russian wife. I have created a well-furnished, almost independent Russian colony. When we get bored or low on supplies, we make forays into the outside world, into rich America."

I remarked that such a style, like a bear hibernating, was similar to his life in Russia, give or take a few details.

"So we're going to have a *philosophical* argument. For that we must move to the living room, or living area, as my landlord has designated it. Let's sit on the sofa — we'll be sophists together," he exclaimed, looking to see if I would laugh.

But we did not in fact pursue the question, it being too portentous for the convivial setting, so Tseitlin's description of America remained the last word: American as sustaining background, as a rich environment nurturing intimate circles of Russianness in its midst.

In my months wandering among the third-wave émigrés, I'd heard that opinion before, but it was startling to hear it from someone I knew to be among the most Americanized of the recent arrivals. My visit to Tseitlin suddenly clarified an idea that had been vaguely present in my mind for a long time. Americans, all of us who are aware of the third-wave émigrés, hopefully regard them as symbols of an essential humanity — we are alike under the skin, we insist, strip away the thin cultural veneer and we would be as one. Or, to put it in more political terms, remove individuals from the communist environment of the Soviet Union and they will take to American-style democracy like fish to water.

It doesn't seem to work. The example of the third-wave suggests that men are *not* essentially the same, or at least that cultural differences are so deeply imprinted that these might as well be considered part of our essential makeup. The political implications are even more disquieting. The third-wave could have been incontrovertible proof of the infinite superiority of the American way of life; but instead, by their ambiguous, sometimes half-hearted acceptance of their new country, they prove only that we are a workable society, with both merits and flaws, if somewhat more of the former.

By the standards of today's world, such a judgment is, in fact, pretty high praise, and most of us would probably rest content with it if not that the third-wave emigration seemed like an opportunity for so much more: unstinting praise from those who came direct from our enemy's camp.

But if we are disappointed, we will recover. We have more urgent concerns anyway. For the third-wave émigrés themselves, however, the decision to leave the Soviet Union and come to America will remain as a most influential factor in their lives, producing, in many of them, a nagging sense of incompleteness. They have placed themselves at a distance from many of the customs and attitudes they knew best, which suited their characters best.

Are the third-wave émigrés better off in America? Yes, without doubt. But that the question should even be raised — and the émigrés raise it themselves continually — is significant. For many, their lot was not incalculably improved, as they had hoped, only calculably. Their fate is to spend the rest of their lives weighing benefits and losses, measuring the price of an ambiguous life in exile against the exorbitant moral cost they would have had to pay to stay in Russia. The decisive item on this balance sheet is the future: as the third-wave émigrés are fond of saying, their children will profit most of all, and their children's children, by which time Russia will have become a dim family legend.

Fyodor Dostoevsky never visited America, but he was not a man to let such a circumstance stand in the way of judgment. In his novel *The Possessed,* he calmly assessed our mode of everyday behavior; he has one of the characters say of his trip to this country, "One has to be born in America, or at least get thoroughly acclimatized, before one can hope to be on the same level with them. Why, even when they asked us for a dollar for something that wasn't worth a penny, we paid it with pleasure, nay, with enthusiasm. We praised everything: spiritualism, lynch law, six-shooters, hoboes. One day when we were traveling a chap put his hand into my pocket, took out my hairbrush, and began brushing his hair with it. [We] just glanced at each other and made up our minds that it was quite all right and that we liked it very much."

Many Russians through the centuries have held similarly negative views about American manners, even if they lacked Dostoevsky's capacity for evocative detail. The irony, of course, is that many Americans have looked with no less condescension on Russian manners. And, sad to say, it's not that far a leap from ethnological contempt to moral judgment — if someone dresses oddly or speaks clumsily, we often assume that he must be morally brutish.

Now that Russians have arrived en masse in the form of the third-wave emigration, matters will presumably be different. We will learn some generosity, some give-and-take in assessing each other's culture. Several restaurants run by third-wave émigrés have opened in New York City, and I decided to visit one. It seemed like a fine place to observe the meshing of cultures. The Russians would hobble their chauvinism while playing the role of hosts; the etiquette of the occasion would check the querulous impulses of American patrons.

The Fiddler on the Roof restaurant was located at Flatbush

and Kingston avenues in Brooklyn; but the architecture, a haciendalike structure of roseate concrete, was strictly Southern California. In this gaudy setting, Fiddler on the Roof incongruously provided a bill of fare most suitable to a *stolovoya*, that cross between a cafeteria and an army mess hall which the Bolsheviks designed to feed the masses. The heart of the menu was *shchi* (heavily greased vegetable soup), *solyanka* (beef and carrot stew), and compote (dried fruit floating in an indeterminate liquid). It did not seem the sort of cuisine to attract a broad clientele, only third-wave émigrés cooking for other third-wave émigrés. But I was in luck. Three well-dressed American couples, with a distinct aura of suburbia about them, were sitting at a corner table. They picked at their food in an investigatory way and continually looked around at the other customers, as if they wanted to observe how fugitives from barbaric communism managed their cutlery.

The restaurant itself seemed to have an informal bipartite arrangement. Beyond the periphery of the customers' tables was an area given over to relatives of the owner, friends and neighborhood cronies. They stood around chatting or smoking in the intense, stabbing manner that Russians favor. Only one or two of them sat down, though there were plenty of seats; and those that did, kept their coats on, as if not wanting to endanger their status as irregulars. Their presence made the act of eating in a restaurant surprisingly ambiguous, broadening the usual horizon of interest beyond the food on one's plate and the waiters who serve it.

In the part of the restaurant devoted to the paying public, activities were in full swing. A band, dressed in the traditional embroidered shirts of Southern Russia, played enthusiastically. It lurched without pause from plangent Russian folk songs to rock, mainly Beatles songs — circa 1960s American music is the state of the art in Russia. At first, the Russians in the restaurant danced only to the Russian tunes. When the band shifted over to its Western repertoire, they yielded the floor to the table of Americans, who proceeded to flaunt their intricate steps. The

Russians seemed cowed. As the evening progressed, however, the Russians by subtle stages counterattacked, till at last they occupied the dance floor continuously. When the music took on a faster tempo, they simply embellished their *kazachok* with random borrowings from the Twist. One soigné couple — he in a velveteen jacket and polka-dotted ascot, she in a pink sheath and high boots — whirled around in a manner that seemed to span the Catskills and the Urals: for every fancy strut and dip, there was a boisterous clapping of hands, and occasionally the woman slapped her palm against her boot like an enthusiastic Cossack. The Russians seated at their tables, where the vodka was now flowing freely, enthusiastically cheered the spectacle.

The Americans had by this time retreated to their table, apparently stunned by the raucous laughter and noise, but they found no haven there. When fueled by vodka, a Russian's pursuit of pleasure acquires an imperialistic urgency: everyone in the immediate area is required to contribute to the joviality. The Americans found themselves forced to respond to convoluted toasts they didn't understand, while the three women in the group found it impossible to fend off the insistent invitations for a few spins around the dance floor, hearty exercises that left them exhausted. The Americans may have come to the restaurant as condescending tourists, out for an evening of ethnological slumming, but now they were in danger of being reduced to minor roles in a Russian opera buffa.

Prodded by his companions, one of the Americans, a burly, bearded giant compacted into a three-piece suit, finally rose to be his camp's champion. With mock courtliness, he walked over to the noisiest Russian table, bowed elaborately, and invited the heavy blond woman to dance. The dance floor cleared for them, and the band leader, sensing a dramatic occasion, came forward to announce in a thick accent, "To honor our American friends, we will play their country's great favorite song, 'Felix.'"

At his command, the band struck up the 1970s classic "Feelings," then stepped up the tempo until the tune was hardly recognizable. The woman never fell behind the beat. Her style of

The Structure of Everyday Life 247

dancing was radically Russian, full of stamping and clapping, with an occasional shout tossed in, but her enthusiasm seemed to keep her in graceful congruity with the American music. The American's elaborate cheerfulness vanished as he increasingly found himself a ploy for his partner's imaginative whirling. He began to sweat from exertion, but the band's imperturbable beat kept him rotating briskly around the floor.

As the crescendo neared, the woman brought forth a brightly colored handkerchief, manipulating it seductively. At first the American played along, grabbing at the handkerchief as it passed before his face; but it always billowed just beyond his grasp. Finally he lunged forward with real exasperation. His partner escaped again, however, and he stumbled and fell to his knees. The audience gasped, then laughed. The American tried to recapture an ironic attitude by kissing the hem of his partner's skirt, but not willing to grant him even that small triumph, she danced nimbly out of reach yet again.

As the crowd applauded this unexpectedly well-played spectacle, a Russian leaped onto the dance floor. Grabbing hold of the blond woman's arm, he raised it in a sign of triumph. "*Soyuz pobedil!* [The Soviet Union is victorious]!" he shouted merrily, and everyone, including the Americans, cheered. Not exactly the meshing of cultures I had hoped to see, but at least some hearty mutual recognition. More, at this moment of the third-wave's history, might have been hard to achieve.